Beyond Access:

Transforming Policy and Practice for Gender Equality in Education

Oxfam GB

Oxfam GB, founded in 1942, is a development, humanitarian, and campaigning agency dedicated to finding lasting solutions to poverty and suffering around the world. Oxfam believes that every human being is entitled to a life of dignity and opportunity, and it works with others worldwide to make this become a reality.

From its base in Oxford in the United Kingdom, Oxfam GB publishes and distributes a wide range of books and other resource materials for development and relief workers, researchers and campaigners, schools and colleges, and the general public, as part of its programme of advocacy, education, and communications.

Oxfam GB is a member of Oxfam International, a confederation of 12 agencies of diverse cultures and languages which share a commitment to working for an end to injustice and poverty – both in long-term development work and at times of crisis.

For further information about Oxfam's publishing, and online ordering, visit www.oxfam.org.uk/publications

For information about Oxfam's development, advocacy, and humanitarian relief work around the world, visit www.oxfam.org.uk

Beyond Access:

Transforming Policy and Practice for Gender Equality in Education

Edited by
Sheila Aikman and Elaine Unterhalter

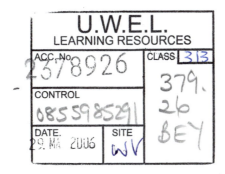

Oxfam

First published by Oxfam GB in 2005

© Oxfam GB 2005

ISBN 0 85598 529 1

A catalogue record for this publication is available from the British Library.

Available from:

Bournemouth English Book Centre, PO Box 1496, Parkstone, Dorset, BH12 3YD, UK
tel: +44 (0)1202 712933; fax: +44 (0)1202 712930; email: oxfam@bebc.co.uk

USA: Stylus Publishing LLC, PO Box 605, Herndon, VA 20172-0605, USA
tel: +1 (0)703 661 1581; fax: +1 (0)703 661 1547; email: styluspub@aol.com

For details of local agents and representatives in other countries, consult our website:
www.oxfam.org.uk/publications
or contact Oxfam Publishing, 274 Banbury Road, Oxford OX2 7DZ, UK
tel +44 (0)1865 473727; fax (0)1865 472393; email: publish@oxfam.org.uk

Our website contains a fully searchable database of all our titles, and facilities for secure on-line ordering.

The views expressed in these chapters are those of the individual authors, and not necessarily those of the publisher or the editors.

Front cover: Mashimoni Squatters Primary School, Kibera, Kenya (Oxfam GB/Geoff Sayer)

Published by Oxfam GB, 274 Banbury Road, Oxford OX2 7DZ, UK.

Printed by Information Press, Eynsham

Oxfam GB is a registered charity, no. 202 918, and is a member of Oxfam International.

Contents

Acknowledgements

Many people have helped to bring this book to completion. Our thanks to all the authors for their contributions and their willingness to work with us on revising material which in most cases was initially produced for different audiences. We are grateful to members of the **Beyond Access: Gender, Education, and Development** project team, in particular Chloe Challender and Rajee Rajagopalan, who have given unstinting help with the preparation of the final text, as well as making the project work at many different levels. We also want to acknowledge the support and enthusiasm that Amy North has brought to the project and the book. Our thanks to Nina Henderson, who contributed to some of the early editorial work, and to Julieanne Porter and Catherine Robinson in the Oxfam GB publishing team for their close and supportive guidance in the editing and production process.

The advisory committee of the Beyond Access project has contributed both critiques and encouragement, each valuable in different ways. We also wish to thank Rachel Hinton, who represents the UK government's Department for International Development (DFID) in the Beyond Access partnership – DFID, Oxfam GB, and the Institute of Education, University of London. Rachel has constantly encouraged our work, and DFID has funded the Beyond Access project from its inception. We are also grateful for the support of colleagues in our respective organisations, and in particular we would like to thank Ines Smyth and Diana Leonard for their comments and encouragement.

Last but not least, we want to thank our families for all their support, without which the book would have been neither started nor completed.

Sheila Aikman (Oxfam GB)

Elaine Unterhalter (Institute of Education, University of London)

Introduction

Sheila Aikman and Elaine Unterhalter

This is a book about transforming policy and practice to promote equitable processes in education, in response to the need for equality, quality, and justice for all. It considers the significance of gender equality in education, and the ways in which gender inequality relates to other sources of division and conflict in society.

We live in a world in which education is characterised by extensive gender inequalities. Two thirds of all those who have no access to education are girls and women. Sixty-five million girls never even start school, and an estimated 100 million do not complete primary education, often because its quality is poor and their opportunities are far from equal to those of boys (Herz and Spurling 2004: 2). More than 542 million women are illiterate, many as a result of inadequate or incomplete schooling. Lack of literacy is generally associated with poverty and discrimination (UNESCO 2003: 87). In an age of enormously expanded access to all levels of education, of high aspirations for political participation, and huge growth of knowledge economies, nearly three quarters of a billion girls and women are being denied education.

The manifest injustice of this state of affairs, and the marked gender inequalities associated with it, prompted the United Nations Millennium Summit in September 2000 to set two Millennium Development Goals (MDGs) to address the problem:

MDG 2: achieve universal primary education, with the target of ensuring that all boys and girls complete a full course of primary schooling by 2015.

MDG 3: promote gender equality and empower women, with the target of eliminating gender disparities in primary and secondary education by 2005, and in all levels of education by 2015.

The MDGs complement other international declarations on gender equality in education, formulated several years ago but not yet realised: the Beijing Platform for Action for gender equality (1995), and the Dakar Education For All (EFA) Framework of Action (2000).

This book examines policies and practices which can contribute towards achieving these goals and declarations. For decades, governments, non-government

1

organisations (NGOs), and individuals have been working to improve girls' access to formal education and the quality of education that they receive in school. Their initiatives have been linked to widely differing aims and expectations of what the education of girls and women can do for economic and political development, social change, and women's empowerment; but these diverse aspirations have often resulted in programmes with significant similarities, supporting both the access of girls to education and greater gender equality and quality beyond the point of access. Considerable knowledge and experience have been accumulated to indicate the policies, strategies, and approaches that improve the access and retention of girls in school in different contexts. But much of this knowledge is not widely shared. We need to learn more from the outcomes of initiatives to promote gender equality in particular economic, social, cultural, and geographical contexts. We need to consider what has made them successful or unsuccessful, in order to develop policies and practices that will transform girls' and women's lives and thus contribute to achieving wide goals for gender equality.

Considerable momentum has built up around the world in support of the commitments expressed in the MDGs. Signatory governments are engaging in debates and negotiations on the question of how to put the goals into practice. There is a huge popular demand for education and for governments to fulfil the promises that they made at the Millennium Summit. During the Global Week of Action for Education in April 2005, hundreds of thousands of activists in 110 countries urged governments and international organisations to recognise education as the key to ending poverty, and to fulfil their millennium commitments. The popular demands are echoed by governments, UN agencies, multilateral financial institutions, and a very wide range of civil-society organisations and coalitions. For Northern donor governments, there is pressure to meet financial commitments made in 2000; for developing-country governments, there is pressure to develop good-quality plans and transparent means of achieving Education For All (EFA).

Parity, equality, equity, and quality

However, while widespread support has been expressed for the challenge of achieving universal primary education by 2015 (MDG 2), the target for MDG 3 (gender parity in primary and secondary schooling by 2005) has not been met. *Gender parity* means that the same proportions of girls and boys enter and complete schooling. When there is no gender parity, there is a gender gap, and a greater proportion of either boys or girls is receiving education. While there are encouraging moves towards increased parity in many countries (for example in Bangladesh and Malawi), in many others the gap in favour of boys is wide (in Mali, Burkina Faso, Niger, Pakistan, Chad, Yemen, and Ethiopia, to name a few).

UNICEF estimates that across all developing countries the gender gap is 10 percentage points (UNICEF 2003). In sub-Saharan Africa, 54 per cent of all girls do not even complete primary education, and only 17 per cent go on to secondary education. At least one in every three girls who completes primary schooling in South Asia cannot read, write, or do arithmetic (Herz and Spurling 2004: 2).

In our view, gender parity is a rather narrow aspiration. A focus on gender parity means measuring quantitative change and counting the numbers of girls, as compared with the numbers of boys, enrolling in school. Concern with parity may be complemented by a focus on other tangible and measurable factors, such as quality of infrastructure and facilities, numbers of textbooks and supplies of teaching/learning materials available to teachers and students, and the measurement of performance through examination results and numbers of girls graduating from primary school. But this is not always the case. Many countries are making progress on gender parity, but the limited concept of parity means that more challenging dimensions of gender equality and equity are often not considered, analysed, and monitored.

This book is concerned with a wider notion of *gender equality*, which is expressed most fully by the Beijing Platform of Action. Gender equality is an aspiration contained in many international conventions and national constitutions; but its precise meaning in relation to education is often unclear. We interpret gender equality in terms of respect for human rights and a set of ethical demands for securing the conditions for all people, men and women, to live a full life. We use the term *gender equity* to characterise institutional and social processes that work for this interpretation of equality. But often *equality* and *equity* are used interchangeably. Some approaches to equality are based on a limited definition, requiring only that resources should be equal: for example, there should be equal numbers of places in school for boys and girls. Other approaches consider that equality entails the removal of deeply embedded obstacles and structures of power and exclusion, such as discriminatory laws, customs, practices, and institutional processes, all of which undermine opportunities and outcomes in education (Unterhalter 2005). Drawing on Amartya Sen's 'capability approach', we consider that achieving gender equality entails developing the freedoms of all individuals, irrespective of gender or other markers of discrimination, to choose actions, aspirations, and attributes that they have reason to value (Sen 1999). Gender equity entails putting in place the social and institutional arrangements that would secure these freedoms. An education system would lack key dimensions of equality in this sense if it was discriminatory or did not develop capabilities in children to achieve an education that was personally and socially attuned to developing freedoms. Some aspects of this equality are the freedom to attend school, to learn and participate there in safety and security, to develop identities that tolerate others, and to enjoy economic, political, and cultural opportunities. Putting gender equity in place in the classroom is a key to connecting schooling and citizenship with human rights. Equity and equality underpin values of care and respect for children and their teachers.

Evidence from the UK, where girls perform as well as (if not better than) boys in examinations, is taken to mean that gender equality has largely been addressed, and quality education has been achieved for all. Focus has shifted to the task of widening access to higher education for all social classes, without attention to gender. But research suggests that women's opportunities to secure graduate and professional employment on a par with men are still constrained by their domestic and family responsibilities (David 2005). Thus gender equality entails more than the attainment of equal numbers in school, or parity in examination results: it implies a fuller meaning of equality, which includes conditions in school and post-school opportunities. We believe that gender equality in education cannot be separated as a goal from gender equality in society as a whole.

Educational quality is crucial for the achievement of gender equality in schooling. Concerns to improve quality include the framing of the curriculum, the content and form of learning materials, the nature of the pedagogy, and teacher–pupil relations. Quality requires gender-sensitive use of human resources, and consideration of gender in the allocation of finances. Quality education entails a concern to include the views of all members of a community, and to take account of local languages and cultures. A quality education is not therefore acquired in isolation from the social setting in which students live. It embraces the notion of education as a transformative process which promotes social change and contributes to building a just and democratic society. A quality education rejects gender discrimination and social injustice. Quality education cannot be achieved without gender equality and equity.

Beyond Access

This book has developed out of the work of our project **Beyond Access: Gender, Education and Development**, a partnership between an NGO (Oxfam GB), a research organisation (Institute of Education, University of London), and a UK government department (the Department for International Development – DFID), working together to contribute to the achievement of Millennium Development Goal 3, by generating and critically examining knowledge and practice regarding gender equality and education, and second by providing appropriate resources to share and disseminate the lessons learned, in order to influence the policies of government departments, national and international NGOs, and international institutions, including UN agencies. The founders of the project were concerned to address the fact that the three constituencies – policy makers, practitioners and activists, and researchers – generally worked in isolation from each other, unaware or unappreciative of each other's work; they feared that this fragmentation of effort would hamper work to achieve and support MDG 3.

The project's concern to maintain dialogue between these three constituencies is reflected in this book. Some of the chapters have developed from the work of MA students at the Institute of Education, where we have both worked. Other chapters are based on the work of NGO coalitions like the Global Campaign for Education, and Elimu Yetu in Kenya. Some chapters were initially presented at a series of Beyond Access seminars which ran from 2003 to 2005 as a discussion forum for policy makers, practitioners, and researchers. Chapter 3 draws on work on measurement commissioned by policy makers in the Commonwealth Secretariat, UNESCO, and UNICEF.

Advancing MDG 3

Because MDG 3 is a key concern of the work of **Beyond Access**, this book addresses several issues related to the MDG project. First, it is concerned to raise the importance of gender equality and ensure that it is not overlooked in the big push towards achieving EFA by 2015. There is no room for complacency: the 2005 target has been missed, and there is a need to question why this has happened and what can be done to ensure that gender equality is recognised as a key element of a rights-based approach to EFA and quality education.

Second, the book challenges the narrow framing of the 2005 target in terms of parity, emphasising the need to engage with all the complexities of gender equality, as it is expressed and manifest both within the education system and in the wider society in which that system operates. Where relations within school and between school and family contribute to maintaining gender inequalities, the MDGs and other international targets have not provided a strong impetus for change. On the contrary, the apparent sequencing of gender targets in the MDGs has put a misplaced emphasis on gender parity, with the result that it seems as if gender equality and equity can be addressed only after the achievement of parity. This presents us all with the challenge of switching the focus of the debate from parity of access to quality, equality, and equity.

Third, the book questions the overwhelming focus of the MDGs on primary education and schooling, which results in the neglect of adult basic education and literacy. Despite the existence of more than 800 million non-literate adults in 2002, of whom 64 per cent are women (UNESCO 2003: 225) and despite widespread agreement that adult education and literacy are crucial for achieving many of the goals currently enshrined in the MDGs, there are no commonly agreed goals or targets for adult education, and very limited resources devoted to it. Governments proclaim their commitment to ensuring adult education and literacy, but their actions belie their words. It has been a low priority for most governments and has been addressed through inconsistent and unco-ordinated programmes of different sizes, durations, and aims, implemented by NGOs and community-based organisations (CBOs). While there *are* good examples of innovative practice – although only a limited number have been documented and disseminated – they remain isolated examples, unable to influence government policy or practice.

Fourthly the book demands that education planners, policy makers, and practitioners adopt a comprehensive approach to HIV/AIDS and gender, because gender inequality is a major driving force behind HIV epidemics. The importance of promoting girls' education in addressing gender inequality cannot be overemphasised, but it should be addressed as part of a holistic approach to gender equality. The development needs of boys should not be neglected in initiatives to combat HIV/AIDS, and there needs to be a strong focus on addressing traditional concepts of masculinity and some forms of male sexual behaviour. At the same time, harmful practices, such as violence at school and the sexual harassment and abuse of girls by teachers, need to be eliminated (Clarke 2005:1).

Advocating the need for a wider framing of the MDGs, contributors to this book illustrate what needs to change in order to bring about gender equality in education. They present factors that make schooling and education gender-inequitable, and they indicate factors that contribute to positive change. It becomes clear from a reading of these chapters that women and girls are not a homogeneous category, and that a one-size policy, approach, or curriculum will not fit all. Women themselves need to participate in decision making about their own education, to ensure that it is flexible and meets a wide range of different needs.

The chapters reveal the complex interrelationships between poverty, cultural and ethnic differences, geographical marginalisation, and gender inequalities, which are obscured by nationally aggregated statistics. For this reason, many of the authors choose to examine initiatives for change in some of the most complex and marginalised contexts, involving some of the poorest girls and women, who experience the most extreme exclusion from State provision. What strategies can be employed, and what lessons can be drawn upon in contexts where governments are fragile and/or communities are nomadic or semi-nomadic? What are the options available in countries where decentralised governments have no budgets for education, and communities are expected to raise their own revenues? These questions need to be considered in relation to countries affected by conflict, as well as those that relate to more stable settings, because there may well be lessons in societies emerging from conflict – for instance, South Africa or Northern Ireland – for countries where conflict is still acute.

A key theme of the book is the interplay between policy and practice. We do not consider policy to be expressed only in official documents and made only by people in leadership positions. We consider that the policy expressed in official documents is made each day by practitioners. Policy making is a diffuse process. Our contributors consider the ways in which official policy is re-interpreted in practice, and how policy is itself a form of practice. Some present examples of practice that offer particularly challenging issues to be considered in the remaking of policy.

The structure of the book

The book is divided into three parts. The first examines the extent of inequality and the nature of the challenge to achieve gender equality in education. It provides a picture of what has been learned, and identifies some changes that are needed if gender equality is to be achieved. The second part presents accounts of government policies and their intended and unintended consequences for women's empowerment. They examine the dynamics of policy making and policy implementation, and pose questions about how policy promotes and secures gender equality in education. The third part examines a range of local settings where gender-equality initiatives have flourished, and raises questions about the policy implications of different forms of practice. The examples in this section present work for gender equality in education by an HIV/AIDS drama group, a faith-based organisation, and a girls-only private school. These are settings outside the remit of conventional work with State institutions and large NGOs, and these chapters raise some key issues that are still unaddressed in policy declarations.

The concluding chapter considers the challenges that remain for policy makers, practitioners, and researchers if they are to advance concerns for gender equality in education as part of work to promote the MDGs.

Part One: The Challenges for Gender Equality in Education

The scene is set in the first chapter, written by **Elaine Unterhalter**, which reviews various approaches to gender, education, and development. Approaches associated with WID (women in development), GAD (gender and development), post-structuralism, and human rights and capabilities variously define the nature of the problem of gender inequality in education and have led researchers from different disciplines to emphasise different aspects of the issues and suggest contrasting policies. This chapter sets subsequent chapters in the context of this framework.

The second chapter, contributed by the **Global Campaign for Education** (GCE), reports on a study of the state of girls' education in nine countries in Africa and Asia which informed a week of campaigning throughout the world on girls' education in April 2003. The research indicates that progress has been made towards gender equality in education in places where a range of factors cohere and reinforce each other. These include a strong political commitment by the government to gender equality, and a policy development process that actively involves an informed body of teachers, parents, and representatives of the women's movement. This combination of forces, working together with strategies that are not isolated or *ad hoc* initiatives but a series of interrelated measures, supported by government and donor resources to sustain implementation, can deliver change.

Where change is not happening or is very slow to take place, a range of measures need to be taken; they include ending the queue for education: all children should have access to school. This is not an end in itself, but a means towards achieving gender equality. Governments need to invest in girls and their education, and invest in poor families and poor schools so that they can offer a high-quality experience for all children.

The GCE analysis is reinforced by the work on new strategies for measuring achievement, documented by **Elaine Unterhalter, Chloe Challender, and Rajee Rajagopalan**. Their chapter questions the limited measures of quality and empowerment currently in use and calls for a wider conception of gender equality, over and above mere attendance at school and completion of primary education. The authors suggest a new form of measurement of progress towards gender equality and education. Using this measure indicates the level of global mobilisation needed to achieve gender equality in and through education.

Part Two: Transforming Action – Changing Policy Through Practice

The chapters in this section take a critical look at contexts and experiences where changes in government policy, together with alliances developed with civil society, have promoted changes in practice, of different types and different degrees, in the direction of greater gender quality. They question the forms of policy and partnership needed to ensure that educational practices intersect appropriately with policy to promote gender equality and quality education.

Janet Raynor shows how policy and practice in Bangladesh are sometimes out of step with each other. The government's attempts to increase the access of girls to secondary education have brought about change in terms of large numbers of adolescent girls now attending secondary school. Raynor argues, however, that it is now time for this programme, which has been greeted with international acclaim, to make modifications to allow the programme to adopt an agenda of empowering girls and women, rather than merely aiming to extend existing gendered roles. Raynor considers the need to improve the quality of girls' education in seriously overcrowded schools, argues for efforts to increase the supply of women teachers to be accompanied by the provision of gender training, and asks why, if the main purpose of education is seen to be enabling girls to take up paid employment, there has been no research into employment opportunities for girls.

The chapter contributed by the Kenyan national education coalition, **Elimu Yetu**, based on its own research in Kenya into the status of girls' education, charts the government's commitments to achieve gender equality through enabling legislation. It counterposes this with the variety of initiatives that members of the coalition have been developing and implementing, both in response to increased government-sanctioned opportunities for increasing gender equality in basic education, and to provide evidence for civil-society's adversarial role in lobbying the government for change. It also emphasises the important role played by civil society in holding government accountable to its commitments, and it offers valuable information about grassroots contexts and issues which demand innovative and context-specific responses.

The chapter by **Ian Leggett** illustrates some of the issues raised in preceding chapters. While national statistics show high rates of gender parity in overall access to education, only by understanding local dynamics and factors external to the school will current policies of building more schools actually achieve progress towards educational equality for girls from groups that are marginalised from the mainstream society. Leggett shows how the national picture of expansion of education in Kenya belies what is happening in one province. He reflects on how a national policy aimed at expanding access where there is demand, but with inadequate resources or acknowledgement of local conditions, falls far short of its objectives. In this case it is the needs of pastoralists and their children that have not been sufficiently acknowledged. Without a comprehensive and imaginative set of initiatives which recognise the depth and breadth of the subordinate status of girls and women and provide specific measures to promote the participation of girls, the policy of expansion is doomed to failure in this province.

From the other side of the globe, **Patricia Ames** contributes a study of Peru which reinforces the message that merely accessing schooling is not enough to ensure a gender- equitable education. Her chapter exemplifies the fact that while national statistics may show 100 per cent enrolment and gender parity, inequalities of access exist for some of the poorest and most disadvantaged groups in society. Research in rural schools identifies a range of external and internal inequities which influence the retention of girls in school and shape expectations of their performance and ability. Teachers' low expectations of rural indigenous children, compounded by their low expectations of girls, in a school environment characterised by aggression and physical punishment, have meant that for girls the social costs of schooling are often too high, and they drop out in large numbers. This cycle of low achievement and high drop-out rates has reinforced girls' low social status.

While the general situation in these Peruvian rural schools is bleak, Ames is careful to maintain that girls are not passive victims of the schooling in their communities; she suggests that a range of strategies could be adopted to improve girls' educational experience dramatically. As earlier chapters confirm, there needs to be a package of integrated measures for change and gender equality, including teacher training, support for schools in poor communities, and social provision that emphasises the importance of investing in girls' education.

The chapter by **Mora Oommen**, on the other hand, evaluates the degree to which women were empowered by the national literacy campaign in India. Although this was a national government initiative, responsibility for its implementation was given to local government and CBOs. This encouraged local ownership and unprecedented voluntary participation. The author argues that the large-scale mobilisation acted as a 'social sanction' for women's participation in the literacy programme, thus breaking through traditional limitations on their participation in the public sphere. To this extent the programme went beyond imparting literacy and questioned a number of social norms constraining women's participation in public life.

From Mali, **Salina Salou and Sheila Aikman** contribute an example of strategies for transforming gender relations in the school and the wider environment. They remind us that poor quality and poor provision of education have a greater negative effect on girls than on boys. In northern Mali, where women's educational attainment rates are very low, few positive examples of what education can do for girls are available to be used to challenge strong patriarchal systems. The chapter examines multiple interventions – school and family animators, curriculum reform, and decentralised decision-making – stressing that several different changes have to take place at the same time for them to have a sustainable impact and improve not only girls' educational experience but also their lives. While education reform at the national level has opened up new opportunities for a skills-based curriculum which reflects the differing cultural and geographical realities of the learners, these realities are also gendered and demand a gender analysis that challenges the continuity of long-established attitudes and practices.

Part Three: The Challenge of Local Practices

The third section of the book highlights a range of innovative approaches being taken at the community and school levels, in response to specific contexts in which women and girls aspire to equality. The chapters show how these approaches and practices are founded on the energy, commitment, and determination of learners and teachers/facilitators.

The challenge of gender inequality is well documented in the fight against AIDS, but the importance of taking a gendered approach to HIV/AIDS education programmes is not well understood. The chapter by **Mark Thorpe** documents a non-formal education approach which used drama in schools to increase young people's understanding of HIV/AIDS prevention in South Africa and Mozambique. To ensure that inequitable relations are not reinforced during and through HIV education itself, they need to be challenged in a process-based approach with specially trained staff who can ensure that young women and men have the space to ask questions and explore issues that closely affect their lives.

Alicia Zents provides an insight into the participation of women in the Pentecostal movement in Burkina Faso. In contexts where African women have a long history of maintaining the vitality of the church, yet occupy a low position in Burkinabé society, Zents examines the extent to which the movement is able to transform concepts of gender, and documents the ways in which women are pushing against the movement's gender hierarchies.

The final chapter in this section considers the case of Loreto Sealdah, a high-prestige girls-only school in India, its ethos of reaching out to girls from underprivileged families, and its philosophy of education for community and solidarity. **Ruth Doggett** discusses the meaning and values that girls (both fee-paying and non-paying 'underprivileged' students) attach to their schooling and its enabling curriculum, which encourages students to identify with their own and others' realities and become active agents of their own lives, able to take on non-traditional roles. The evidence suggests that the fee-paying students were better able to do this than the non-paying students, who were more aware of external constraints on their future options.

The Conclusion highlights some of the intersections and disjunctures of policy and practice, assesses the nature of change that has been achieved, and considers some of the key challenges that the chapters have highlighted which need to be addressed if MDG 2 and MDG 3 are to be achieved. It emphasises the importance of multi-sectoral initiatives and a respect for human rights in support of gender equality in education, to ensure high-quality education and consequently a better quality of life. A multi-sector approach entails partnerships, and many of the chapters illustrate the importance of partnerships outside the education sector for initiating and sustaining gender equality. While the book indicates that there are no 'quick fixes' to the deep-rooted and often widely accepted forms of gender discrimination that limit girls' educational opportunities, it also demonstrates the imperative need for political will at all levels if change is to be achieved. It shows how dramatic actions, such as the abolition of school fees, can have a major impact in terms of increased numbers of girls in school, and how training or other forms of structured reflection on gender inequality by teachers, officials, and NGOs can yield significant results.

Sheila Aikman is the Global Education Policy Adviser with Oxfam GB, and co-ordinator of the DFID-funded 'Beyond Access' Project. She formerly taught at the Institute of Education, University of London, in the Department of Education and International Development. She has conducted long-term ethnographic field work on indigenous education with indigenous peoples of Peru and has published widely on intercultural bilingual education, language policy, and gender.

Elaine Unterhalter is a senior Lecturer in Education and International Development at the Institute of Education, University of London. She was born and educated in South Africa and has written a number of books and articles on gender in South Africa. She has also done work on India, Bangladesh, and global institutions. With Sheila Aikman, she has co-ordinated the Beyond Access project since 2003.

References

Clarke, D. (2005) 'Planning and Evaluation for Gender Equality in Education in the Context of HIV and AIDS', paper presented at Beyond Access Seminar 5 on 'Partnerships for Gender Equality', Dhaka, 31 January –2 February 2005 (www.ungei.org)

David, M. (2005) 'A Feminist and Critical Perspective on Family-Education Partnerships for Gender Equality and Quality Basic Education', paper delivered at Beyond Access Seminar 5, 31 January-1 February 2005, Dhaka. Full text can be found at http://k1.ioe.ac.uk/schools/efps/GenderEducDev/Miriam%20David%20paper%20final.pdf

Herz, G. and B. Sperling (2004) 'What Works in Girls' Education: Evidence and Policies from the Developing World', Council on Foreign Relations

Sen, A. (1999) *Development as Freedom*, Oxford: Oxford University Press

UNESCO (2003) *Gender and Education for All: the Leap to Equality*, Global Monitoring Report 2003/4

Unterhalter, E. (2005) 'Gender equality and education in South Africa: measurements, scores and strategies' in L. Chisholm and J. September (eds.) *Gender Equity in South African Education, 1994-2004*, Pretoria: HSRC

Part One

The Challenges for
Gender Equality in Education

1 Fragmented frameworks?
Researching women, gender, education, and development

Elaine Unterhalter

This chapter critically reviews contrasting frameworks which present different ways of understanding the nature of the challenge to achieve gender equality in education. Different meanings of gender equality and schooling have consequences for our understanding of two Millennium Development Goals (MDGs): MDG 2, which is concerned with gender equality in schooling, and MDG 3, concerned with the empowerment of women. Different meanings entail different actions, and, as will be shown, organisations have interpreted *gender, education, development, empowerment*, and *equality* in very different ways. These interpretations are underpinned by different approaches to research and analysis: how one undertakes research on gender and women will determine the conclusions. This chapter examines different meanings of the challenge for gender equality in education and evaluates the implications of each approach for policy and practice.

Four approaches to gender equality in education

Table 1 summarises the four approaches and main phases of thinking and action concerning gender education, development, and equality that have prevailed since approximately 1970. (For a fuller discussion of some of the theoretical issues raised, see Unterhalter 2003a, 2005a.)

In practice there are considerable overlaps between the four approaches, but I have separated them out analytically to emphasise some of their key differences. The WID (women in development) framework, with its stress on expansion of education for girls and women, linked to efficiency and economic growth, is the framework with the longest history and the most powerful advocates in governments, inter-government organisations, and NGOs. It is the framework that views gender in relatively uncomplicated ways and generates clear policy directives regarding, for example, the employment of more women teachers to reassure parents about girls' safety at school.

The GAD (gender and development) framework considers gender as part of complex and changing social relations. Influential for more than twenty years

Table 1: Gender, education, and development: contrasting frameworks

Framework	Linked theories	Understandings of gender	Understandings of development	Understandings of education	Understandings of equality
Women in Development (WID): from 1970s to the present	Modernisation; human-capital theory	Gender = women, girls	Growth, efficiency, good governance, social cohesion	Schooling	Equality of resources. Sometimes termed *parity*.
Gender and Development (GAD): from 1980s to the present	Structuralism; Marxism	Constructed social relations, power	Challenging inequity and oppression	Conscientisation	Redistribution of power. Sometimes termed *equity*.
Post-structuralism (from 1990s to the present)	Post-colonial theory	Shifting identities	Struggling with the past in the present to shape multi-faceted identities and new narratives	Deconstructive	Stress on difference
Human development (from 1990s to the present)	The capability approach	Inequality and capability denial	Development as freedom	A basic capability	Equality of rights and capabilities

among women's organisations concerned with development, GAD has only slowly made an impact on the thinking of some governments and education NGOs. Because GAD is alert to complex processes entailed in the reproduction and transformation of gendered relations, it is less easily translatable into simple policy demands. However, GAD approaches have had some impact on practice, particularly with regard to teachers' understanding of work in a gendered classroom, women's organisations' linking of education-related demands to wider demands for empowerment, and the ways in which advocates of gender equality work in institutions.

The post-structuralist approach questions the stability of definitions of gender, paying particular attention to fluid processes of gendered identification and shifting forms of action. While the issues raised by this approach have not influenced government policies directly, they have put on the agenda the affirmation of subordinated identities, and they have made some impact on the development of learning materials and forms of organisation that recognise the complexity of social identities.

The final framework analysed is concerned with human development and human rights in development. In some ways this is a meta-theory, working at a higher level of abstraction, and suggesting not concrete policies or forms of practice but rather a framework in which these can be developed ethically. However, the human-development approach also differs significantly from the other three with regard to how gender and education are understood, and some of the processes entailed in developing policy. It thus allows us to see the three other approaches in a somewhat different light.

I now want to look in more depth at the assumptions and research base of each approach, drawing out its policy and practice implications, its achievements, and some associated problems and questions.

Bringing girls and women into school: the dominance of the WID approach

The WID framework, with its emphasis on bringing women into development, and thus girls and women into school, has links to aspects of liberal feminism in Northern contexts. It stresses the importance of including women in development planning to improve efficiency, but not necessarily challenging the multiple sources of women's subordination. Histories of the WID approach point to its beginnings in the early 1970s with the work of Ester Boserup, which illustrated how women, who do the bulk of farming in Africa, were neglected in rural development projects (Boserup 1970; Moser 1994).

WID has had the strongest resonance for analysts of education in governments and inter-government organisations. The most influential policy thinking on gender, education, and development in the 1990s drew on this approach, expressed most clearly in a collection of papers edited by King and Hill and first published in mimeographed form in 1991 for the World Bank. This was to have enormous influence on governments, and on large-scale development assistance projects. King and Hill emphasised the importance of counting girls and women inside and outside schooling, overcoming the barriers to access, and realising the *social* benefits of their presence in school: increased GDP per capita, reduced birth rates and infant mortality, and increased longevity (King and Hill 1991; 1993). This analysis was framed in key policy documents throughout the 1990s, including the World Bank's *Priorities and Strategies in Education* and UNESCO's *Delors Commission Report* (World Bank 1995; Delors 1996). Its influence is still evident in key passages of important strategy documents from the World Bank, including *Engendering Development* (2001), and DFID's *Girls' Education: Towards a Better Future for All* (DFID 2005).

In the WID approach, 'gender' is equated with women and girls, who are identified descriptively in terms of biological differences. 'Education' is understood as schooling. 'Development' or 'empowerment' is linked with economic growth or social cohesion and sometimes improved governance. Herz and Sperling's influential analysis *What Works in Girls' Education*, written in 2004 in response to the failure to meet the MDG on gender parity in schooling, uses some forms of WID analysis, identifying the benefits of girls' education in terms of faster economic growth, more productive farming, smaller and better-educated families, and reduced infant and child mortality. While the report also argues that the education of girls will result in benefits to them, such as higher earning potential, better protection from HIV and domestic violence, and greater political participation, the assumption is that these personal benefits are acceptable because they fit with accepted social benefits (Herz and Sperling 2004). Intrinsic benefits from education that might be more personal and private are not acknowledged.

Questions of exploitation, subordination, and social division are generally not considered in this framework. The slogan *'If you educate a woman you educate the nation'* nicely captures the thinking that underpins the mainstream policy support for WID. The education of women is for others, not for themselves. The benefits of women's education are to be realised in the household, often the site of the harshest discrimination. Some critiques draw attention to WID's narrow assumption that 'education' is always delivered in formal schools; that gender is not a political relationship, but merely a set of descriptive categories; and that the concerns of individual women are not to be taken into account (Unterhalter 2000; Fine and Rose 2001; Brighouse and Unterhalter 2002).

The WID approach to the challenge of gender inequality in education is to get more girls into school. A great deal of the empirical work using this framework has concentrated on counting the numbers of girls in or out of school and measuring the breadth of the gender gap between girls and boys in enrolments or achievement (UNESCO 2003; UNICEF 2000–2004). This work has been carried out by government ministries, including census departments. District household surveys have been a key instrument in collecting data on school attendance. Additional surveys have looked at how household relations affect decisions about sending girls to school and keeping them there (Hadden and London 1996; Filmer and Pritchett 1999; Alderman, Orrazo and Patterno 1996). Analysis has also concentrated on quantifying the benefits of girls' and women's schooling in terms of reduced birth rates and improved uptake of immunisation (Klansen 1999; Subbarao and Raney 1995; Gage *et al.* 1997). Much of this work has been undertaken by researchers working for multilateral organisations, including the World Bank, UNICEF, and UNESCO. Generally these researchers are economists, and very often research teams have been led by international experts who employ local research assistants for fieldwork.

Some work mixes qualitative and quantitative data to consider gender in relation to achievement at school (Nath and Chowdhury 2001). In the Caribbean this work has studied how boys underachieve because of their relations with female teachers and other boys (Kutnick *et al.* 1997; Parry 1997). While the qualitative research provides some of the insight about social relations that is difficult to discern in the quantitative work, the assumptions that underpin it are the same: that is, the importance of bringing girls into school and assuring achievement for girls and boys.

This quantitative work on gender, access, retention, and achievement tends not to deal with other dimensions of inequality, particularly race, ethnicity, caste, and disability. While some acknowledgement is made of differences between rural and urban girls, there is little engagement with the complexity of social division. This resonates with the way in which writers in the WID framework interpret equality. Within this framework, equality is generally understood in terms of equal numbers of resources: for example, places in school for girls and boys, male and female teachers employed, or equal numbers of images of women and men in textbooks. Studies thus concentrate on describing the gender gap, that is the inequality in numbers of boys and girls at school (UNESCO 2003), the lack of female teachers (King and Hill 1994; Herz and Sperling 2004), and the numbers of boys and girls in children's textbooks (Joshi and Anderson 1992; Obura 1991). This approach pays little attention to gendered processes of learning, the conditions in which women teachers work, the way their work is regarded by their societies, or the meanings that children make and take from the images they see in textbooks. Chapters in this book by the Global Campaign for Education (Chapter 2) and Elimu Yetu (Chapter 5) are examples of a WID approach.

Policies associated with the WID approach have concentrated on improving access for girls, through giving them stipends or abolishing school fees, providing food in return for attendance at school, developing the infrastructure of training or accommodation to ensure that more women teachers are employed, digging latrines, and providing water. Some associated practice has entailed mobilising teachers and communities to encourage girls to enrol in school and ensure that they pass examinations. These are often seen as ends in themselves. In Malawi and Kenya, the abolition of school fees led to hundreds of thousands of girls enrolling in school – with little provision to support them. WID practice is not much concerned with the content of what girls learn, how they learn, or whether gender inequalities face them after their years in school are over. Generally WID analysts will comment on the content of schooling when it has a bearing on access, but not more generally. For example, Herz *et al.* highlight the importance of girls' studying science in Kenya because it encourages parents to send their daughters to school, not because learning science might provide intrinsically useful knowledge (Herz *et al.* 1991). The stress in WID practice is on bringing girls into school and ensuring that they learn appropriately. The framework is not concerned to raise questions about the gendered practice of teachers in relation to children's learning styles, management practices in school, or gendered structures of power in society.

The WID framework is not able to explain more complex aspects of gender equality and inequality in school. GAD critiques of WID, discussed below, have taken issue with some of these limitations. However, it must be acknowledged that WID's simple messages about policy and practice, despite – or possibly because of – their lack of analytical complexity, have galvanised huge programmes by government and inter-government organisations, mobilised additional funding, and led to some important legal changes with regard to the provision of education. Despite the many limitations of WID's failure to look beyond the school gate, the policy achievements associated with the framework in the past two decades must be acknowledged.

The gendered power structures of school and society: drawing on GAD in education

In opposition to WID, the GAD (gender and development) approach emerged in the late 1980s, emphasising the significance of gendered power structures of inequality in a range of contexts. GAD theorists argued that inequality needed to be challenged politically and could not merely be ameliorated by a process of inclusion, by the provision of welfare support, or by a belief in the greater efficiency of projects or programmes that included women (Moser 1993). GAD grew mainly out of women's organisations (primarily but not exclusively those of poor rural and urban women). It was also linked to debates about feminism in the third world, and the contributions of critical theorists in development studies who highlighted the inadequate ways in which women and gender were conceptualised in the work of mainstream development theory (Kabeer 1994; Elson 1995; DAWN 1995; Randall and Waylen 1998; Molyneux 1998; Rai 2002). In some ways this work resonated with the approach of socialist feminists in Western Europe. (Radical feminism, with its trenchant critique of the politics of the family, had considerable impact in North America, Western Europe, and Australia, but was less significant politically in developing countries, although there are some notable exceptions, particularly in Latin America.)

GAD work focused on the sexual division of labour inside and outside the household, on forms of political mobilisation, and changing gendered structures of power. As a form of political analysis and action, GAD paid relatively little attention to issues concerning formal schooling. Partly because education is so centrally concerned with the State, which provides an ambiguous partner for transforming gendered social relations (Stromquist 1995), the writings of influential GAD theorists tended not to deal with formal education.

A key element in GAD analysis was to make a distinction between practical gender needs and strategic gender interests. Practical gender needs are concerns with immediate day-to-day requirements like food, water, and shelter. Strategic gender interests are concerns with challenging the deeply entrenched forms of gender discrimination in the legal system, sexual violence in the family, the lack of political representation, and discrimination in the workplace (Moser 1993; Kabeer 1994; Molyneux 1998). Although there was considerable debate about the link between gender needs and gender interests, GAD theorists considered the importance of developing programmes that could operate at both levels to bring about significant changes and redistribution of power to achieve greater equality (Molyneux 1998; Elson 2002). Very little writing on gender, education, and development engaged with these GAD debates, and it is unclear whether education can be categorised as a practical gender need or a strategic gender interest. Indeed, in writings critical of the WID approach and influenced by GAD theories, the two tended to be conflated (Chisholm and Unterhalter 1999).

A second central concern of GAD writers was the debate about empowerment that had some bearing on understandings of equality. Use of the concept grew out of feminist movements that stressed the importance of enhancing agency among the poorest. However, initial attempts to give empowerment conceptual coherence suffered from a number of difficulties. These included how to specify the social context (an important concern for GAD analysts); how to work with changing meanings of empowerment, often linked to agendas about privatisation very different from those of the women's movement; how to engage with questions of justice; and how to define the nature of agency or relate women's interests strategically to the agendas of those in power (Yuval Davis 1994; Rowlands 1997; Kabeer 1999; Rai 2001; Brighouse and Unterhalter 2002).

In an important paper which addresses the need for a clearer conceptualisation, Kabeer discusses how empowerment might be measured. She distinguishes three different dimensions that need to be examined when considering women's choices (singly or collectively). Firstly, empowerment entails choice with regard to access to resources; secondly it entails agency in decision making and negotiating power; and thirdly it comprises achievements of outcomes of value. Kabeer argues that an adequate assessment of empowerment requires triangulation of measurement of all three sources (Kabeer 1999).

- First, translating this into a definition of what is implied in measuring gender empowerment in education would entail measuring access to schooling up to a certain level. (Note that here access includes retention – that is, the capacity to retain access – and achievement – that is, capacity to gain knowledge from schooling.)

- Secondly, measuring empowerment would imply measuring agency in how decisions about education are made, thus placing more emphasis on gender equality with regard to decision making about education by adult women. It might consider decision making about access to schooling in households, as well as decision making in schools or in education ministries, or in local authorities, like village education councils in India with devolved responsibilities for some aspects of education management.

- Lastly, measuring empowerment would also need to be analysed with regard to achievements that flow from education – not just narrowly defined notions of reading and writing up to a certain level, or GDP per capita, but more complex notions of *well-being*.

It is evident that this approach differs somewhat from WID, because access to resources and decision making, not simple inclusion, is at issue. Similarly there are different inflections to GAD, particularly the varying stresses on resources and distribution, not merely agency.

The discussion of empowerment identifies some key areas that are relevant to GAD theorists' understandings of equality. In contrast with the WID interpretation of equality based on equality of resources, GAD theorists consider equality in terms of the removal of the structural barriers to gender equality: unfair laws; labour-market practices; management regimes in institutions; barriers to women's decision making in all settings; inequitable processes with regard to the distribution of time, money, and schooling. The process of remedy was sometimes seen as 'empowerment', but was also called 'equity', an approach to instituting fairness. This might entail inequalities in resources, for example in affirmative-action programmes. Thus equality was an ideal of equal power, participation, and distribution, but the process of achieving it might sometimes look inequitable because of historical and contextual issues that could not be excluded from analysis.

The literature that draws on a GAD framework to analyse education policy has tended to focus more on the gendered politics of aid and national policy than on ethnographic work on gender relations in schools and communities (Swainson 2000, Hossain *et al.* 2002; Sato 1997; Oda 2000; Stromquist 1997, 2000). Some GAD-influenced studies have considered levels of sexual violence in school (Leach *et al.* 2003; Mirembe and Davies 2001), and gender, school management, and school improvement, highlighting the substantial difficulties that women face in management (Davies 1998; Chisholm 2001; Coleman, Haiyan, and Yanping 1998). Analyses of the gendered politics of community involvement in education indicate the ambiguity inherent in decentralisation policies in societies where there are severe constraints on women's participation in decision making (Subrahmanian 2005; Vavrus 2003). GAD ideas were influential in the design and delivery of adult literacy projects such as REFLECT (Archer and Cottingham 1996). GAD aspirations were given a particular organisational form in the emergence of NGOs and new social movements from the mid-1980s, with a particular focus on aspects of gender inequality, often including components of adult education in their forms of mobilisation. The ways in which these organisations linked education to other forms of social development illuminated issues of empowerment and the interlinking of practical needs and strategic interests (Basu 1995; Stromquist 2000; Unterhalter and Dutt 2001; Khandekhar 2004). Contributions to this book by Raynor (Chapter 4), Leggett (Chapter 6), Ames (Chapter 7), Sanou and Aikman (Chapter 9), Thorpe (Chapter 10), and Zentz (Chapter 11) all use elements of a GAD approach.

In contrast to the prevalence of economists in research associated with WID, writers working on education within a GAD framework draw on history, sociology, anthropology, politics, and development studies. Generally GAD research has not been conducted for commissions from large multilateral organisations, but represents small-scale projects, often by academics living in developing countries. Two notable exceptions were the studies in six countries in Africa carried out by a team led by Christopher Colclough in partnership with FAWE, studying gendered social relations and girls' access to schooling (Colclough, Rose, and Tembon 2001; Colclough *et al.* 2004). This study, by a multidisciplinary team with some contributions by economists, contained some elements of a WID approach; but, because it also contained detailed data gleaned from interviews in communities, it was able to present a finely nuanced analysis.

The research commissioned by UNESCO for the 2003 Global Monitoring Report (GMR), synthesised in Chapter 3 of that report, also takes a predominantly GAD-type perspective, looking in considerable detail at gendered relations in schools and post-schooling, not only at barriers to access (UNESCO 2003). These two studies, particularly at the level of detailed analysis, represent a hybrid of WID and GAD positions; however, as evinced in the Executive Summary to the GMR, WID is the framework that is seen to have more wide-ranging policy leverage.

It is notable how little of the GAD-inspired literature on gendered relations in education deals with schools and classrooms. In high-income countries, gender and education, as an area of political engagement and academic debate, was centrally influenced by the women's movement in the 1970s. While many of the demands of the women's movement in these countries had resonance with demands in Third World countries, there were a number of key differences. Among these, one of the most important was the significant participation of highly educated women in feminist organisation: in many Third World contexts, highly educated women were generally a minority in feminist mobilisation, although there are some important exceptions to this observation, most notably in Egypt and Iran.[1] A second difference lay in the fact that in high-income countries feminists frequently occupied important, though often fragile, positions in the leadership of trade unions, including teachers' unions, in established political parties, and as policy makers, particularly at local and district levels. These were generally not spaces available to a feminist leadership elsewhere in the world. When women did gain senior positions, it was not very frequently on terms associated with a politics concerning gender equality.

The articulation of concerns about gender and education in developing countries often linked with the mobilisation of grassroots women's organisation, but was given institutional form by education ministries and powerful donors in development assistance, which often had very little connection with this popular constituency (Swainson 2000). By contrast in Western Europe, North America, and Australia, gender and education was given political and theoretical coherence largely by teachers in schools and teacher-education institutions who were directly involved in the women's movement. A number of these later moved on to work in higher education, continuing to research in schools. The political and academic work was thus organically linked with practice. Many of the issues of concern to these activist teachers and researchers, such as gender bias in the curriculum, co-educational or single-sex schools, the formation of femininities (and later masculinities) in schools, approaches to sex education, levels of sexual harassment at school and university, and the intersections of race and gender discrimination, were issues that arose out of practice (Lees 1993; Weiner 1994; Kenway *et al.* 1998; Arnot, Weiner, and David 1999; Epstein and Johnson 1998; Paechter 2000; Francis and Skelton 2001; Arnot 2002; Leonard 2001). In some contexts, remarkable spaces opened in the education bureaucracy for women who had a particular combination of knowledge about gender and connection with the women's movement. Termed *femocrats* in Australia, but recognisable in a number of different contexts of institutional leadership, they were sometimes able to secure considerable resources for gender equality in education, although often at grave personal cost (Blackmore 1995; Morley 1999).

For this group of writers, the analysis of liberal feminists, so influential with regard to WID elsewhere in the world, had very little to say, largely because access was not the problem, except to some areas of higher education. Even this ceased to be a major barrier in the 1990s, as access to higher education by previously excluded groups was widely encouraged in the drive to build high-skilled economies. While girls' achievement at school initially seemed to be lower than that of boys, by the 1990s there was a moral panic about boys' underachievement (Epstein, Elwood, and Maw 1998; Kenway and Kraack 2003).

Much more influential for these writers were theorists who could help to analyse the persistence of inequalities of gender, class, and race/ethnic identity, despite universal access and high levels of achievement by girls. Thus Bernstein's work on class, Bourdieu's work on habitus, Foucault's analysis of power, concerns with the simultaneous exclusions and inclusions of citizenship, a number of feminist post-structuralist accounts regarding the negotiations of meaning, and feminist analysis of embodiment generated the most useful theoretical and political insights. In contrast with writings on gender, education, and development, this literature has been more theoretically engaged with debates in sociology, cultural studies, and women's studies, and more focused on practice. Concomitantly it has taken rather less account of education in relation to economics, political philosophy, or the changing nature of households, although there are important exceptions to this generalisation (Crompton 1999; Moller Okin 1999; Walkerdine, Lucey, and Melody 2000).

The work of theorists using GAD in education has not generated the simple 'what works' messages associated with WID. GAD influence on policy and practice can be seen at two levels. Firstly, GAD thinkers have developed critiques of policy making that are concerned with the gendered processes of decision making. Gender budgeting and gender mainstreaming are both planning tools that have been developed in an attempt to make gender central to the concerns of policy makers, rather than seeing it as a quick solution to a range of social problems (Jahan 1995; Kabeer 2002; Budlender and Hewitt 2002). Gender mainstreaming seeks to legitimise gender equality as a fundamental value that is reflected in development choices and institutional practices for a society as a whole; to advance gender equality from central, key ministries; and to facilitate the presence of women as decision makers (UNDP 2002). UNICEF and DFID have developed gender-mainstreaming guides for policy makers, taking particular account of education (UNICEF 2003; Derbyshire 1998). Gender budgeting seeks to identify the gendered expenditure of a departmental budget, focusing on elements that can be seen to yield specific benefits to women and girls. Some evaluative work on gender mainstreaming and gender budgeting has been published, showing some of the uneven processes and outcomes entailed (Razavi and Miller 1995; Derbyshire 1998; Goetz 1997; Schalkwyk 1998), but studies of gender mainstreaming and gender budgeting in education have yet to be undertaken. These concerns with attending to gendered processes in organisations may well be amenable to further adaptation for schools and their management committees. Gender training, which often underpins gender mainstreaming work (Williams *et al.* 1999), has much potential for use in the development of teacher-education modules that consider gender.

While WID has been successful in generating simple messages and clear policy directives, the achievement of GAD has been to highlight the complexity of institutional change. GAD researchers and policy activists have demonstrated the importance of having appropriate processes in place to redress imbalances in gendered power in organisations. They reveal how much care and time needs to be allocated to redressing deeply entrenched and sometimes unacknowledged gender inequities in schools, education ministries, political decision making, families, and the labour market.

Problematising universal categories: the challenge of post-structuralism to gender, education, and development

While WID and GAD emerged out of development politics and practice, post-structuralism (and related ideas, loosely grouped together as 'post-colonial theory'), was primarily an approach located in universities or among groups of highly educated critics. The approaches that they developed were applied as a form of critique to a range of development practice and the methodologies associated with thinking about the Third World. Commentaries highlighted problems in the universalisation of a notion of 'third-world woman' and 'development', and the power relations masked and perpetuated by development-assistance rhetoric (Mohanty 1988; Marchand and Parpart 1995; Spivak 1999). An important strand of the literature presents schooling as a space that disrupts and diminishes the power of local or indigenous knowledges (Tuhiwai Smith 1999; Kowakole 1997). A key question posed by writers who used this framework, which is largely absent from most WID and GAD discussions of gender, education, and development, concerns questions of methodology and the 'colonial gaze': the process by which research participants 'become gendered', in accordance with certain ascribed meanings of the term and the silencing and erasure of women from many conventional sources for data collection (Spivak 1999).

Post-structuralist thinkers have raised critical questions about identity and shown how the meaning of gender entails fluid and shifting processes of identification in tension with the fixed structures noted by GAD analysts. For these writers, the process of education is partly a process of recognising this fluidity and critiquing the process of marginalisation of non-mainstream identities. Thus in this framework equality is not the major concern, as a key political and theoretical objective is the recognition of difference (Mannathoko 1999).

Relatively little work has used a post-structuralist framework to consider gender and education in development settings, in contrast to the rich literature on this theme in Western Europe, North America, and Australia. However, the complexity of the challenges posed by the HIV/AIDS epidemic has generated work that considers the gendered and sexualised identities of learners and teachers (Pattman and Chege 2003; Pattman 2004), and ways in which meanings associated with school spaces can subvert concerns with gender equality (Kent 2004). The fluid identities of educated women in Africa and India have also been documented (Stambach 2000; Narayan 1997).

Generally post-structuralist writers on gender, education, and development have been employed in higher education, either working in or closely connected with Western European and North American institutions. It is here that their influence has been most pronounced in course content and in the focus of what is published. While their influence on government and NGO policies has not been large, their analysis of the importance of identities has had resonance with political mobilisation to address subordinated identities, for example gay and lesbian identities in South Africa, or Dalit identities in India (Gevisser and Cameron 1995; Khandekhar 2004).

Equality of what in education? Rights and capabilities

The WID framework draws primarily on economic analyses, GAD on sociological approaches, and the post-structuralist approach on insights from literary theory and cultural studies. Each has had a different constituency with regard to policy making and practice. The generally acknowledged context to the work in all three approaches is the global compact on human rights, gender equality, and education, specifically the Universal Declaration of Human Rights, the Convention on the Rights of the Child, and the Jomtien and Beijing Declarations. While WID and GAD theorists use these documents to legitimise their concerns, some post-structuralist writers are critical of their universal aspirations and the disjuncture between declared intent and actual practice. However, questions posed in political philosophy regarding the nature of rights, needs, and capabilities and their implications for thinking about gender and education are outside the scope of all three frameworks.

These questions have been addressed in the formulation of the 'capability approach' by Amartya Sen and Martha Nussbaum, who have posed questions concerning the definitions of rights to education and the political foundation of the demand for gender equality (Sen 1999; Nussbaum 2000). The capability approach considers that the evaluation of equality, for example in education provision, needs to be based on an understanding of human capabilities – that is, what it is that each individual has reason to value. This contrasts sharply with the human-capital approach, influential in WID analysis, which stresses that the evaluation of education provision is about some aggregated benefit to society or future society. While human-capital theory has little to say about injustices and inequality in the household, the workplace, or the State, the capability approach is centrally concerned with these, but relies not on outlining the structures of inequality (as GAD does), but on positing a strategy based on an ethical notion of valuing freedoms and affirming rights as ethical obligations of each person to another.

Sen and Nussbaum have expounded their views of the significance of education as a key capability (Saito 2003; Nussbaum 2004). Sen drew on this analysis in a key speech to the Commonwealth Education Ministers' conference in 2003, when he explained how education capabilities and enlarged capabilities for women underpinned other freedoms (Sen 2003). The concern of the capability approach with multi-dimensionality, linking provision of education with health services, income, aspects of trade, and governance, has been a key influence on UNDP's *Human Development Reports* (Fukuda and Parr 2003). Research using the approach is characterised by multidisciplinary approaches which mix economics, political philosophy, education, and health.

The capability approach is not without important critics, particularly with regard to its failure to take account of injustices of recognition, not solely distribution (Fraser 1997), its inability to engage with dimensions of group-based social mobilisation for democratisation and gender equality (Young 2000; Stewart 2004), and its tendency to universalise, which may not take sufficient account of particular contexts.

To some extent, empirical work drawing on the approach shows how issues of recognition and social context can be accommodated. Research on women, gender, education, and the capability approach considers the ways in which evaluations of literacy can be enhanced by drawing on the approach (Alkire 2002). This approach might also be used in relation to evaluating policy to overcome gender violence in the context of HIV in South Africa (Unterhalter 2003), and it might inform an understanding of education linked to gender equality (Walker 2004). Contributions by Oommen (Chapter 8) and Doggett (Chapter 12) in this book, while not working explicitly with a capability framework, still express concerns with rights and the enlargement of freedoms that resonate with work linked to the capability approach.

There are some clear policy implications of the approach. Governments using the capability approach have an obligation to establish and sustain the conditions for each and every individual, irrespective of gender, ethnicity, race, or regional location, to achieve valued outcomes. These may entail ensuring that each person acquires a certain level of educational attainment, but they undoubtedly entail ensuring the freedoms that allow valued outcomes to be articulated and achieved (Gasper 2004; Unterhalter 2005b). Thus, for example, failing to ensure conditions where sexual violence in and on the way to school can be identified and eradicated would be a failure to ensure freedom for valued outcomes. While GAD writers have tended to describe the structures that generate these problems, the capability approach contains an ethical injunction with regard to formulating policy for change. Similarly, failure to ensure opportunities for a particular group to participate in decision making about valued outcomes, again well documented in GAD literature, would also be a limitation on freedoms or capabilities. Sen's capability approach highlights the importance of diverse social settings where capabilities will be articulated. He emphasises the importance of free forms of discussion and association in articulating capabilities. Sen writes about development as freedom because the freedom to think, talk, and act concerning what one values is a meaning of development closer to a concern with human flourishing than narrower notions of a certain level of GDP per capita, or a pre-specified level of resource.

The capability approach attempts to overcome some of the difficulties with the universalism in the concept of rights by highlighting the importance of securing the conditions for individuals articulating 'valued beings and doings'. The stress on securing conditions for social justice sets this approach apart from WID, with its stress on practical strategies, GAD with its focus on disempowering structures, and post-structuralism with its emphasis on identities. A combination of the capability approach with other analytical frameworks seems a useful way forward for future policy work.

Conclusion

This chapter has identified four frameworks in which the debate about gender, education, and development has been set. It can be seen that while each has a distinctive set of concerns, demands, policy implications, and favoured researchers, in particular settings there is considerable overlap. The policy paper produced by the Global Campaign for Education for the Commission on the Status of Women in New York in 2005 articulated many key WID demands for an end to user fees and expanded access to school. But it also highlighted GAD concerns with gendered processes of learning in school and gender inequalities outside school. It presents a view of multiple actors in development that has some resonance with the post-structuralist critique and emphasises the importance of girls' learning linked to outcomes that they value, which resonates with the capability approach (GCE 2005). It may be that the failure to meet the 2005 MDG will catalyse new thinking, bringing together the richness of the insights associated with the different frameworks, and thus generating new forms of action that go beyond the fragmented achievements of the past.

Elaine Unterhalter is a senior lecturer in Education and International Development at the Institute of Education, University of London. She has written a number of books and articles on gender in South Africa and has also done work on India, Bangladesh, and global institutions. With Sheila Aikman, she has co-ordinated the Beyond Access: Gender, Education and Development project since 2003.

Note

1   My thanks to Niloufar Pourzand for clarification on this point.

References

Alderman, H., P. Orazem, and E. Paterno (1996) 'School Quality, School Cost, and the Public/Private Choices of Low-Income Households in Pakistan', Impact Evaluation of Education Reform Working Paper No. 2, World Bank Development Research Group, Washington, DC: World Bank

Alkire, S. (2002) *Valuing Freedom. Sen's Capability Approach and Poverty Reduction* Oxford: Oxford University Press

Archer, D. and S. Cottingham (1996) *Reflect Mother Manual*, London: Action Aid

Arnot, M., G. Weiner, and M. David (1999) *Closing the Gender Gap: Postwar education and social change*, Cambridge, Polity Press

Arnot, M. (2002) *Boyswork: Teacher initiatives and gender equality*, London: Open University Press

Basu, A. (1995) (ed.) *The Challenge of Local Feminisms: Women's Movements in Global Perspective*, Boulder: Westview Press

Blackmore, J. (1995) 'Policy as dialogue: Feminist administrators working for educational change', *Gender and Education*, 7/3: 293–314

Boserup, E. (1970) *Women's Role in Economic Development*, New York: St Martin's Press

Brighouse, H. and E. Unterhalter (2002) 'Primary Goods, Capabilities and the Millennium Development Target for Gender Equity in Education', paper presented at conference, 'Promoting Women's Capabilities: Examining Nussbaum's Capabilities Approach', Cambridge

Budlender, D. and G. Hewitt (2002) *Gender Budgets Make More Cents: Country studies and good practice*, London: Commonwealth Secretariat

Chisholm, L. and E. Unterhalter (1999) 'Gender, education and the transition to democracy: research, theory and policy in South Africa, c 1980–1998', *Transformation*, 39: 1–26

Chisholm, L. (2001) 'Gender and leadership in South African educational administration', *Gender and Education*, 13/4

Nath, S.R and A.M.R. Chowdhury (2001) (eds.) *A Question of Quality: State of primary education in Bangladesh*, Vol. II: Achievement of Competencies, Dhaka: Campaign for Popular Education and University Press

Colclough, C., P. Rose, and M. Tembon (2000) 'Gender inequalities in primary schooling: the roles of poverty and adverse cultural practices', *International Journal of Educational Development*, 20/1: 5–28

Colclough, C., S. Al Samarrai, P. Rose, and M. Tembon (2004) *Achieving Schooling for All in Africa: Costs, commitment and gender*, Aldershot: Ashgate

Coleman, M., Q. Haiyan, and L. Yanping (1998) 'Women in educational management in China: experience in Shaanxi province', *Compare* 28/2

Crompton, R.(1999) *Restructuring Gender Relations and Employment*, Oxford: Oxford University Press

Davies, L. (1998) 'Democratic practice, gender and school management' in P.Drake and P. Owen (eds.) *Gender and Management Issues in Education: An international perspective*, Stoke-on-Trent: Trentham

DAWN (1995) 'Rethinking social development: DAWN's vision', *World Development* 23/ 11: 2001–4

Delors, J. (1996) *Learning: the Treasure Within*, Paris: UNESCO Publishing

Derbyshire, H. (1998) *Mainstreaming Gender Equality in Project Implementation*, London: DFID

DFID (2005) *Girls' Education: Towards a Better Future for All*, London: Department for International Development

Elson, D. (1995) (ed.) *Male Bias in the Development Process* (2nd edition), Manchester: Manchester University Press

Elson, D. (2002) 'Gender justice, human rights and neo-liberal economic policies' in M. Molyneux and S. Razavi (eds.) (2002) *Gender, Justice, Development and Rights*, Oxford: Oxford University Press

Epstein, D. and R. Johnson (1998) *Schooling Sexualities*, Buckingham, Open University Press

Epstein, D., J. Elwood, and J. Maw (1998) *Failing Boys: Issues in gender and achievement*, Buckingham, Open University Press

Filmer, D. and L. Pritchett (1999) 'The effect of household wealth on educational attainment: evidence from 35 countries', *Population and Development Review* 25(1): 85–120

Francis, B. and C. Skelton (2001) (eds.) 'Men teachers and the construction of heterosexual masculinity in the classroom', *Sex Education* 1/1: 1–17

Fraser, N. (1997) *Justice Interruptus. Critical reflections on the 'postsocialist' condition*, New York: Routledge

Fine, B. and P. Rose (2001) 'Education and the post Washington consensus' in B.Fine, C.Lapavitsas and J.Pincus (eds.) *Development Policy in the 21st century. Beyond the post Washington consensus*, London: Routledge

Fukuda Parr, K. and A.K.S. Kumar (2003) (eds.) *Readings in Human Development. Concepts, measures and policies for a development paradigm*, New York: UNDP

Gage, A., E. Sommerfelt, and A. Piani (1997) 'Household structure and childhood immunization in Niger and Nigeria', *Demography* 34/2: 195–309

Gasper, D. (2004) *The Ethics of Development*, Edinburgh: Edinburgh University Press

Gevisser, M. and E. Casmeron (1995) *Defiant Desire: Gay and lesbian lives in South Africa*, London: Routledge

Global Campaign for Education (2005) 'Girls Can't Wait', Briefing Paper available online at www.campaignforeducation.org/documents/news/2005/Mar/b10%20brief%20final.doc (accessed 18 March 2005)

Goetz, A.M. (1997) (ed.) *Getting Institutions Right for Women in Development*, London: Zed

Hadden, K. and B. London (1996) 'Educating girls in the Third World: The demographic, basic needs and economic benefits', *International Journal of Comparative Sociology*, 37/1–2: 31–46

Herz, B. *et al.* (1991) 'Letting Girls Learn: Promising Approaches in Primary and Secondary Education', World Bank Discussion Paper No. 133, Washington DC: World Bank

Herz, G. and B. Sperling (2004) 'What Works in Girls' Education: Evidence and Policies from the Developing World', Council on Foreign Relations

Hossain, N., R. Subrahmanian, and N. Kabeer (2002) *The Politics of Educational Expansion in Bangladesh*, IDS Working Paper 167, Brighton: University of Sussex

Jackson, V. and R. Pearson (1998) (eds.) *Feminist Visions of Development. Gender Analysis and Policy*, London: Routledge

Jahan, R. (1995) *The Elusive Agenda. Mainstreaming women in development*, London: Zed

Joshi, G. P. and J. Anderson (1994) 'Female motivation in the patriarchal school: An analysis of primary textbooks and school organisation in Nepal and some strategies for change', *Gender and Education* 6/2

Kabeer, N. (1994) *Reversed Realities*, London: Verso

Kabeer, N. (1999) 'Resources, agency, achievements: reflections on the measurement of women's empowerment', *Development and Change*, 30: 435–64

Kent, A. (2004) 'Living life on the edge: examining space and sexualities within a township high school in greater Durban in the context of the HIV epidemic', *Transformation*, 54

Kenway, J. *et al.* (1998) 'The education market: the view from the school', *The Primary School in Changing Times*, London: Routledge

Kenway, J. and A. Kraack (2002) 'Place, Time And Stigmatised Youthful Identities: Bad Boys In Paradise', Special Issue of *Rural Sociology on Rural Youth* www.unisa.edu.au/cslplc/publications/preprint_Kenway2 (accessed 24/06/03)

Khandekar, S. (2004) 'Women's movement' in A. Robinson Pant (ed.) *Women, Literacy and Development*, London: Routledge

King, E.M. and M.A. Hill (1993) (eds.) *Women's Education in Developing Countries: Barriers, Benefits and Policies*, Washington: World Bank

Klasen, S. (1999) 'Does Gender Inequality Reduce Growth and Development? Evidence from Cross-Country Regressions', Policy Research Report on Gender and Development Working Paper No. 7, Washington DC: World Bank

Kolawole, M.E.M. (1997) *Womanism and African Consciousness*, New Jersey: Trentham Books

Kutnick, P., V. Jules and A. Layne (1997) *Gender and School Achievement in the Caribbean*, London: Department for International Development (Education Research Serial No. 21)

Leach, F. *et al.* (2003) *An Investigative Study of the Abuse of Girls in African Schools*, London: DFID

Lees, S. (1993) *Sugar and Spice: Sexuality and Adolescent Girls*, London: Penguin

Leonard, D. (2001) *A Woman's Guide to Doctoral Studies*, Buckingham: Open University Press

Longwe, S. (1997) 'The evaporation of gender policies in the patriarchal cooking pot', *Development in Practice* 7/2: 148–56

Mannathoko, C. (1999) 'Theoretical perspectives on gender in education: the case of Eastern and Southern Africa', *International Review of Education*, 45 (5/6): 445–60

Marchand, M. and J. Parpart (1995) (eds.) *Feminism, Postmodernism, Development* London: Routledge

Mirembe, R. and L. Davies (2001) 'Is schooling a risk? Gender, power relations and school culture in Uganda', *Gender and Education* 13/4: 401–16

Molyneux, M. (1998) 'Analysing women's movements' in Jackson and Pearson (eds.) 1998

Moller Okin, S. (1999) (ed.) *Is Multiculturalism Bad for Women?*, Princeton: Princeton University Press

Mohanty, C. (1988) 'Under Western eyes: feminist scholarship and colonial discourse', *Feminist Review*, 30

Morley, L. (1999) *Organising Feminisms*, London: St Martin's Press

Moser, C. (1993) *Gender Planning and Development*, London: Routledge

Narayan, U. (1997) *Dislocating Cultures. Third world feminism and the politics of knowledge*, New York: Routledge

Nussbaum, M. (2000) *Women and Human Development*, Cambridge: Cambridge University Press

Nussbaum, M. (2004) 'Women's education: a global challenge', *Signs* 29: 325–55

Obura, A.(1991) *Changing Images: The portrayal of girls and women in Kenyan textbooks*, Nairobi: African Centre for technology Studies

Oda, Y. (2000) 'Gender and policy in public education of the Philippines', *Journal of International Co-operation in Education* 3/2: 157–71 (in Japanese)

Paechter, C. (2000) *Changing School Subjects. Power, Gender and Curriculum*, Buckingham: Open University Press

Pattman, R. (2004) 'Resources for Gender Equality and Education in the Context of HIV', paper presented at Beyond Access Seminar 3, Oxford, UK, April 2004

Pattman, R. and F. Chege (2003) *Finding our Voices: Gendered and Sexual Identities and HIV/AIDS in Education*, Nairobi: UNICEF

Rai, S. (2001) *Gender and the Political Economy of Development*, Cambridge: Polity Press

Randall, V. and G. Waylen (1998) (eds.) *Gender, Politics and the State*, London: Routledge

Razavi, S. and C. Miller (1995) *From WID to GAD. Conceptual Shift in the Women and Development Discourse*, Geneva: United Nations Research Institute for Social Development

Rowlands, J. (1997) *Questioning Empowerment. Working with women in Honduras*, Oxford: Oxfam GB

Saito, M. (2003) 'Amartya Sen's capability approach to education: A critical exploration', *Journal of Philosophy of Education*, 37/1: 17–33

Sato, Y. (1997) 'Development assistance in poverty and WID: experience of Japan', *International Cooperation Study* 13/2: 9–24

Schalkwyk, J. (1998) *Capacity Building for Gender Mainstreaming: UNDP's Experience*, Gender in Development Programme (GIDP), UNDP

Sen, A. (1999) *Development as Freedom*, Oxford: Oxford University Press

Spivak, G. (1999) *A Critique of Postcolonial Reason*, London: Harvard University Press

Stambach, A. (2000) *Lessons from Mount Kilimanjaro*, New York: Routledge

Stewart, F. (2004) 'Groups and Capabilities', paper presented to 4th Capability Approach Conference, Pavia

Stromquist, N. (1995) 'Romancing the State: gender and power in education', *Comparative Education Review*, 39/ 4: 423–54

Stromquist, N.P. (1997) *Literacy for Citizenship. Gender and Grassroots Dynamics in Brazil*, New York: State University of New York Press

Stromquist, N. (2000) 'Voice, harmony and fugue in global feminism', *Gender and Education,* 12/ 4: 419–34

Subbarao, K. and L. Raney (1995) 'Social gains from female education', *Economic Development and Cultural Change* 44/1: 105–28

Subrahmanian, R. (2005) 'Education exclusion and the development state', in R. Chopra and P. Jeffrey (eds.) *Education Regimes in Contemporary India*, Delhi: Sage

Swainson, N. (2000) 'Knowledge and power: the design and implementation of gender policies in education in Malawi, Tanzania and Zimbabwe', *International Journal of Educational Development* 20/1: 49–64

Tuhiwai Smith, L. (1999) *Decolonizing Methodologies: Research and indigenous peoples*, London: Zed Books

UNDP (2002) *Gender Mainstreaming. Learning and Development Pack*, New York: UNDP (on line at www.sdnp.undp.org/gender/, accessed October 2003)

UNESCO (2003) 'Global Monitoring Report', Paris: UNESCO

UNICEF (2003) *Gender Mainstreaming Kit*, available online at www.un.org/womenwatch/ianwge/gm_facts/ (accessed 18 March 2005)

Unterhalter, E. (2000) 'Transnational visions of the 1990s: contrasting views of women, education and citizenship' in M. Arnot and J. Dillabough (eds.) *Challenging Democracy. International perspectives on gender, education and citizenship*, London: Routledge

Unterhalter, E. (2003a) 'Gender, education and development: competing perspectives' in L.M. Lazaro Lorente and M.J. Martinez Usarralde (eds.) *Studies in Comparative Education. Estudios de Educacion Comparada*, Valencia: Martin Impresores

Unterhalter, E. (2003b) 'The capabilities approach and gendered education: an examination of South African complexities', *Theory and Research in Education* 1/1: 7–22

Unterhalter E. (2005a) 'Gender equality and education in South Africa: Measurements, sources and strategies' in L. Chisholm and J. September (eds.) *Gender Equity in South African Education 1994–2004*, Cape Town: HSRC Press

Unterhalter, E. (2005b) 'Global inequality, capabilities, social justice: the millennium development goal for gender equity in education', *International Journal of Education and Development*, 26: 111–22

Unterhalter, E. and S. Dutt (2001) 'Gender, education and women's power: Indian state and civil society intersections in DPEP (District Primary Education programme) and Mahila Samakhya', *Compare* 31/1: 57–73

Vavrus, F. (2003) *Desire and Decline: Schooling and Crisis in Tanzania*, New York: Peter Lang

Walker, M. (2004) 'Girls' Lives and Capabilities', paper presented at the 4th Capability Approach Conference, Pavia

Walkerdine, V., H. Lucey and J. Melody (2000) *Growing up for Gender and Class in the 21st Century*, Basingstoke: Macmillan

Weiner, G. (1994) 'Feminisms and education', in *Feminism and Education*, Buckingham: Open University Press

World Bank (1995) *Priorities and Strategies in Education*, Washington DC: World Bank

World Bank (2001) *Engendering Development. Through gender equality in rights, resources and voice*, New York: Oxford University Press

Young, I.. (2000) *Inclusion and Democracy*, Oxford: Oxford University Press

Yuval-Davis, N. (1994) 'Women, ethnicity and empowerment', *Feminism and Psychology*, special issue: 'Shifting Identities Shifting Racisms', Vol. 4/1: 179–98

2 Ensuring a fair chance for girls

Global Campaign for Education

This chapter is based on a report by the Global Campaign for Education, entitled 'A Fair Chance: Attaining Gender Equality in Basic Education by 2005' (GCE 2003). The report drew on secondary research conducted in nine countries: Bangladesh, Cambodia, Ethiopia, India, Malawi, Mali, Nepal, Nigeria, and Pakistan. Using evidence from case studies and the wider literature, the first section of this chapter considers the causes of gender inequality in basic education, and more specifically the additional barriers that girls face when enrolling in school and attending classes. The second section investigates what has been done to close the gender gap. It cites four main success factors for eliminating gender inequalities, and analyses the interventions within integrated strategies that have been particularly effective. The third and concluding section considers what needs to be done now to make gender equality in education a reality.

The success stories from our case-study countries have several factors in common. In particular, they have discarded a project-by-project approach in favour of comprehensive plans to tackle all of the main factors that keep girls out of school. The success of their ambitious approaches has been guaranteed by high-level political support; organised backing from powerful women and other gender advocates and civil-society organisations within the country in question; the participation of key education stakeholders, including teachers and communities; realistic resource allocations; and, in the case of most low-income countries, sustained and co-ordinated donor support. In several of our case-study countries, political commitment to girls' education was closely linked to wider struggles to empower women and overcome gender injustice. Moreover, programmes specifically aimed at increasing the enrolment of girls have been most effective when they are accompanied by a nationwide effort to expand access for all children, for example by removing school fees, constructing more schools, and hiring more teachers. As long as education opportunities are costly or in short supply, access will continue to be 'rationed', with those who are wealthy, urban, and male at the front of a very long queue.

Why do fewer girls than boys go to school?

Girls face many barriers in their attempts to gain an education. In most developing countries, the economic benefits that families will receive are usually much lower than the social returns, and considerably lower than the returns from boys' education. The precise causes and consequences of gender inequality in basic education vary from country to country, but there is a common set of constraints that must be tackled. The most important are endemic poverty; the unaffordable costs of schooling; the burden of household labour; shortage of school facilities, especially in rural areas; negative and even dangerous school environments; cultural and social practices that discriminate against girls, including early marriage and restrictions on female mobility; and limited employment opportunities for women. Even when girls do manage to gain access to school, their self-confidence is not reinforced by the content of the curriculum, which tends to perpetuate gender stereotypes. Girls are trapped in a vicious circle. Because they face such difficulties at school, many of them struggle to complete their education and to pass key national examinations. As a result, their parents are less inclined to invest heavily in their education. The story of Kanchi from Nepal (see Box 1) illustrates how endemic poverty is preventing girls from realising their full potential at school.

Son preference

Cultural and social beliefs, attitudes, and practices prevent girls from benefiting from educational opportunities to the same extent as boys. There is often a powerful economic and social rationale for investing in the education of sons rather than daughters. In most countries, both the public and private sectors continue to be dominated by men. Consequently, the chances of a young woman, especially from a poor rural background, finding a 'good job' remain extremely limited. In Ethiopia, for example, only 18 per cent of senior officials and managers, and 25 per cent of technical and associated professionals, are women (Rugh 2000). In Mali, parents commonly regard girls' education as a 'lost investment', because it is the future husband's family who reap the returns, not the girl's own family.

However, it is important to emphasise that parental decision making with regard to schooling is complicated and multidimensional. Parents' preferences often change quickly when the direct and indirect costs of educating girls fall significantly. Recent surveys in the highly conservative Pakistani provinces of North West Frontier and Baluchistan, where until recently more than 40 per cent of villages had no government-funded schools that were open to girls (Rugh 2000: 15), show that the same parents increasingly aspire for both sons and

---

Box 1: Kanchi's story

Kanchi is eight years old. She lives with her family in a village in south-east Nepal. They belong to the community of *mushars* ('the mice eaters'). Her family is considered 'untouchable'. They live as landless squatters on government-owned land, or on the edge of the landlord's farm. Her father and mother are agricultural labourers. They survive on the grain that they receive as compensation for their work of harvesting and winnowing.

Children start working from an early age: as soon as they are able to walk, they are assigned duties. The younger ones either work as domestic servants or they help with carrying firewood, herding the goats and cattle, and taking the midday meal to their parents in the field.

There are nine people in Kanchi's family. She started school with the help of a local NGO, but she stopped attending because her parents could not afford the school books that she needed. The costs of the books are reimbursable, but her parents do not know this. Her community faces another problem in educating its children: most are not citizens and therefore do not have birth certificates, which are required in order to enrol in school. The upper castes and local landlords who control the government bureaucracy are opposed to their obtaining citizenship, because they fear that this will enable them to buy land and free themselves from their abject status as bonded labourers.

Kanchi says: *'My father has been trying to find the money to buy my schoolbooks'.* But her parents are more determined to send their second son to school. When asked how she will manage to find the money for his education, Kanchi's mother says, *'I will try all means. After all, he is a son.'*

Another daughter in the family also no longer attends school, because she must stay at home to cook, clean, and look after the younger ones while their mother is away at work. The eldest sister is married. At the age of 18, she has a son, aged two and a half. She encourages Kanchi to study, and wishes that she too had had the chance.

(Source: GCE 2003)

---

daughters to become doctors, civil servants, teachers, and business people. Parents' attitudes also change fast when the private returns to girls' education increase. However, most developing countries made only limited progress in expanding female employment opportunities during the 1990s. Given the very direct link between education and obtaining a good job, this has been a major disincentive for parents to educate girls.

Early marriage

The low value attached to girls' education reinforces early marriage, and vice versa. In the late 1990s, the median age of marriage was 17.1 in Malawi; 16.1 in Mali; 16.5 in Nepal; 17.2 in Nigeria; and 15.6 in Ethiopia (Demographic and Health Surveys, various). In Nepal, 40 per cent of girls are married by the age of 15. Too often, marriage is seen as a higher priority than education. In Mali, for example, parents' unwavering expectations of marriage for their daughters are combined with cultural traditions that dictate that the woman enters into her husband's family upon marriage and, is in many ways, 'lost' to her parental family (GCE 2003).

However, marriage does not always work against girls' education. For example, where a girl's family receives dowry, there are incentives to educate daughters. In Muslim countries such as Bangladesh, being educated can help to secure a husband from a higher social class. In the Punjab and Pakistan, however, the necessity to give dowry impedes education, because many families have to choose between saving money for their daughters' dowry and saving it to pay for their education.

In some African countries, girls are withdrawn from school in order to participate in circumcision ceremonies in preparation for marriage. Many parents also withdraw their daughters from school because local and national authorities are failing to protect them from sexual abuse, creating a very real fear of their becoming pregnant or contracting HIV. A significant proportion of female drop-out in the higher grades of secondary school is due to pregnancy in many countries, especially in East and Southern Africa.

School is too expensive

The direct costs of sending all children to school are usually too high for poor parents. While primary-school tuition fees have now been abolished in many countries, nearly all developing countries still require parents to pay charges of various kinds; in many cases, these charges are far higher than the tuition fees. They include charges for books, stationery, exam fees, uniforms, contributions to 'building funds', levies imposed by the school management committees, informal 'tips' to teachers, and travel costs.

In Tanzania, before the removal of school fees, it cost about half of the annual income of poor rural families to send one child to primary school for one year (Penrose 1998: 104; Watkins 2000: 178). Secondary-school tuition fees alone cost the equivalent of three months' minimum wage (Tomasevski 2003). Parents in 234 villages in rural India cited 'unaffordability' as the single most important factor keeping children out of school (PROBE 2000).

Girls have too much to do at home

'Needed at home' and/or 'need to earn money' are major reasons why poor girls drop out of school in most countries. 'Opportunity costs' refer to labour time lost to the parent when the child goes to school. These opportunity costs are usually much higher for girls than for boys, since girls are expected to do more domestic work than boys. For example, poor girls in rural India are expected to clean the house, wash clothes and utensils, and collect water before school; and collect firewood, cook the evening meal, look after siblings, feed cattle, and fetch water after school. Ethiopian girls of primary age work for 14–16 hours a day (Watkins 2000: 191). A study in Egypt showed that boys do only 15 per cent of the chores (Rugh 2000: 31).

In the case-study countries, there are very few Centres for Early Childhood Development to relieve older sisters of their child-care obligations. In the context of HIV/AIDS in high-prevalence countries in Africa, the burden of work at home for girls is particularly acute, because they are increasingly required to stay at home to nurse sick relatives, look after siblings, and do domestic tasks normally done by adults. In addition to their domestic chores at home, girls are expected to do work around the school and in the fields, which leaves them very little time to study and complete homework. In Nepal, girls contribute at least 50 per cent more labour than boys.

Government schools are too few and too far

In Mali, the average distance to school exceeds 7 km in rural regions; in the capital region, the average distance is less than 1 km (Watkins 2000: 193–4). Ministry of Education planners do not always take girls' enrolment targets into consideration when determining how many schools should be built. The need to travel long distances to school is a particular barrier for girls, especially (but not only) in countries where a cultural premium is placed on female seclusion. For reasons of safety and security, most parents are reluctant to let their daughters walk long distances to school. In Egypt, another study found that girls' enrolment dropped off sharply when schools were located more than 1.5 km away, while in Pakistan the threshold was 1 km (Rugh 2000: 31).

In parts of sub-Saharan Africa and South Asia, the compelling shortage of secondary-school places has fuelled the expansion of private schools. In many countries, particularly in South Asia, the burgeoning private sector has attracted mainly male students. In some countries (including India and Nepal), the expansion of private secondary schools has resulted in expanded enrolments of girls in government secondary schools. Although the private sector is relieving governments of the burden of providing secondary-education facilities, there is clearly a danger that the rapid expansion of private education is creating a two-tiered system which entrenches inequalities based on social class, caste, and gender.

Schools fail to protect the basic rights and dignity of girls

Schools in most countries are not girl-friendly, and girls often suffer sexual harassment, bullying, and other forms of intimidation, sometimes even rape. These abuses often meet with silence and inaction on the part of local and national authorities.

Failure to provide adequate physical facilities, such as toilets and running water, is an inconvenience for boys, but a disaster for girls. During menstruation, most girls will not attend school if there are no toilet facilities. Also, sexual harassment may occur unless separate toilets for girls and boys are provided. If toilets are provided, they are often poorly serviced and maintained.

Teachers frequently pay more attention in class to boys than girls. A study in Nigeria showed that while positive interactions between teacher and student were almost equally divided between boys and girls in the early years of schooling, by the sixth grade teachers were significantly more positive towards boys than towards girls, spending more time on the former (Rugh 2000: 57). This tends to perpetuate the already low self-esteem of many young girls.

In some countries, including large parts of India, gender segregation persists in the classroom. Teachers routinely use biased language which reinforces distinctions of class, caste, and gender. Children from poor and lower-caste backgrounds are particularly discriminated against and are sometimes subject to beatings and forms of verbal abuse (Subrahmaniam 2003; Ramachandran 2003). They are not helped by the fact that most teachers in India belong to upper castes.

Schools fail to motivate or encourage girls

It is widely believed that the limited number of female teachers in both primary and secondary schools is a major constraint on girls' education. The presence of female teachers tends to make schools more girl-friendly and provide role models for girls.

Most countries in our study had long-established quotas for the recruitment of women teachers, yet none had managed to fill these quotas, primarily because governments have failed to develop effective incentives to encourage female teachers to work in rural areas. Teacher deployment in some countries is so blatantly corrupt that it is impossible for rational and objective staffing practices to be adopted. Access for young women to teacher-training colleges is still severely limited.

Across the developing world, typically less than one-quarter of primary-school teachers are women. In rural and remote areas, there are usually even fewer female teachers. In Nepal, nearly 66 per cent of primary-school teachers in Kathmandu are women, but only 15 per cent in the Far West Region. The number of female teachers in the upper primary grades is also much lower than that of males. This reflects the failure of girls to progress through secondary school to obtain teaching qualifications.

Considerable progress has been made in designing more gender-sensitive curricula. However, the use of textbooks with stereotypical images of women and men is still common in many countries. Women are consistently depicted solely as mothers and housewives, while men are portrayed in adventurous and decisive roles such as property owners. Seven out of our nine case-study countries now have gender-sensitive curricula at primary level. But the challenge is not merely to transform the content of the curriculum, but also to improve teacher training so that teachers are adequately equipped to deliver it.

NGOs have powerfully demonstrated and advocated the need for education that enhances children's capacity and self-confidence to address real-life challenges. For girls, knowledge and self-confidence in sexual and reproductive-health matters can be transformative; in the context of the AIDS epidemic, it has become an issue of life or death. But promoting awareness of students' rights as citizens and as women is equally important. Most fundamentally, as captured by the South Asian concept of 'joyful learning', education perhaps does most to empower girls when it affords children the confidence to express themselves as individuals.

The long list of constraints that result in sizeable gender gaps in many countries looks formidable. However, a number of countries, including Bangladesh and Malawi, have made remarkable progress during the past decade or so towards increasing girls' enrolments in both primary and secondary school and dramatically reducing, and indeed eliminating altogether, the gender gap in enrolments and achievements. The next section explores how they have done so.

What has been done to close the gender gap?

Our research suggests that the countries that have made the greatest progress in eliminating gender inequalities have four main things in common.

- First and most important, there has been strong political commitment to supporting women in both development and education.

- Related to this, policy development has been informed and influenced by the demands of strong women's networks, and other key stakeholders such as teachers and parents.

- Third, alongside overarching efforts to provide free and universal access for all groups, comprehensive strategies have been implemented which specifically tackle the key causes of gender inequality in education. Each strategy comprises a package of inter-related measures, rather than isolated and *ad hoc* interventions.

- And finally, both governments and donors have been willing to allocate the resources necessary to sustain implementation.

Taking women and education seriously

Eliminating gender inequality in education will not work unless it is part of a much broader nationwide mobilisation with ambitious goals to ensure that women fully and equally participate in all aspects of economic, social, and political development. This creates an enabling environment for Ministries of Education and education NGOs to work together to achieve gender equality in education. Effective 'gender and development' strategies include active labour-market policies that promote skills and tackle pervasive discriminatory practices in the workplace; reform of patriarchal inheritance laws; tackling violence against women; greater political involvement of women at both national and local levels; and raising the legal age of marriage. Supporting the economic empowerment of women through small-enterprise and micro-enterprise development, especially through the provision of credit, is also critically important. In other words, a 'package deal' is required: one which covers all aspects of gender inequality and not merely the denial of educational opportunities.

Signing up to international agreements such as those reached in Jomtien and Dakar is of course important, but it is the manner in which governments, working with civil society, translate these well-intentioned goals into action that is most critical. Until gender equity becomes a visible and popular cause, governments and elites are likely to continue neglecting it.

Indigenous struggles for democratisation have been very important in empowering women and ensuring that gender is increasingly mainstreamed in all key areas of policy. Veteran Nepali activist Shahana Pradhan describes the deep links between the democracy movement and the girls' education movement in Nepal:

> *I came into politics, not because I was interested in politics, but as a young girl I wanted to be educated and attend school along with my brothers… We joined the first political rally against the Ranas [the monarchs]. We were immediately arrested, and upon inquiry our strong and assertive demand was a school for girls … By 1947, the Nepal Mahila Singh [Nepal Women's Association] had been*

formed by a very large number of women, with the major objective of bringing about social and political changes through education. Therefore, 'Education for Women' was its initial objective. By 1949, there was an [increasing] sense of responsibility among parents about sending girls to school. There was a mushroom growth of schools after democracy was established in 1951.
(Belbase 1998: 187)[1]

Mainstreaming gender within EFA strategies

To achieve gender parity, education-sector plans must respond to poor people's needs, and they must include a comprehensive attack on all forms of educational inequality – recognising that girls typically face more than one source of disadvantage (gender, class, caste, ethnicity, physical disability, etc.). It is also important to develop locally appropriate strategies to overcome the multiple economic, cultural, and social barriers that keep girls out of schools (see Box 2).

In practice, this has happened in relatively few countries. Most EFA programmes have focused on easing general constraints on access, but without planning specific steps to ensure that girls benefit equally from the new opportunities created (falsely assuming that gender inequalities would be automatically redressed by the expansion of free primary education). Or they have focused on separate girls' programmes without doing anything to address the overwhelming constraints on access – such as high costs and shortages of schools and teachers – that place all disadvantaged groups, especially poor, rural girls, at a permanent disadvantage. Another problem is that politicians have found it easy to dismiss 'gender' as a foreign concept, partly because women's groups, NGOs, and other civil-society members who could act as champions for girls' education have been excluded from policy dialogue between governments and donors. In Pakistan and Nigeria, it has been a long struggle to get politicians and policy makers to mainstream gender in major donor-supported education projects. A key factor behind recent progress has been the co-option of gender advocates from the NGO sector into influential policy-making positions in government, bringing with them not only their own commitment but also their capacity to reach out to, and mobilise, wider civil-society networks. Clearly there is no universal solution, because these constraints vary so much from one country to another. However, a balanced package addressing *all* aspects of gender inequalities in education is essential.

Priority measures for integrated strategies

Governments and NGOs have adopted a range of policies, programmes, and projects in order to improve girls' education. Comparative analysis suggests that within an integrated strategy, the following interventions have been especially

---

Box 2: Getting girls into school the BRAC way

The approach of the Bangladesh Rural Advancement Committee (BRAC) to non-formal primary education has been instrumental in proving that gender and poverty are not necessarily impediments to education. An innovative approach to curriculum design and school management encourages attendance by poor children, and by poor girls in particular, who are typically excluded by the formal system. Crucially, BRAC has succeeded in channelling poor children into the mainstream, by qualifying them to enter the formal system on graduation. The success of the approach lies in the way in which it has evolved to respond to poor people's needs, while tackling sensitive problems of gender relations with locally appropriate strategies. Not only are BRAC schools thus attractive to children and parents, they are also accessible in terms of the direct costs and opportunity costs to parents of sending their children to school.

BRAC's success in widening educational access for poor students, and poor girls in particular, can be attributed to the responsiveness and flexibility of the approach. From the outset, the programme has evolved to be relevant to the needs and interests of the community. Parents must request a school for their village and support the programme by finding a location for it, setting school hours, and attending monthly parent–teacher meetings. A committee of three parents, a local leader, and a teacher has overall responsibility for school management. Teachers are usually women with secondary-school education, recruited from the local community. They receive initial and refresher training, in short but intensive sessions. Local community involvement ensures that parents remain committed to and involved with the school, and that the school remains responsive to the learning needs of its pupils. The curriculum is practical, including issues relating to everyday life, and the fact that school hours are set to allow for other activities helps to minimise the opportunity costs of sending children to school. Unlike in the formal sector, there are no hidden costs for poor families who send their children to BRAC schools.

(Source: Hossain in Subrahmanian 2002)

---

effective: free primary education, increased incentives, more accessible schools, tackling sexual harassment and discrimination against pregnant pupils, developing a network of community schools, introducing bridging programmes to mainstream non-formal education, and promoting early childhood education and care.

Free primary education for all

The whole or partial abolition of primary-school fees has been a central element of recent strategies for Universal Primary Education (UPE) in many countries, including Kenya, Tanzania, The Gambia, Malawi, Ethiopia, Uganda, Bangladesh, Cambodia, India, and Nepal. Removing these fees has signalled government commitment to education as a right, and has helped to release enormous pent-up demand for education, causing massive increases in both girls' and boys' enrolments. In Malawi, for example, the number of primary school pupils soared by 50 per cent, from 1.9 million to 3 million, in just one year. In Bangladesh, total enrolment in primary and basic education rose from nearly 12 million in 1990 to 18 million in 2001.

The very success of free primary education has in turn created new financial and administrative challenges. Ministries face urgent needs to train and employ more teachers and to supply more classrooms and learning materials at primary level, in order to reduce class sizes to reasonable levels: in government primary schools in Bangladesh, class numbers often reach 200. They must simultaneously respond to unprecedented demand for secondary-school places, which remain in severely short supply in most African and South Asian countries. If this problem is not quickly addressed, there is a real risk of recreating inequalities at the next stage of education, and perhaps ultimately undermining demand for primary education.

The 'hidden costs' of sending children to school remain high in most countries. Efforts to regulate or abolish 'unofficial' charges levied by school committees and head teachers have achieved mixed results. In Tanzania, a new block grant to schools was introduced in 2002 to reduce the risk of schools imposing additional charges to compensate for lost income from official fees. However, ensuring that these grants actually reach the schools is difficult.

All of these challenges reinforce the need for donors to deliver a better-coordinated and more generous response when governments take the fundamental step of abolishing fees. Otherwise, it is very difficult to see how the education MDGs can be attained.

Parental incentives to educate girls

Incentive schemes have been introduced in many countries to reduce the overall costs of primary and secondary schooling for girls. Incentives are both in cash and in kind.

Primary-school stipends: Small stipends have been offered to needy girls in many countries to support their primary schooling. In Nepal, for example, nearly 40,000 poor girls have received small scholarships (Rupees 250 per annum) in order to support their primary schooling. The impact of this programme has been significant in terms of increasing girls' intake and retention, and reducing their drop-out rates.

Improved nutrition: Feeding programmes are also increasingly common. One of the main problems facing the drought-stricken countries of sub-Saharan Africa has been the inability of children to attend school on account of hunger.

Even if they do attend, they have limited concentration. In Malawi, the World Food Programme introduced a pilot feeding programme for primary-school children in 2000. Initially, only the 'most needy' children were targeted, but in response to the overwhelming levels of poverty, it was decided to provide free meals for all children. This illustrates the difficulty of targeting by 'need' or 'gender' in a situation of general deprivation. In-school feeding programmes (at pre-school and primary schools) in Central and Southern Africa have also become an important means of supporting children affected by HIV/AIDS. The provision of free school meals has a major impact on school attendance. Under the Food for Education programme for primary-school children from poor families in Bangladesh, parents have to guarantee 75 per cent attendance of their supported children and a minimum of 40 per cent marks in the end-of-year examinations, in return for food. In mid-2002, this scheme was converted into a cash grant. Both boys and girls benefit. The impact of the programme on schooling attendance has been very positive.

Secondary-school scholarships: A major challenge facing countries that have achieved UPE is to respond to the demand created by the increased numbers of those who do manage to complete primary school. In most countries, only children from better-off families are able to afford secondary school and, without financial incentives for poorer children, this will continue to be the case. Although girls' enrolments at primary level have improved, they are often less likely than boys to complete primary school and move on to secondary school. The same applies to the transition from secondary to tertiary education.

Ensuring girls' safety and dignity at school

> *While societal and family issues are important, the presence of a vibrant and happy school in the neighbourhood can dramatically change the way communities view education for their children.*
> (GCE 2003)

The low quality of basic education has been recognised as a fundamental constraint on attempts to expand girls' education in virtually every country. From a gender-equality perspective, quality means creating a functioning and positive school environment in which girls can learn. We have reviewed a number of interventions that have attempted, with very limited success, to make schools 'girl-friendly', reduce female drop-out, and improve girls' learning attainment. Given the immensity of the task and the difficulty of making an impact, we recommend that governments start with the basics: by eliminating the sexual intimidation and harassment of girl pupils, and providing basic facilities for their safety and dignity. Unless and until these prerequisites are in place, more ambitious targets for improving quality are unlikely to be achieved. Governments that are serious about getting girls into school must prioritise the provision of toilets and running water above other infrastructural improvements.

Dealing with sexual harassment and intimidation of girl pupils is an uphill struggle in most countries, because it means challenging deeply entrenched male attitudes towards female sexuality; but, by the same token, it is very difficult to see how schools can ever become 'girl-friendly' as long as such attitudes and practices are allowed to persist.

Box 3: Challenging sexual harassment

A primary school in Addis Ababa, the capital of Ethiopia, has more than 1000 pupils. Harassment of female students, child labour, abduction, and rape are some of the harmful practices in the school. Solutions to these problems have been proposed by the school's Girls' Club. Teachers, NGOs, community members, students, and the police force are also involved in challenging harassment. Teachers give lectures on some of the harmful practices, both to other staff members and to the students.

Female teachers provide sex education and discuss the problems that arise for girls and women. In one incident, a girl in Grade 3 had stopped attending school. The fact was reported to the Girls' Club. The members followed it up and found that the girl had been raped at the school by an 18-year-old student in Grade 4. The girl was brought back to school, and the boy was taken into police custody the same day. The girl's father was contacted and brought in for discussions with the Director.

In another incident, a girl was forced to marry against her will. The Girls' Club intervened and succeeded in getting a divorce for her. The girl was able to resume her studies. Another girl was forced to quit school because of repeated harassment. After a year's absence, she was approached by teachers and club members, who persuaded her to continue her lessons. Girls are encouraged to participate in all extra-curricular activities, including sports. The Family Planning Club provides sex education, especially for girls who are older but are still in lower grades.

(Source: GCE 2003)

In many countries, girls who get pregnant, often as a result of unwanted encounters with teachers or male pupils, are penalised by being forced to drop out of school (while the baby's father seldom faces any kind of sanction). Pregnant girls are reportedly expelled from school in Liberia, Mali, Nigeria, Swaziland, Tanzania, Togo, Uganda and Zambia, while the rules have been changed in Bolivia, Botswana, Chile, Côte d'Ivoire, Guinea, Kenya, and Malawi (Tomasevski 2003: 165). However, even where laws and regulations have been enacted to guarantee young mothers the right to continue their education, it is equally important that school management provides a sympathetic and constructive environment in which girls can return after giving birth. Botswana has found it necessary to deal with many obstacles in order to encourage girls to return, including relaxing age limits and procedures for re-admission (FAWE 2000, quoted in Tomasevski 2003).

Community schools

The emergence of various kinds of community school has had a major impact on efforts to redress gender inequalities in education in a growing number of countries. Community schools have been developed in different shapes and forms, mainly in South Asia and Africa over the past two decades. They differ from government schools in that they are mainly funded by contributions and are managed by the local community. They also tend to be located in the more remote areas, where populations have had little contact with 'modern' schooling (Hyde 2003).

The success of the BRAC model (see Box 2) has inspired the development of similar community schools in a growing number of countries elsewhere in Asia, and also in Africa. For example, UNICEF has supported the development of community schools in Uganda, Guinea, Zambia, and Egypt. The government provides classrooms and pays the salaries of teachers, while UNICEF trains the facilitators. Schooling is free of charge, and children are not required to wear uniforms. The project has had high levels of school attendance and low rates of drop-out, while student performance is generally better than in State primary schools. Evaluations show that, despite often very different country contexts, learning outcomes of community schools are frequently better, and certainly no worse, than in government schools. Furthermore, relationships between teachers, students, and communities appear to be good, and these schools provide opportunities for basic education for children who might otherwise have had none at all.

However, a number of common problems have also been identified: community schools tend to be introduced in poor areas with low access to schooling, lacking transport and communication; the community is compelled to provide significant (and often onerous) support for the construction and management of the schools and payment of the teachers. The teachers/instructors are often less qualified, and/or paid less, than teachers in government schools. Sponsors of community schools have attempted to use age, and geography, as criteria to restrict access to the schools (in order to maintain small class sizes), whereas the communities often want a more inclusive approach.

Para-teachers

In India, as in several francophone African countries, the present expansion of government schools is being made possible by the employment of 'para-teachers', who come from the local communities, are paid less, enjoy fewer benefits or career-development opportunities, and have less training and lower qualifications than professional teachers in State schools. This presents a dilemma for government policy, because the use of such teachers does enable schools to function, but at the risk of developing a 'second tier' of education. Systematic evaluation is needed to ascertain the impact of these schemes on quality and equity.

Bridging (accelerated) programmes

The main aim of bridging, or accelerated, programmes has been to get children back into school. They share some of the characteristics of community schools, but tend to be more remedial in their approach.

Box 4: Mahila Shikshan Vihar, Jalore

Situated in the Jodhpur District of Rajasthan, the Mahila Shikshan Vihar (MSV), Jalore, is an institution with a difference. Young women are motivated to take part in a residential, intensive education programme. Most have either dropped out of school or have never attended one. Women are divided into eight groups, consisting of 9–12 students, according to their educational level and pace of learning. Teachers work with the groups, teaching, testing, and preparing them to take the Grade V exam. There is one teacher for every group of 10–12 women, moving along at the pace of the learners. These young women learn at such a fast pace that it leaves the teachers exhausted. They seem to have boundless energy for games, music, theatre, cycling, and even driving the solitary auto-rickshaw parked on the campus. They manage their own cooking, washing, and cleaning, and they maintain the school premises, including the kitchen and the garden. In the evenings and late at night, these bright young women can be seen huddled together, studying, teaching, and learning. Twenty-four hours seem too short. It almost seems as if they were trying to catch up on every minute of their lost childhood – and enjoying every bit of it. The Jalore MSV can leave a visitor feeling dizzy.

(Source: GCE 2003)

The idea of attaching bridging courses to a government school would seem sensible and likely to reinforce the importance of the mainstream. However, such schemes should not be accepted as permanent solutions. The aim should be to get the education system functioning properly, so that the need for such programmes is gradually reduced and eventually eliminated.

Promoting early childhood education and care

Pre-school children benefit greatly from attending Early Childhood Development and Care (ECDC) centres. The benefits include improved socialisation and improved learning. Such facilities also free up older girls to attend class, instead of looking after younger siblings. Community-based pre-schools have been established on a pilot basis in Cambodia, in order to promote girls' enrolment in Grade 1, with excellent results. However, cost considerations have prevented most countries from significantly expanding this type of educational provision. A study of early-learning childhood-development programmes in Kenya concluded that 'in addition to increasing the future productivity of children, low cost ECDC programmes would be likely to produce the twin effects of releasing the mothers' time for market work and allowing older girl siblings to participate in school. ECDC programmes may be seen as optimal investments that affect both the current and future welfare of households with small children' (Lokshin *et al.* 2000: 22).

Involving communities

A lot has been done to raise community awareness of the importance of educating girls. Participatory methods are now commonplace and used by NGOs and governments alike to promote grassroots participation in education. Lok Jumbish (meaning People's Movement) was jointly established by an NGO and the government of Rajasthan in northern India in the early 1990s to respond to very low enrolment of girls, high drop-out rates, teacher absenteeism, and lack of schools close to home. A highly effective and innovative approach has evolved on the basis of widespread participation and experimentation. Huge strides have been made in increasing enrolments and encouraging more girls to stay on at school. UNICEF also has two major awareness-raising programmes. The Meena Initiative in Bangladesh uses a multimedia approach to raise the profile of girls, as well as stressing the importance of education. The Sara initiative in East, Central, and Southern Africa was modelled on 'Meena'. Materials produced are used in both formal and non-formal settings. Both programmes have been supported by bilateral donors. However, although Meena is considered to be a success in the South Asian context, adapting the same set of materials from one cultural environment to another has been problematic.

Involving and nurturing gender advocates

In Malawi, local women's groups played an important role in lobbying for special attention to be given to female education (Swainson 1998: 35). In particular, the organised political power of the League of Malawi Women greatly enhanced the influence of gender advocates within the Ministry of Education and Ministry of Community Services. In addition, the first woman Minister of Education, appointed in 1993, 'played a central role in steering through the pregnancy and school uniform reforms ... she was ideally placed as a gender advocate to introduce what were culturally-sensitive and controversial measures, such as those dealing with schoolgirl pregnancy' (Swainson 1998: 37).

Similar conclusions can be derived from experience in Bangladesh. According to Jahan (1998: 33-4), the government's commitment to girls' education was galvanised in the mid-1990s by a substantially strengthened women's movement, which effectively 'articulated women's demand for equal access to, and control over, all social resources and services'. Their leverage was increased by the actions of international bodies, resulting in commitments to women's education and gender equity that were signed by the government. A recent assessment of three Sector Wide Approaches (SWAPs) to donor aid for education suggests that their success in promoting gender-equity goals could be greatly increased if donors made more active efforts to reach out to, consult, and support indigenous gender networks. Donors should 'work on the assumption that gender equality is an inseparable part of the sustainable development agenda, which already has the support of many key players in education in the partner country; [and] ensure that support to "champions of reform" extends to these "gender champions"' (Norton *et al.* 2000: 15).

Beyond rhetoric: making gender equality in education a reality

Setting clear operational targets

Clear, time-bound targets for the elimination of gender gaps in access and completion must be supported by the commitment of necessary resources and proper management systems. Gender targets should be incorporated into the performance targets, appraisal systems, and career incentives of every education worker, from government ministers down to classroom teachers.

Bilateral and multilateral donors should also translate the education MDGs into clear outcome-targets for their own support for girls' education. While the trend towards comprehensive sector-development plans and budgetary support may make it difficult or impossible to identify how much aid has been committed to 'girls' education' *per se*, donors could set specific targets for the numbers of out-of-school girls whom their aid programmes will have assisted to enter and complete school by 2010.

The size of the challenge

Gender-enrolment parity has already been largely achieved in Latin America, the Caribbean, East Asia, and the Pacific. South and West Asia still pose the greatest challenge, followed by the Middle East, North Africa, and sub-Saharan Africa.

In sub-Saharan Africa, the overall female net enrolment rate will have to almost double from its current level in order to meet the 2015 target. Among the group of French-speaking African countries where gender inequalities are particularly acute, female enrolments will have to increase by more than 200 per cent (assuming zero repetition), compared with around 120 per cent for males. In Southern Africa, on the other hand, female enrolments will have to increase by only six per cent to meet the 2015 target, mainly because of the impact of HIV/AIDS on the school-age population.

What must be done?

Clearly, there is no single formula that can be applied to all countries. The need for diverse and creative national policy responses is underlined in Table 1, which shows the major recommendations made by the local researchers for eight case-study countries in the Fair Chance Report.

Table 1: Recommended initiatives to improve girls' access to education in eight countries

Priority Gender Interventions	Nepal	Cambodia	Malawi	Nigeria
NFE/Bridging for Adolescent Girls		●		
Female Literacy		●	●	
Gender Sensitive Curriculum and Practice	●			●
Integrate Life Skills into Curriculum		●		
Protection Against Sexual Harrassment at School			●	
Support for Children Affected by HIV/Aids and Pregnant School Girls				●
Improve Separate Toilets at School for Girls and Boys			●	
Day Care Facilities	●		●	
Compulsory Education				
Mentoring for Girls				
Incentives (fee subsidies, cash or kind) for Pupils	●			●
Participation in Community/School Management	●			●
Improve and Expand Teacher Training for Women Incentives for Women Teachers		●		

However, there are also certain basic concerns that must be addressed in nearly all countries. In order to achieve the 2005 and 2015 Millennium Development Goals for education, governments and donors must work together as follows.

End the education queue

In Ethiopia, almost two-thirds of rural girls have never been to school. Gender gaps are often greatest in countries where overall net enrolments are low. By failing to provide enough free school places to accommodate all of the boys *and* all of the girls, governments create an education queue in which the poorest and least privileged groups, including girls, are almost certain to come last (Filmer 1999). The following steps are needed to eliminate this queue:

- Build enough schools and hire enough teachers to guarantee that all communities are served by a school within safe walking distance for girls.

- Remove school fees, which guarantee the continuing exclusion of poor rural girls (in Uganda, following the introduction of free primary education, the number of girls enrolled increased from 1.4 million in 1996, to 3 million in 1999).

- Expand 'bridging' schemes developed by NGOs to attract hard-to-reach children into the school system.

- To avoid recreating the queue at secondary level, governments must plan to rapidly extend free and universal access to secondary schools. Currently, only one in five girls in Africa and two in five girls in South and West Asia get the chance to go to secondary school.

Offer extra help for poor families to keep girls in school

Positive action must be taken so that girls – especially those who are poor, lower-caste, and living in remote rural areas – can benefit from educational expansion in equal measure – or greater measure – than boys. In particular, extra assistance, such as a free school meal, or stipends linked to regular attendance, helps poor families to keep daughters in school for longer. It is also an inexpensive and effective way to redistribute resources towards poor communities, since a relatively small up-front investment by governments enables poor girls to acquire a lifelong asset which helps them to escape the poverty trap. Stipends for secondary-school girls have been particularly effective: they not only increase secondary enrolments, but also create strong incentives for girls to enter and complete primary school. In Bangladesh, districts where secondary-school bursaries were introduced experienced a sharp decline in child marriages, as well as soaring girls' enrolments. Governments need to involve communities and civil-society groups in developing incentive packages that are appropriate to local circumstances, and the costs of implementing such programmes in all districts need to be factored into donor and government plans.

Launch a rescue plan for schools in poor communities

> *The problem today is not that parents do not want to send their daughters to school. The tragedy is that they would like to send them, but the absence of a proper functioning school and the poor quality of education comes in the way of realising their aspirations.*
> (India report)

Many schools in poor, rural areas (and urban slums) lack even the basics needed to function. All schools need a trained, motivated teacher who turns up every day to teach, and enough books and desks for all the pupils. Construction of safe and private toilet facilities for girls should be mandatory. Strong sanctions against the sexual abuse and harassment of girl pupils must be enacted and enforced.

A first priority should be improving the status, pay, and support of teachers, especially those who are posted to rural or 'difficult' areas. Long-established quotas for gender parity among rural teachers should be backed up with efforts to extend and improve teacher training facilities in the rural areas as well as the urban areas, with additional incentives and career-development opportunities for female teachers willing to take up posts in the rural areas.

While learning outcomes are unacceptably low in many countries, it is essential that reforms are rooted in the local realities. Experience of the last 20 years shows that attempts to import learner-centred learning methodologies without taking local cultures into account have often been problematic.

Encourage a range of education provision

The scale and urgency of the action necessary to meet the targets of gender parity and gender equality make it essential that NGOs are strongly supported in playing a complementary role in developing sustainable education provision. Sadly, not every country has an NGO of the size and vision of BRAC in Bangladesh, but much more can be done to expand and mainstream the provision by NGOs of basic education, especially for hard-to-reach groups. These schools need to develop clear pathways into and links with the formal system, so that the non-formal sector does not become a ghetto for girls and poor students. Greater flexibility is needed, so that eventual transfer to State schools is facilitated and encouraged. Some of the new, wide-ranging education-sector development plans currently being implemented in many countries do not pay enough attention to this key role of NGOs, nor have NGOs been sufficiently involved in the design and management of these sector plans.

Engage with civil society

Experience shows that a top–down approach to girls' education is not only ineffective, but it may create resistance and resentment that will ultimately be counter-productive – a leading cause of 'implementation failure' in girls' education (Ramachandran 1998). Acting with urgency must not be confused with acting in haste, or used as an excuse for shutting out the participation of parents, teachers, and gender experts in designing reforms.

The participation of communities, teachers, and women's groups in the policy-making process is crucial to developing appropriate, well-informed responses to local complexities, and generating the broad-based support needed to implement them successfully.

Governments and donors must open the door to robust and regular exchange with civil-society groups, instead of the usual one-off 'consultations'; they must also provide timely access to information and support civil-society efforts to build advocacy skills.

Break the glass ceiling

Expanding primary-school opportunities for girls is obviously a first priority for the countries furthest off track for achieving the 2005 goal. But, given the very severe shortages of secondary-school places in most developing countries, a sole focus on attaining UPE may have the unintended effect of turning the primary-school leaving exam into a 'glass ceiling' that few girls are able to break through. To avoid creating a new education queue at secondary level, governments must plan for the rapid extension of free and universal access to secondary schools.

Given the unemployment crisis in most countries, school leavers stand little chance of finding a job in the formal sector, unless they have performed well in their secondary-school leaving examinations. Moreover, many of the health and productivity benefits of educating girls are not fully unlocked until secondary education is attained. This illustrates the importance of balanced investment by donors and governments in increasing girls' access, completion, and achievement at secondary level.

In a large majority of countries, gender inequalities are most severe at universities and other higher-education institutions. It is often forgotten that the gender-parity goal includes equity at tertiary level by 2015. Expanding the output of female graduates from these institutions is essential in order to ensure that women can begin to occupy the full range of professional and managerial jobs, and in doing so, can break down dominant patriarchal views about gender and employment. Increasing the numbers of educated and qualified women can act as a powerful and positive influence on girls.

Counter the impact of HIV/AIDS

The AIDS epidemic has very serious implications for the attainment of gender equality in basic education, especially in sub-Saharan Africa. The three main areas of impact are lower enrolment growth, increased teacher morbidity and mortality, and increased numbers of orphans and other children directly affected by the epidemic. Girls are likely to be particularly badly affected by the impact, because they will be expected to look after sick parents and other family members, and take over some of their household activities. Girl orphans are also thought to be more vulnerable than boys and are, therefore, very likely to drop out of school. Given that AIDS-related mortality is expected to be highest among young female adults, this has far-reaching implications for female teachers and any attempt to increase the number of female teaching staff. It is essential, therefore, that in high-prevalence countries, comprehensive strategies are developed by Ministries of Education with their partners to both prevent and mitigate the impact of the epidemic on students and teachers, particularly females.

Invest more in girls

Countries that have achieved success in girls' schooling are the ones that have dramatically increased their own spending on basic education until it constitutes as much as 20 per cent of their budget, or 3 per cent of their GDP. Yet even at this high level of government commitment, low-income countries will still need substantial help – in the order of US$ 5.6 bn per year in external resources – in order to achieve the education MDGs (UNESCO 2002). However, the total value of bilateral education aid in 2000 was 30 per cent lower in real terms than in 1999. The nine countries in this study alone face a financing gap of about US$ 1bn per year. Until the financing gap is closed, the gender gap cannot be closed.

Aid not only needs to be increased: it needs to be intelligently targeted towards countries that face the greatest numerical and financial challenges in attaining the 2005 and 2015 goals, and whose governments show real and demonstrated commitment to redressing gender inequalities. Sustained, long-term financial aid is required to enable governments to commit external resources to meet salary costs and other recurrent expenditures. If the payment of teachers' salaries relies exclusively on domestic resources, this is likely to be a major constraint on the expansion of basic and secondary education. The impact of increased financing for education for all through the Fast Track Initiative (FTI) will be limited unless it includes funding for programmes to get girls into school.

FTI financing estimates also need urgent revision, to take into account the cost of implementing measures which can help to achieve gender equity – including the removal of fees and charges, the introduction of nation-wide subsidy or incentive schemes for the poorest families, and positive steps to improve conditions for both teachers and students. We know what needs to be done to provide all girls with their right to a basic education, and we know what it will cost. We also know what a high price there is to be paid for failure. We must now mobilise this ambition and all the available resources to implement and achieve what we know to be right.

The Global Campaign for Education, founded in 1999, brings together major NGOs and teachers' unions in more than 150 countries around the world to promote education as a basic human right. The elected GCE Board takes policy decisions and oversees the development of campaign strategy, and a World Assembly meets every two years. It works to mobilise public pressure on governments and the international community to fulfil their promises to provide free, compulsory, public, basic education for all people; in particular for children, women, and all disadvantaged, deprived sections of society.

Note

1   However, the repression of civil society after 1960 impeded the development of the women's movement, and for the next 30 years government action on girls' education was largely restricted to token measures. Since the reinstatement of multi-party democracy in 1990, growing freedom of association has made space for cross-party groups such as the Women's Security Pressure Group (WSPG) to put pressure on the government for policy reforms in all areas relevant to women. Significant progress on girls' enrolment and retention is finally being made.

References

Belbase, L.N. *et al.* (1998) 'The Nepal experience' in V. Ramachandran (ed.) 1998

FAWE (2000) 'Botswana re-entry policy', *FAWE News* 8/3, July–September

Filmer, D. (1999) *The Structure of Social Disparities in Education: Gender and Wealth,* Policy Research Report on Gender and Development, Working Paper No. 5, Washington DC: World Bank

GCE (2003) 'A Fair Chance: attaining gender equality in basic education by 2005', Global Campaign for Education

Hossain, N., R. Subrahmanian, and N. Kabeer (2002) *The Politics of Educational Expansion in Bangladesh,* IDS Working Paper 167, Brighton: Institute of Development Studies

Hyde, K.A.L. (2003) 'Expanding Educational Opportunities at Primary Level: Are Community Schools the Answer?', draft report (processed), Nairobi: sponsored by the Rockefeller Foundation

Jahan, R. 1998. 'The Bangladesh experience', in V. Ramachandran (ed.) 1998

Loskin, M.M., E. Glinskaya, and M. Garcia (2000) 'The Effect of Early Childhood Development Programs on Women's Labour Force Participation and Older Children's Schooling in Kenya', World Bank Development Research Group, Washington, DC: World Bank

Norton A., M. Sibbons, D. Smawfield, and A. Gibbard (2000) 'Mainstreaming Gender through Sector Wide Approaches in Education – Synthesis Report', London: Centre for Aid and Public Expenditure, Overseas Development Institute and Cambridge Education Consultants

Penrose, P. (1998) *Cost Sharing in Education: Public finance, school and household perspectives*, DFID Education Research Serial No. 27, London: Department for International Development

PROBE Team (2000) *Public Report on Basic Education in India*, Delhi: Oxford University Press

Ramachandran, V. (ed.) (1998) *Bridging the Gap between Intention and Action: Girls' and women's education in South Asia*, New Delhi: ASPBAE and UNESCO

Ramachandran, V. (2002) 'Gender and Social Equity in Primary Education: Hierarchies of Access', New Delhi

Rugh, A. (2000) *Starting Now: Strategies for helping girls to complete primary*, SAGE Technical Report No. 1, Washington DC: Academy for Educational Development

Subrahmanian, R. (2002) *Gender and Education: A review of issues for social policy*, UNRISD Social Policy and Development Paper No. 9, Geneva: United Nations Research Institute for Social Development

Subrahmanian, R., Y. Sayed, S. Balagopalan, and C.Soudien (2003) 'Education inclusion and exclusion: Indian and South African perspectives', *IDS Bulletin* 34/1, January

Swainson, N., S. Bendera, R. Gordon, and E.C.Kadzamira (1998) *Promoting Girls' Education in Africa: The design and implementation of policy interventions*, Education Research Serial No. 25, London: Department for International Development

Tomasevski, K. (2003) *Education Denied: Costs and Remedies*, London: Zed

UNESCO (2002) *EFA Global Monitoring Report: Education for All – Is the world on track?* Paris: UNESCO

Watkins, K. (2000) *The Oxfam Education Report*, Oxford: Oxfam GB

3 Measuring gender equality in education[1]

Elaine Unterhalter, Chloe Challender, and Rajee Rajagopalan

Developing an understanding of how to improve gender equality in education is not a simple matter. One of the many challenges that it poses is the nature of the information base. Qualitative work has provided insights into how social relations inside and outside schools shape gender inequalities and can contribute to change; but generally this work is based on small-scale, in-depth research. Qualitative work can deepen knowledge about the nature of gender inequalities, but it cannot provide an overview of their extent, or an indication of where additional resources to address their consequences would best be deployed. For this purpose, quantitative work is needed – but there are major problems with the methods by which gender inequality in education is currently measured. This chapter critically reviews the existing measures of gender equality in education used by international agencies and governments. It goes on to propose alternative forms of measurement which seem to us better able to capture the aspirations of Education For All and the understanding that gender equality requires forms of counting that themselves go beyond mere statistics about access.

Current measures of gender equality in education

The mobilisation of resources for Education For All (EFA) after the Jomtien conference in 1990, and the follow-up meeting at Dakar in 2000, resulted in more punctilious collection of gender-disaggregated data on primary gross enrolment ratios (GER) and net enrolment ratios (NER). **GER** is the number of children enrolled in school, expressed as a proportion of the children of a specific age cohort (say 5–11) who should be enrolled in school. GER can sometimes be more than 100 per cent if there are large numbers of under-age and over-age pupils in school. **NER** is the number of children in the appropriate age group enrolled in school, expressed as a proportion of the official age group required to be in school. GER and NER, even when disaggregated by sex, only give us a picture of the number of children on the school register. They can tell us nothing about whether children attend regularly, once registered; whether they complete grades successfully; or whether passing a grade means that children have acquired knowledge that they can use outside the school context. In addition, because in many countries children's births are not registered, NER is often based on estimations.

Acronyms used in this chapter

EDI	Education Development Index, used in GMR
EFA	Education For All
EMIS	Education Management Information System
GDI	Gender Development Index, used by UNDP
GEEI	Gender Equality in Education Index
GEI	Gender-related EFA index, used in GMR
GER	Gross Enrolment Ratio
GMR	Global Monitoring Report (UNESCO)
HDI	Human Development Index
MDG	Millennium Development Goal
NER	Net Enrolment Ratio

Generally GER and NER data are based on the Education Management Information System (EMIS) of education ministries, and are passed to the UNESCO Institute for Statistics for the compilation of international datasets. EMIS is only as good as the relations of trust, truthfulness, and accuracy that underpin the system. In some contexts local officials do not know the reasons why they collect data for EMIS. They may have difficulties in reaching areas that are socially or geographically distant to collect information; they may believe that underestimating or overestimating children on the school register may bring additional facilities to a locality. Carr Hill *et al.* (1999) emphasise the fragility of the data on which many national and international conclusions are based. When participatory activities are held in villages to identify children who are not at school, more robust data are assembled. However, there are difficulties in translating local mobilising actions into official data on GER and NER, although in some countries this form of micro-planning is used by governments as well as NGOs.

Throughout the 1990s, GER and NER in many countries showed a gap between girls' and boys' levels of enrolment. This gender gap came to be seen as a major source of concern, demonstrating that in many countries fewer girls than boys were enrolled in primary and secondary schools (although it should be noted that there can be gender parity – equal numbers of boys and girls in school – when there is low GER or NER). So great was the concern with reaching gender parity that this became the chief indicator for the Millennium Development Goal 3 on the empowerment of women (Millennium Commission 2000).

Recent developments in measuring gender equality in education

The gender-related EFA index (GEI), developed by UNESCO for use in its Global Monitoring Reports (GMR), is an attempt to indicate the extent to which boys and girls are equally present at different levels in the education system (primary, secondary, and adult education). However, a country can have a GEI of 1, indicating complete equality between boys and girls, but still have low rates of access, retention, and achievement for girls and boys. For example, in 2003 Myanmar had a GEI of 0.949, with only 84 per cent primary NER; and Kuwait had a GEI of 0.966 with a primary NER of 83 per cent (UNESCO 2003: 288-9). Gender parity on its own cannot tell us much about gender equality in relation to accessing education, progressing through school, and living in a gender-equitable society after school.

From the late 1990s, gender-disaggregated data have become available on progression through school (that is, the completion of primary and secondary school), with data often available by district. These data give richer insight than mere enrolment figures can provide on whether or not an education system is delivering gender equity in progression. Generally the statistics show that with the exception of a very few countries – for example, Angola, Benin, Ethiopia, Guinea, and Mozambique – once girls gain access to school, their rate of repetition is less than or the same as that of boys, and so girls in school do as well as boys (UNESCO 2003: 336-43). However, an assessment of research evidence on gender and learning achievement in developing countries found considerable variation between countries. In some countries, girls achieved as well as boys, while in others their learning achievement was at a markedly lower level (UNESCO 2000a).

In GMR, 'gender' is viewed as merely the numbers of boys and girls entering and progressing through a school system. These forms of measurement give no indication of gendered power relations in schooling, which have a marked impact on progression and achievement. This approach to measuring gender equality does not provide information on the ways in which gender equality or inequality link with other dimensions of human flourishing, for example health, access to decision making, the labour market, or income. In fact, these figures can give an impression quite at odds with the literature based on qualitative research

---

Box 1: Case study – Bangladesh

In Bangladesh, which saw a rapid increase in the numbers of girls in school throughout the 1990s, the Campaign for Popular Education (CAMPE) established *Education Watch* in 1999. This initiative, run by civil-society organisations, monitors progress in the quality and availability of primary education.

Data on enrolment were collected household by household from 312 villages in 64 districts. In total, 45,548 households were visited during the survey. In addition, school records were scrutinised for information on completion and attendance (885 schools were assessed). The quality of the educational experience was measured by carrying out individual interviews with more than 3,350 children (11–12 years old) through the Assessment of Basic Competencies Test, independent of the set curriculum. The test assessed the 53 competencies that the Bangladesh government had specified as central to the curriculum. Those children achieving a minimum level of competency in the four separate areas of reading, writing, arithmetic, and life skills/knowledge were classified as having received a 'basic education'. Only 29.6 per cent of pupils who had completed primary school attained all the competencies tested. This figure contrasts sharply with Bangladesh's high enrolment figures. Bangladesh has a gross enrolment ratio of 100.2 per cent – yet CAMPE's findings expose the fact that educational access does not necessarily ensure high quality. This lack of educational quality works to the disadvantage of girls. Boys performed better than girls in CAMPE's assessments of learning achievements. Even in non-formal schools, considered to be relatively gender-sensitive, girls' results were lower than boys'.

(Source: CAMPE 1999)

---

in a country. In South Africa, for example, quantitative data show high levels of gender equality in access and progression, but qualitative data highlight danger at school from sexual harassment and violence, girls' anxiety about their futures, and considerable discrimination against many women teachers (Unterhalter 2005a).

The UNESCO GMR has tried to develop a definition of quality in schools, linking it analytically with equality. Koïchiro Matsuura, Director-General of UNESCO, in his Foreword to the 2005 GMR, commented that 'Quality must pass the test of equity: an education system characterized by discrimination against any particular group is not fulfilling its mission' (UNESCO 2004). However, the 2004 GMR itself pays little attention to gender dimensions of quality and does not suggest what the 'test of equity' might be. The GMR focuses instead on four proxy measures for quality, only one of which has data with a gender dimension. The measures used are pupil/teacher ratios, teachers' qualifications, expenditure on education, and learning achievements. Only this last has been measured with respect to girls and boys. The failure of the GMR to link quality substantively

---

Box 2: Case study – Jordan

The limitations of quantitative measures of gender parity are exemplified by the case of Jordan. Jordan has achieved gender parity at all levels of education – and indeed has a ratio of women to men students of 1.06 at tertiary level – yet women struggle to become economically or politically empowered in adulthood. Women hold only 8 per cent of parliamentary seats. Women's estimated annual earned income is very low: $1896, compared with men's annual earned income of $6118 (UNDP 2004). The ILO estimates that women make up less than one quarter of the labour force in Jordan (ILO 2003–2004). Indicators of women's income and workforce participation in Jordan are among the lowest in the world, despite the fact that their access to education equals that of their male contemporaries. This highlights the limited scope of the gender-parity indicators. The complex reasons behind women's lack of empowerment in Jordan and many other Arab States include patriarchal family structures, restrictive social and gender relations within society, and actual State policies (Khoury and Moghadam 1995). So while on paper girls and boys in Jordan appear to have equal opportunities, in practice it is clear that social, cultural, and economic norms limit the opportunities available to adult women.

---

with equity is a problem of both measurement and analysis. The assumption of the report is that girls and boys enter schools which are unmarked by gender with regard to quality. The gender-neutral ways in which quality has been assessed offer no opportunity to understand the similar or different achievements of children.

In an attempt to bring together information on access, quality, and the gender gap, UNESCO developed the Education Development Index (EDI) from 2003. The EDI constituents and related indicators are as follows:

- **universal primary education:** net enrolment ratio;

- **adult literacy:** literacy rate of the group aged 15 and over;

- **gender:** gender-specific EFA index (GEI, the arithmetical mean of the Gender Parity Indices for the primary and secondary gross enrolment ratios and the adult literacy rate);

- **progression:** survival rate to grade 5.

The problem with the EDI with regard to gender is threefold:

- Its main gender component, the GEI, is concerned with parity, which, as discussed above, gives insufficient insight into context. Men and women, or girls and boys, may have gender parity in literacy or access to schooling but have low levels of participation.

- The EDI does not take account of gender in children's survival in schooling. It primarily considers gender in relation to access and not achievement.

- The EDI weights each of its four components equally. Thus enrolments, and gender parity in enrolments, are weighted equally with achievements. However, research in many countries shows that enrolling children in school is only the first hurdle. Ensuring attendance and completion are much harder tasks, and this is particularly the case for girls, whose progress is constrained by many factors linked to safety, hygiene, nutrition, and family responsibilities (Watkins 2000; Tomasevski 2003). Weighting access as equivalent to achievement underestimates the EFA challenge that confronts governments, but it is particularly serious because of its failure to assess gender-related aspects of school achievement adequately.

Towards an alternative measure

There are three major problems with the existing measures of gender equality and inequality in education. Gender parity and the gender gap are inadequate measures of gender equality, because they do not acknowledge context. Existing measures of quality obscure the gender question. And the EDI fails to take full account of the significance of gender inequality in achievement. These problems have led the Beyond Access project to develop a new measure which expresses more accurately the aspiration for gender equality in education.

The approach has been developed as a contribution to the debate about the need for a publicly accountable criterion of justice in terms of gender equality in education. Thus the approach is offered partly in the hope that it will elicit useful critical discussion. It draws on work undertaken by Amartya Sen and Martha Nussbaum, who distilled a general approach to human flourishing based on capabilities and human rights (Sen 1999; Nussbaum 2000). These ideas have been operationalised in the UNDP's *Human Development Reports*, which have developed the Human Development Index and the Gender Development Index (GDI) (Fukuda Parr and Kumar 2003; UNDP 1995–2004). A number of writers explore capabilities in relation to aspects of education (Alkire 2002; Unterhalter 2003; Unterhalter and Brighouse 2003; Terzi 2004; Walker 2004; Unterhalter 2005b).

A key idea when measuring capabilities (which might be termed *valued doings and beings*) is that they are multi-dimensional. Measuring capabilities entails measuring functionings – that is, what people achieve, for example completing five years at school – and measuring the freedoms or opportunities that people have to achieve them (Sen 1999: 74). Measuring gender equality in education is not only about recording the gender gap in enrolments of girls and boys in school (gender parity), but about measuring some of the other cross-sectoral aspects of gender equality and equity in relation to health, wealth, and decision making which all have a bearing on gender equality in school. A second aspect of capabilities is that, while the concept has particular strengths with regard to other measures of equality – for example, people's expressed desires, or aggregated utility (the greatest good for the greatest number) – the more one needs to draw comparison at a cross-country level, the less fine-grained are the capabilities that can be measured, and the more one has to rely either on measures of resources (like access to school) or on other routinely collected data that can act as some kind of proxy for capabilities (Unterhalter and Brighouse 2003; Unterhalter 2005a).

There are many problems with developing a quantitative measure of gender equality in education. It represents the interrelationship between countries or regions as competitive – creating a culture of winners and losers – when in fact they are deeply interlinked and in need of each other's support. It sets up an arbitrary board of scorers, who usually have little experience of delivery, to judge performance. And it tends to extinguish the processes of working towards achievement. These are compelling reasons not to proceed down this path of analysis, relying either on scorecards or on quantitative measures of gender equality. However, alongside these arguments must be considered the confusion that results from not knowing which countries or districts are improving gender equality in education; which areas need resources, and why we deem this to be the case; and in what areas countries can learn from each other. These reasons, based on harnessing available resources to work together on developing a methodology for measurement of a problem of global significance, seem to mitigate to some degree the negative dimensions described above (Unterhalter 2005c).

However, it should be stressed that the utilisation of this or any other version of measurement of gender equality in education should not be a substitute for detailed quantitative and qualitative research. A key dimension that requires consideration in any form of measurement is an analysis of social and cultural relations and the opportunity for dialogue, debate, and the exploration of differences, particularly with regard to the public–private interface. Such work must be conducted rigorously to provide a corrective to the simplifications and crude assumptions of any approach based on scorecards or league tables. Only in-depth analysis will furnish the detailed knowledge of local contexts and actions necessary to take forward any of the very general directions that measurements of gender equality in education might point to.

The Gender Equality in Education Index

Bearing these issues in mind, we developed the Beyond Access Project scorecard for gender equality in education, which we have renamed the *Gender Equality in Education Index (GEEI)*. The GEEI puts together data gathered by UNICEF on girls' attendance at school, by UNESCO on girls' achievement in primary school and access to secondary school, and by UNDP on the gender development index (GDI). The GDI is a measure that consists of the distribution of female to male life-expectancy in a country, literacy and enrolment in school, and estimated earned income. The three indicators (life-expectancy, education, and income) are equally weighted when compiling the index, although the education index gives two-thirds weight to the adult literacy index and one-third weight to the gross enrolment rate (UNDP 2003: 343-4).

The Beyond Access GEEI has been developed to assess both access and retention in broader ways than hitherto. It includes not only the numbers of girls who attend and remain in primary school, but also an assessment of whether those girls are able to translate that attendance and retention into future secondary schooling, healthy lives, and reasonable incomes. Four widely used measures have been used to develop the GEEI for girls' access to and retention in school:

- girls' net attendance rate at primary school

- girls' survival rate over five years in primary schooling

- girls' secondary Net Enrolment Ratio (NER)

- a country's gender development index (GDI).

These measures were selected because they indicate access to primary schooling (net attendance rate), derived from household surveys; retention in primary schooling (survival rates); the potential of the education system to generate teachers and managers who are concerned to achieve gender equality (girls' secondary NER); and the possibilities for these women to survive and flourish as adults (GDI).

The Beyond Access scorecard is not an unweighted index. In compiling our index, we weighted girls' survival over five years in primary school and the capacity of women to survive into adulthood, retain literacy, and earn a decent livelihood (signalled by the GDI) as twice as important as attendance in primary schools. We weighted girls' enrolment in secondary school, which we believe points to the emergence of a cadre of women who will work in social development with some orientation towards gender equality and equity, as 50 per cent more important than attendance. (See Appendix for a more detailed explanation of how the GEEI is calculated.)

There are a number of critiques of the GDI as a measure of gender equality. Charmes and Wieringa point out that the GDI measures general welfare, rather than gender inequality. In fact, the values for the GDI are very similar to those for the HDI, particularly for countries with high human development (Charmes and Wieringa 2003). They also point out that the choice of measuring health by using life-expectancy, a very long-term measurement, is not likely to offer a precise indication of women's health for the current time period – unlike, for instance, infant and child mortality rates. Other critics point out that statistics of earned income do not include the work that women do in the subsistence economy (Elson 1999). Brandolini (2004) argues that the calculations for the HDI and GDI are problematic, because it is implied that gains in one dimension, for example in schooling or income, can be traded off against losses in another, for example longevity. These are substantial criticisms, but in our view they do not negate the usefulness of the GDI as an easily accessible measure of some aspects of gender in relation to human well-being, which is why we have used it in the GEEI.

The UNDP's Gender Empowerment Measure (GEM) might have been a better measure of how girls and women are able to translate their education into earning and political decision-making. The GEM is an average of three indices: women's share of parliamentary representation; their economic participation through share of positions as legislators, senior officials, managers, and professionals; and their share of earned income. There are criticisms of the GEM. For example, the number of seats in parliament occupied by women does not fully indicate how much power women actually have. Emphasising women's earned income in the formal sector undervalues women's earnings in the informal sector or care economy ,where a great many exchanges that are of value to women and their societies take place. However, despite these limitations, the GEM does provide a proxy measure of the level to which women are visible in key political posts, earn equivalent amounts to men in the formal sector, and have professional employment. Unfortunately, however, the GEM has not been calculated for many countries, and if it has been calculated recently there are no time-series data, so comparisons cannot be made. Because GDI has generally been calculated for the early 1990s and 2000s for most countries, it has therefore been used in GEEI instead of GEM.

Tables 1–3 present the GEEI for Commonwealth countries in Africa, Asia, and Latin America between c. 1993 and 2003. They are based on work commissioned from the Beyond Access project by the Commonwealth Secretariat, UNESCO Bangkok, and UNICEF Regional Office for South Asia (Unterhalter *et al.* 2004; Unterhalter, Rajagopalan, and Challender 2005; Unterhalter and McCowan 2005).

Table 1: GEEI for Commonwealth Africa, c. 1993–2001

	GEEI % c.1993	Rank	GEEI % c.2003	Rank	Percentage increase/ decrease
Mauritius	89	1	81	1	-9
Botswana	73	2	78	2	7
Zimbabwe	73	2	42	7	- 42
Swaziland	68	4	60	5	-11
South Africa	64	5	66	4	3
Namibia	62	6	72	3	16
Zambia	42	7	36	11	-14
Lesotho	37	8	42	7	14
Kenya	36	9	26	12	- 28
Ghana	34	10	39	9	15
Tanzania	33	11	39	9	18
Cameroon	33	11	15	16	- 55
Nigeria	26	13	20	14	- 23
Uganda	24	14	54	6	125
Mozambique	20	15	20	14	0
Malawi	20	15	26	12	30

Source: Unterhalter *et al.* 2004

The changes in GEEI for Commonwealth countries in Africa from the early 1990s to approximately 2003 tell a devastating story. Of the top six countries in approximately 1993, only Botswana, South Africa, and Namibia have made gains. These gains are not large, and the highest-scoring countries in Africa rank well below countries like Sri Lanka in Asia and most of the countries in Latin America (see Tables 2 and 3). Zimbabwe's GEEI has declined more than 40 per cent. There have been similar large declines in countries lower down the ranking order. Cameroon has declined by more than 50 per cent in GEEI, Nigeria by 23 per cent, and Kenya by 28 per cent. Although there was a small decrease in GEEI in Trinidad (see Table 3) and in Philippines and Pakistan (Table 2), in no other region were there spectacular declines in GEEI like those observed in Africa. The combination of debt, decline in social-sector provision, war, and repressive governments has had devastating effects on gender equality in education. The data in Table 1 show that only in Uganda, where there was huge government and civil-society mobilisation for gender equality in education, were there significant gains; but the task ahead even for Uganda is still considerable (see Table 4).

Table 2: GEEI for Asia, c. 1993–2001

	GEEI % c.1993	Rank	GEEI % c.2001	Rank	Percentage increase/ decrease
Korea, Rep. Of	100	1=	100	1=	0
Singapore	100	1=	100	1=	0
Japan	100	1=	100	1=	0
Kazakhstan	91	4	91	9	0
Malaysia	89	5	94	4=	6
Kyrgyzstan	88	6=	94	4=	
Georgia	88	6=	88	11	
Armenia	84	8=	94	4=	12
Azerbaijan	84	8=	84	12=	
Fiji	83	10	94	4=	13
Uzbekistan	81	11	81	15=	
China	79	12	89	10	13
Tajikistan	78	13=	84	12=	8
Mongolia	78	13=	81	15=	4
Philippines	75	16	68	18	-9
Sri Lanka	68*	17=	94	4=	38
Indonesia	68	17=	76	17	12
India	28	19	41	20	46
Bangladesh	23	20=	48	19	109
Pakistan	23	20=	20	23	-13
Nepal	20	22=	36	21	80
Lao, PDR	20	22=	26	22	30

Sources: Unterhalter, Rajagopalan, and Challender 2005; Unterhalter and McCowan 2005

Table 2 shows Asia divided into two halves with regard to gender equality in education. A large number of countries, predominantly in South East Asia, and some in Central Asia, already have relatively high GEEI. Sri Lanka made spectacular gains in GEEI in a decade of low economic growth. The most populous countries in the region – Bangladesh, India, and Pakistan – score low on GEEI. Some countries – Bangladesh, Nepal, and Lao PDR – have made huge gains in GEEI, but are still in the lower half of the table.

Table 3: GEEI for Latin America, c. 1993–2004

	GEEI % c.1993	Rank	GEEI % c.2003	Rank	Percentage increase/ decrease
Trinidad	100	1	94	3	-6
Cuba	88	2	94	3	7
Jamaica	88	2	91	6	3
Chile	86	4	97	2	13
Guyana	84	5	84	9	0
Panama	83	6	94	3	13
Costa Rica	78	78	89	7	14
Ecuador	71	8	72	12	1
Venezuela	70	9	86	8	23
Paraguay	58	10	76	11	31
Dominican Republic	42	11	72	12	71
Bolivia	33	12	81	10	145
El Salvador	33	12	69	14	109
Nicaragua	33	12	46	15	39
Guatemala	26	15	39	16	50

Source: Challender and Unterhalter 2004

Table 3 shows that while many countries in Latin America have much higher levels of GEEI than do countries in Asia and Africa, two countries – Nicaragua and Guatemala – with histories of war and repression continue to have low GEEI, despite considerable gains during the decade. There have also been enormous gains in El Salvador and Bolivia. But Table 3 also tells another story that resonates for Africa and Asia. Countries with relatively high GEEI in 1993 did not reach 100 per cent by 2003, and Trinidad, despite its natural resources and high levels of industrialisation, experienced a fall in GEEI. Raising GEEI requires constant attention; it does not automatically follow from a relatively high score that forward momentum will be maintained. In fact it might be as hard to move from 80 to 100 per cent GEEI as from 33 per cent to 81 per cent, as Bolivia did.

What does the GEEI tell us?

Similar trends can be discerned across all three regions from the GEEI. Countries with long and devastating histories of war or repressive government are at or near the bottom of the league. Conversely, countries with long histories of democratic government are at the top. Countries which, despite a history of war and undemo-cratic government, have paid attention to reconstruction also come near the top (Namibia and South Africa; Malaysia and China; Chile and Cuba). Countries with high levels of women's mobilisation or political participation, such as Uganda, Fiji and Chile, score higher than countries where there has been minimal or only 'top–down' mobilisation on these issues. Countries with vast regional inequalities (Kenya and Ghana; Indonesia and India; Chile and Venezuela) score considerably lower than countries where regional inequalities are not an issue on this scale (Mauritius and Botswana; Korea and Malaysia; Trinidad and Cuba).

Other interesting issues emerging from the tables include the large overall rise in GEEI in Latin America over the course of the 1990s: in 1990 the median GEEI score was 71; in 2000 it was 87. However, there is a sharp division in these increases: the two lowest scorers have remained in this position, with relatively small rises. Thus, Nicaragua's score rose from 33 to 46 and Guatemala's from 26 to 39 between 1990 and 2000. Meanwhile, several countries just above them in the GEEI in 1990 have experienced meteoric rises in their GEEI: for instance Bolivia and El Salvador, which more than doubled their scores between 1990 and 2000.

Larger economies do not equate with higher scores. The largest economy in Latin America, Brazil, was ranked joint tenth in 2000. Of the two lowest scorers, Nicaragua is classified by the World Bank as a low-income economy, and yet Guatemala – a middle-income economy – appears below it. This trend is also apparent on the Africa Scorecard: South Africa, with the largest economy on the continent, is not the country with the highest GEEI. While it is no surprise that Asian countries such as Japan, Korea, and Singapore, which have a high GDP per capita, come at the top of the scorecard for GEEI, it is notable that countries with relatively low GDP per capita, such as Sri Lanka and China, score so highly.

The division of the GEEI for Asia into two very distinct halves is also interesting. There is a big gap between the lowest-ranking 'high scorer', the Philippines, on 67 per cent, and the highest-ranking 'low scorer', Bangladesh, on 47 per cent. While in Africa there are many low-scoring countries, a regional disjuncture of this form is not evident. Another notable aspect of the Asia scorecard is that countries which have or have had communist governments for long periods (China, the former Soviet republics, Mongolia, and Vietnam) and countries which have had many decades of government commitment to the expansion of education (South Korea) score far higher than countries such as India and Pakistan which have had less co-ordinated policies on mass education. Bangladesh, which has mobilised huge local and international resources to improve education, scores far more highly than other countries in South Asia, where policy on education has been less clearly directed.

What does the GEEI tell us about how far the world needs to go to meet the two Millennium Development Goals that relate to education: MDG 2 and MDG 3?

Tables 4–6 compare the rate of improvement in GEEI for countries in Africa, Asia, and Latin America between c. 1993 and 2001 and estimate the level of further improvement that would be needed in order to reach a GEEI score of 95 per cent. A GEEI score of 95 per cent would indicate net girls' primary attendance of 90 per cent and above, girls' primary survival rate of 90 per cent and above, girls' secondary NER of 60 per cent and above, and GDI of 0.800 and above (equivalent to the gender-equality levels in life-expectancy, education, and income of Korea, Singapore, and Japan in 2003).

Table 4 shows the extensive mobilisation of resources that will be needed in Africa to reach a GEEI of 95 per cent. Every single country will have to increase the level of effort expended between 1993 and 2003. Countries at the top of the scorecard, like Namibia, Botswana, and Mauritius will need to invest two to three times the amount of effort in gender-equality programmes. South Africa will need to achieve 14 times the level of improvement attained in the first decade of democracy. But the majority of the countries will need to invest hundreds of times the level of resources and effort mobilised in the previous decade.

Table 4: GEEI scores for Africa, c.1993–2003, and improvements needed to reach GEEI 95 per cent by 2015

	GEEI % c.1993	GEEI % c.2003	Percentage increase/ decrease	% increase needed to reach GEEI of 95
Mauritius	89	81	-9	17.28
Botswana	73	78	7	21.79
Zimbabwe	73	42	-42	126.19
Swaziland	68	60	-11	58.33
South Africa	64	66	3	43.93
Namibia	62	72	16	31.94
Zambia	42	36	-14	163.89
Lesotho	37	42	14	126.19
Kenya	36	26	-28	265.38
Ghana	34	39	15	143.59
Tanzania	33	39	18	143.59
Cameroon	33	15	-55	533.33
Nigeria	26	20	-23	375.00
Uganda	24	54	125	75.93
Mozambique	20	20	0	375.00
Malawi	20	26	30	265.396

Table 5: GEEI scores in Asia, c. 1993–2003, and improvements needed to reach GEEI 95 per cent by 2015

	GEEI % c.1993	GEEI % c.2003	Percentage increase/ decrease	% increase needed to reach GEEI of 95
Korea, Rep. of	100	100	0	0
Singapore	100	100	0	0
Japan	100	100	0	0
Kazakhstan	91	91	0	4.40
Malaysia	89	94	6	1.06
Kyrgyzstan	88	94		1.06
Georgia	88	88		7.95
Armenia	84	94	12	1.06
Azerbaijan	84	84		13.09
Fiji	83	94	13	1.06
Uzbekistan	81	81		17.28
China	79	89	13	6.74
Tajikistan	78	84	8	13.10
Mongolia	78	81	4	17.28
Philippines	75	68	-9	39.70
Sri Lanka	68*	94	38	1.06
Indonesia	68	76	12	25
India	28	41	46	131.70
Bangladesh	23	48	109	97.91
Pakistan	23	20	-13	375.00
Nepal	20	36	80	163.89
Lao PDR	20	26	30	265.39

Table 5 shows that while many countries in Asia will have to sustain the gains of the previous decade, some relatively high scorers will have to double or treble the level of mobilisation (Indonesia and Mongolia). Countries in the bottom half of the scorecard will either have to equal the very high level of mobilisation of the previous decade (Bangladesh), or double or treble it (Nepal and India). Lao will need levels of mobilisation ten times as great as the previous decade, while Pakistan will need 300 times greater mobilisation (although there is some doubt about the figures reported in this case).

Table 6: GEEI scores for Latin America, c.1993–2003, and improvements needed to reach GEEI 95 per cent by 2015

	GEEI % c.1993	GEEI % c.2003	Percentage increase/ decrease	% increase needed to reach GEEI of 95
Trinidad	100	94	-6	1
Cuba	88	94	7	
Jamaica	88	91	3	1
Chile	86	97	13	4
Guyana	84	84	0	13
Panama	83	94	13	1
Costa Rica	78	89	14	8
Ecuador	71	72	1	32
Venezuela	70	86	23	11
Paraguay	58	76	31	25
Dominican Republic	42	72	71	32
Bolivia	33	81	145	17
El Salvador	33	69	109	38
Nicaragua	33	46	39	107
Guatemala	26	39	50	144

Table 6 shows that working to achieve the two education MDGs will entail for many Latin American countries sustaining the growth of the last ten years in relation to gender equality, or slightly increasing resources for this area. El Salvador will need to increase momentum by 40 per cent, not losing the significant gains of the previous decade. Nicaragua and Guatemala, however, will have to nearly treble the gains that they made from 1993.

Conclusion

The GEEI presents an alternative means of measuring gender-equality gains and losses in and through education. GEEI calculations show catastrophic falls in many countries in Africa through the 1990s, and they indicate that maximum mobilisation of resources is needed for that continent to halt this under-acknowledged disaster and achieve good levels of gender equality. While the extent of the task in Africa is enormous, huge challenges also remain to increase GEEI in many countries in Asia and Latin America. Reaching the targets for

MDG 2 and MDG 3 by 2015 is not impossible, given the talent and wealth of the world. This assessment of GEEI gives some indication of the size of the task and the levels of mobilisation needed. This task falls not only to the people who live in the countries with low GEEI. The MDGs are challenges to global collaboration and resource mobilisation. The numbers point to the heightened levels at which we need to work together.

Appendix: Calculating the GEEI

The GEEI was constructed by using four measures deemed useful as indicators of girls' access to and retention in school, and women's health and levels of income after school. The indicators selected were girls' primary attendance, girls' survival rate over five years of primary schooling, girls' secondary NER, and the Gender Development Index (GDI).

Data from the EFA Monitoring Reports, UNICEF's *State of the World's Children*, the Human Development Reports, World Bank reports, and countries' own EFA assessments were used. Occasionally, where there were no figures available, secondary literature was consulted.

Net primary attendance rates, survival at school, secondary NER, and GDI levels were given a value based on the following assessments shown in Table 7.

Table 7: Criteria for scoring achievements with regard to access and achievement in girls' education

Score	Criteria to achieve the score
5	Excellent conditions. Already at (or extremely well positioned to achieve) gender equity in 2015 and likely to fulfil the aspirations of the Beijing Declaration.
4	Very good conditions. Substantial achievement with regard to gender equity and well on the path to achieving 2015 goal with regard to access. Some gains needed in order to improve retention.
3	Good conditions. Progress towards 2015 evident, but further work necessary on access and retention.
2	Poor conditions. Progress towards 2015 slow. Considerable and intensive work needed on access and retention.
1	Very poor conditions. 2015 goals unlikely to be reached without massive mobilisation on all fronts to secure access and achievement.

Using these criteria, the scoring system illustrated in Table 8 was developed with regard to the indicators.

Table 8: GEEI scores and indicators

Score	Net girls' primary attendance	Girls' primary survival rate	Girls' secondary NER	GDI
5	90% and above	90% and above	60% and above	0.800 and above
4	80–89%	80–89%	50–59%	0.700–.799
3	70–79%	70–79%	40–49%	0.600–.699
2	60–69%	60–69%	30–39%	0.500–.599
1	59% and below	59% and below	29% and below	Below 0.499

Raw scores on the basis of this table were then weighted as follows:

Net girls' primary attendance (raw score x 1.25)	Girls' primary survival rate (raw score x 2.5)	Girls secondary NER (raw Score x 1.75)	GDI (raw score x 2.5)	GEEI (sum of weighted measures divided by 4)

Detailed calculations of the GEEI for Africa and Asia are to be found in earlier papers (Unterhalter *et al.* 2004; Unterhalter, Rajagopalan, and Challender 2005).

Elaine Unterhalter is a senior lecturer in Education and International Development at the Institute of Education, University of London, where (with Sheila Aikman) she has co-ordinated the Beyond Access: Gender, Education and Development project since 2003.

Chloe Challender is Editor for the Beyond Access project. She has worked for NGOs and the UK Treasury on international development issues, especially children's rights, for several years.

Rajee Rajagopalan is a part-time research assistant on the Beyond Access project. Previously she worked as administrator of the International Development Unit at the Institute of Education, University of London.

Note

1   This paper is based on work commissioned from the Beyond Access project in 2004–05 by the Commonwealth Secretariat, UNESCO Bangkok, and UNICEF Regional Office for South Asia. We are grateful to all three organisations for permission to publish this chapter, which draws on reports prepared for them. A further paper, with a detailed consideration of these issues as they apply in South Asia, is to be published by UNICEF in 2005.

References

Alkire, S. (2002) *Valuing Freedom. Sen's Capability Approach and Poverty Reduction*, Oxford: Oxford University Press

Brandolini, A. (2004) personal communication, December 2004

CAMPE (Campaign for Popular Education) (1999) *Hope not Complacency: State of Primary Education In Bangladesh*, Dhaka: the University Press

Carr-Hill, R., M. Hopkins, A. Riddell, J. Lintott (1999) 'Monitoring the Performance of Educational Programmes in Developing Countries', London: Department for International Development

Challender, C., and E. Unterhalter (2004) 'A Scorecard for Latin America' in *Equals* Issue 8, online at http://ioewebserver.ioe.ac.uk/ioe/cms/get.asp?cid=7746&7746_0=10870

Charmes, J. and S. Wieringa (2003) 'Measuring women's empowerment: an assessment of the Gender-related Development Index and the Gender Empowerment Measure', *Journal of Human Development* 4/3: 430

Elson, D. (1999) 'Labour markets as gendered institutions: equality, efficiency and empowerment issues', *World Development* 27?3: 611–27

Fukuda Parr, S. and A.K.S. Kumar (eds.) (2003) *Readings in Human Development,* New York: Oxford University Press

ILO (2003–2004) 'Key Indicators of the Labour Market' (Geneva, 2003), www.ilo.org/kilm

Khoury, N. F. and V. M. Moghadam (1995) *Gender and Development in the Arab World – Women's Economic Participation: Patterns and Policies,* Tokyo: United Nations University Press and London/New Jersey: Zed Books

Millennium Commission (2000), 'The Millennium Development Goals', online at www.un.org/millenniumgoals

Nussbaum, M. (2000) *Women and Human Development*, Cambridge: Cambridge University Press

Sen, A. (1999) *Development as Freedom,* Oxford: Oxford University Press

Terzi, L. (2004) 'On Education as a Basic Capability', paper presented at the 4th International Conference on the Capability Approach, University of Pavia, Italy, 2–7 September

Tomasevski, K. (2003) *Education Denied: Costs and Remedies,* New York: Zed Books

UNDP (1995–2004) *Human Development Reports,* New York: UNDP

UNESCO (2000) 'Status and Trends. Assessing Learning Achievement', Paris: UNESCO, on line at http://unesdoc.unesco.org/images/0011/001198/119823e.pdf (consulted March 2005)

UNESCO (2003) *Education for All Global Monitoring Report 2003–4: Gender and Education for All,* Paris: UNESCO

UNESCO (2004) *Education for All Global Monitoring Report 2005: The Quality Imperative,* Paris: UNESCO

Unterhalter, E. (2003) 'The capabilities approach and gendered education: An examination of South African complexities', *Theory and Research in Education* 1/1: 7–22

Unterhalter, E. (2005a) 'Gender Equality and Education in South Africa: Measurements, Scores and Strategies'

Unterhalter, E. (2005b) 'Global inequality, capabilities, social justice: The millennium development goal for gender equality in education', *International Journal of Educational Development* 25: 111–222

Unterhalter, E. (2005c) 'Mobilisation, meanings and measures: reflections on girls' education', *Development* 48/1

Unterhalter, E. and T. McCowan (2005d) 'Girls' Education and the Millennium Development Goals: What do the indicators show us?', paper presented at UNGEI Technical Meeting, Bangkok, February 2005

Unterhalter, E., and H. Brighouse (2003) 'Distribution of What? How will we know if we have reached EFA by 2015?', paper presented at the 3rd Conference on the Capability Approach, University of Pavia, Italy, September

Unterhalter, E. *et al.* (2004) 'Scaling Up Girls' Education: Towards a Scorecard on Girls' Education in the Commonwealth', on line at http://k1.ioe.ac.uk/schools/efps/GenderEducDev/Where%20are%20we%20scaling%20up%20 from%20FINAL%20FINAL.pdf

Unterhalter, E., R. Rajagopalan, and C. Challender (2005) 'A Scorecard on Gender Equality and Girls' Education in Asia, 1990–2000', UNESCO Bangkok, online at www2.unescobkk.org/elib/publications/gender_equality_asia/index.htm

Unterhalter, E., R. Rajagopalan, and C. Challender (forthcoming) 'A Scorecard for Girls' Schooling in Latin America'

Walker, M. (2004) 'South African Girls' Narratives on Learning: Insights from the Capability Approach', paper presented at the 4th International Conference on the Capability Approach, University of Pavia, Italy, 2–7 September

Watkins, K. (2000) *The Oxfam Education Report,* Oxford: Oxfam

Part Two

Transforming Action:
Changing Policy through Practice

4 Educating girls in Bangladesh: watering a neighbour's tree?

Janet Raynor

There is an old Bengali saying which observes: *'Caring for a daughter is like watering a neighbour's tree'*. It reflects the view that it is a waste of resources to invest in a daughter who will be 'lost' to another family through marriage. It is one of the arguments that have been used in the past to justify girls' exclusion from school in Bangladesh. However, various recent education initiatives by both government and NGOs have placed stronger emphasis on girls' education, leading to a widely praised increase in access over the last ten years. They include a secondary stipend programme which started on a small scale in 1982 and became a nationwide programme in 1994. The expansion of girls' education in Bangladesh – and how it is perceived – is the subject of this study, with the government's secondary Female Stipend Programme (FSP) used as a case study.[1]

The study examines attitudes towards girls' education and educated girls and women in Bangladesh. It explores attitudes towards the programme, and the programme's effects on social attitudes. Many reports on the various forms of the FSP offer a quantitative analysis, showing the success of the project in terms of access or retention (Sarker, Chowdhury, and Tariq 1995; Khandker and Samad 1996; *Daily Star* 2003a; *New Nation* 2004b). However, few reports offer insight into the ways in which lives and attitudes are being affected. Little attention has been paid to the impact of the programme at the family or individual level, or how stated values compare with observed behaviour. This study examines these aspects, exploring the attitudes of girls and boys, mothers and fathers, teachers and education officials, and project personnel. Specific focus areas include the following:

- **Perceptions:** does girls' education strengthen traditional gendered roles or lead to empowerment? Is it seen to be beneficial or detrimental to the individual girl, to boys and men, and to society as a whole?

- **Purpose:** in the past, girls in Bangladesh have been denied formal education. Is girls' education regarded now as a need, a right, or a luxury, and what is its perceived purpose?

- **Culture:** is maintenance of cultural values seen to be more important than formal education for girls? Do dominant social groups use 'culture' as an argument to preserve the *status quo*?

Background to the study

Working in education in Bangladesh over the past 12 years, I have come into regular contact with people who were in some way connected to or affected by the FSP. This was particularly so during 1998–99, when I was involved in a secondary-level programme in eastern Bangladesh, where discussions arising in informal meetings with those involved in secondary education indicated that there was a general lack of understanding of the rationale behind the FSP, and that there were various forms of resistance to it. This resistance might take the form of, for example, an influential village leader and member of a School Management Committee insisting that it was a waste of resources to educate a girl from a rural area, because she would be unable to use that education to find suitable employment. A government education official declared to a group of teachers that the programme discriminated against boys and was therefore unacceptable. Others, however, were very supportive of the project. These attitudes seemed worth exploring, because the success of the project depends to a large extent on how 'acceptable' it is within the context in which it is operating.

The Bangladeshi context

Bangladesh has a population of approximately 138.5 million people, making it the ninth most populated country in the world (CIA 2003), and (barring a few island nations) the most densely populated country in the world. Since its independence from West Pakistan in 1971, it has been devastated by war and natural disasters, and has attracted much international aid. Until 2003, it was ranked as having 'low human development', but it has recently edged into the medium development range, ranking 138 out of 177 countries in the 2004 UNDP Human Development Index, which indicates that there has been some positive development (UNDP 2004).

However, in terms of the UNDP's Gender Empowerment Measure, Bangladesh ranks 76th out of the 78 countries included (UNDP 2004). Although under the 1972 constitution women and men have equal rights (Government of Bangladesh 1996), and although various legal measures have been taken to improve the position of women, in practice little has changed – especially for poor women and girls in rural areas (Mannan 2002; Koenig *et al.* 2003). When the government of Bangladesh (GoB) ratified the 1979 Convention on the Elimination of All Forms of Discrimination against Women (CEDAW), it 'maintained reservations on all articles calling for women's equal rights in the family' (Jahan 1995a: 102). The 1980 Prohibition of Dowry Act has done little to reduce dowry practice, with the incidence of dowry substantially increasing since the 1970s (Esteve-Volart 2003), and 247 reports of dowry violence – including 122 deaths – in the last three months of 2004 (*Daily Star* 2005). Similarly, in 1961 family ordinance laws set a minimum age for marriage and restricted men's rights to polygamy and divorce, but in rural areas these laws are often overlooked (Jahan 1995a; Khan 2001). The International Centre for Research on Women's Demographic Health Survey 1996–2001 lists Bangladesh as the country with the second-highest rate of child marriage, with an estimated 75 per cent of girls married before they reach the age of 18 (ICRW 2003), although the Bangladesh Bureau of Statistics gives a figure of 47 per cent (cited in UNESCO Bangkok 2003). Sweetser, in a report exploring gender relations, non-formal education, and social change, notes a marked generational difference in attitudes towards women. She gives examples of attitudes displayed by the older men, which included their disapproval of 'modern trends' of women or girls going to school, working in the fields, arranging their own marriages, riding bicycles and motorcycles, taking up seats on buses, and being served in a shop first. One man seemed to sum it up by saying: 'All the degradation in the world starts with the loosening on the restrictions on women' (Sweetser 1999:16). In such a context, there could well be a struggle for girls' and women's rights to participate in education, and any empowerment that it might be seen to lead to.

Education in Bangladesh

One of the first documents advocating formal education for girls in Bangladesh (then part of India) is 'Wood's Education Despatch' of 1854. In that document, 'female education' was promoted because it enhanced the educational and moral tone of the people (excerpts annexed in Jalaluddin and Chowdhury 1997). What educational provision there was for girls focused on 'education for enlightened motherhood' (Chanana 1994): they were being trained to be mothers, rather than – for example – being prepared for paid employment or for tertiary education. The 1974 Qudrat-e-Khuda Education Commission Report of the newly independent Bangladesh firmly asserted that 'women's education should be such as to be of help to them in their domestic life', and stressed that subjects such as 'child-care, the nursing of the sick, preservation of health, food and nutrition' must be included. It also suggested that girls should be channelled into 'vocations specially suitable to them', such as primary-school teaching, nursing, and typing (Jalaluddin and Chowdhury 1997: 290). For more than 100 years, formal education for girls was not designed to bring about fundamental change in society.

The Female Stipend Programme

The stipend programme has brought about change. Adolescent girls are now visible in large numbers, going to and from school in rural areas – in itself a fundamental change.

The FSP offers an allowance to encourage families to send girls to school, and to help to meet the costs of education. The first form of the FSP for secondary-level girls was set up by Bangladesh Association for Community Education (BACE) in 1982. According to Mr Azizul Huq, Director of BACE (personal interview), the initiative was '100 per cent Bangladeshi', the prime mover being Dr Mohammed Abdus Sattar, at that time Secretary for Population Control and Family Planning in the Ministry of Health and Population Control. The pilot project was reportedly inspired by population-related literature which suggested that girls' enrolment in secondary education would delay marriage and increase contraceptive use, and thus reduce fertility levels. It was initially supported by USAID, and later by the Asia Foundation, before being taken up by NORAD in 1992. There were remarkably positive results, with female enrolment almost doubling in some project areas, and drop-out rates being dramatically reduced (Haq and Haq 1998). Based on the success of the pilot projects, a nationwide programme was launched in 1994 under the umbrella term of *Nationwide Female Stipend Programme*. All rural districts became part of the programme, with funding from NORAD, the World Bank, the Asian Development Bank, and the government itself.

Under the programme, girls in rural areas in Classes 6–10 are eligible for the stipend, conditional on their maintaining a minimum of 75 per cent attendance, obtaining a minimum of 45 per cent in annual school exams, and remaining unmarried up to the Secondary School Certificate (SSC) examination in Year 10. The award consists of an allowance, free tuition, a book allowance for Year 9, and SSC examination fees in Year 10. The stipend is not large: girls receive a sum equivalent to no more than US$ 1.00 a month, and schools get US$ 1.50–2.00 a semester in tuition fees. It is paid to all girls who meet the eligibility criteria, regardless of family wealth. Means-testing was introduced as an experiment in the 1980s, but proved to be too problematic (Valad 1995). However, there is continuing pressure from donors for the introduction of means-testing to increase the sustainability of the programme, and to target impoverished families (Mahmud 2003).

The model has been praised internationally as a means of achieving Millennium Development Goals. For example, a conference in Shanghai in May 2004 on 'Reducing Poverty, Sustaining Growth', co-hosted by the World Bank and the Chinese government, focused on successful examples of scaling up anti-poverty interventions, and the FSP was one of them. The conference – and Bangladesh's success in promoting girl's education – attracted much positive media attention (for example, Agence France Presse 2004; *Daily Star* 2004; *New Nation* 2004c), along with claims that Bangladesh had already achieved the Millennium Development Goals *of eliminating gender disparity in education* (emphasis added). What is meant here is *parity of enrolment*; that is, equal numbers of boys and girls in school.

In terms of increasing enrolment, the FSP has undoubtedly been a success. Rising from about 700,000 beneficiaries in the first year of the nationwide programme, the number peaked in 2001 at more than 4 million as more girls completed primary school, more schools joined the programme, new girls joined the programme, and more girls stayed on at higher levels. There has been a drop since 2002: the numbers were down to about 2.25 million beneficiaries in 2004. This drop is largely due to stricter criteria for awarding stipends. There have been various reports of widespread corruption, with well-informed unofficial estimates of the number of 'irregular' awards being as high as 50 per cent (BANBEIS 1998, 1999, 2001; FSSAP 1999, 2004; Mahmud 2003; World Bank 2003; FESP 2004; and discussions with project personnel). The corruption issue is not the focus of this study, but it is real and should be noted. However, it is an undeniable fact that girls are now in secondary school in Bangladesh in large numbers, and that gender parity of enrolment was apparently achieved in 2000.

It should be noted that – as Figure 1 shows – while there have definitely been increases in girls' enrolment, and most significantly since the introduction of the FSP, there has also been an increase for boys, perhaps in part because of the FSP. It should also be noted that the increase in girls' enrolment cannot simply be ascribed to the FSP: it is one of many education initiatives in Bangladesh, but the FSP is also seen as having had a positive impact on the enrolment of girls in primary schools (Thein, Kabir, and Islam 1988; Chowdhury, Choudhury, and Nath 1999; Ahmed and Ahmed 2002). Most of the more recent statistical data shown here were collected for a study commissioned by DFID Bangladesh, on which this section draws heavily (Raynor and Chowdhury 2004). The 2003 figures given here are provisional only, and they show only those who enrolled at the beginning of the academic year, with no indication of how many girls actually completed the year. We must wait to see what impact the 'tightening up' has had on the overall enrolment of girls, but there has almost certainly been a drop in girls' enrolment in 2004 and 2005 (Thornton *et al.* 2005).

The FSP was, and still is, based within a Women in Development (WID) framework, with a focus on what women can do for development, rather than vice versa – an example of what Unterhalter describes as programmes that 'utilise women as a tool for a greater good' (Unterhalter 2000:17). Herz's (1991) World Bank Discussion Paper *Letting Girls Learn* is a fairly representative example. It focuses on the education of girls, cites early forms of the FSP as a 'promising approach' in education, and represents the thinking of at least one of the major external agencies involved in the FSP. It was written when plans for the nationwide programme were being considered. It lists the standard WID justifications for greater investment in girls' education, such as healthier, better-educated children and reduced population growth. In what can be seen as an extension of the attitude expressed in the adage about 'watering a neighbour's tree', Herz

Figure 1: Growth of secondary-school enrolment in Bangladesh, 1970–2003

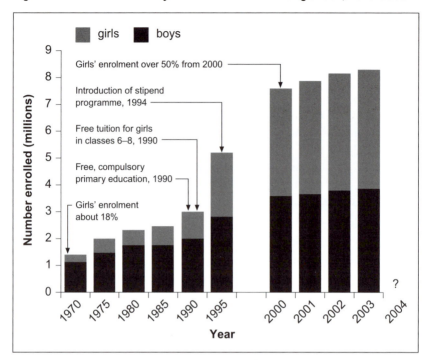

Sources: BANBEIS 2002; BANBEIS 2003, and discussions with BANBEIS personnel 2004. Note: the columns on the left are at five-year intervals; those on the right relate to one year.

recommends financial incentives and subsidies for girls' education, arguing that they are 'economically justifiable because the parents who pay ... have little to gain, but society benefits greatly from the presence of educated women' (*op. cit.*, p. xiii). FSP policies, like the instrumentalist WID policies from which they are drawn, take account of women's productive and reproductive roles, but do not go beyond them. For example, the FSP focus on delayed marriage is for fertility control, rather than representing a rights-based approach to the prevention of child marriage.

Although current official government policy strongly promotes girls' and women's education, private resistance may work against that public policy. Some research indicates that her father's education and assets may actually have a negative impact on a girl's schooling in Bangladesh. This finding comes from a comparative study of four countries – including 826 households in 47 villages in three sites in Bangladesh – exploring factors that influence the bargaining power of household members. The authors speculate that 'wealthier Bangladeshi fathers may attach a higher premium to marrying their daughters off earlier' (Quisumbing and

Maluccio 2000:54), although this goes against the widely held belief that poverty is a driving factor in early marriage. There have also been public outbreaks of (male) resistance to certain education programmes, particularly in the east of the country, and particularly around 1994, when the stipend programme was introduced (Sultan 1994, Jahan 1995b, Momen 1995, and Kabir 1996 all report such cases). However, these were reports of responses to education programmes with some sort of overt empowerment agenda such as the teaching of legal rights, and all were linked to programmes for women rather than girls.

While twenty years ago girls were visible to some extent in primary classes, very few girls were allowed to attend secondary school: they tended to be withdrawn at or around puberty (Sattar 1982). Most recent figures indicate that girls' enrolment – primary and secondary – is now about equal to that of boys. Bellamy (2004) indicates that girls' net primary enrolment had risen to nearly 90 per cent by 2000 – compared with 48 per cent in 1996 (BANBEIS 1999) – and gives the 2000 secondary Gross Enrolment Rate as 45 per cent for boys and 47 per cent for girls. Thus, if figures are correct, Bangladesh has succeeded in providing equal access to girls and boys at primary and secondary levels. However, there are strong reservations about the quality and relevance of education in Bangladesh for both boys and girls (Sen 2002; Mahmud 2003); this has particular consequences for girls, who are still less likely to complete secondary school, gain an academic qualification, or enter secure paid employment (Ahmed 2000; *Daily Star* 2003b; UNESCO Bangkok 2003; World Bank 2003). Parity of enrolment is no mean achievement, but Bangladesh still has a long way to go in terms of meeting the EFA goals of quality and equality in education (World Education Forum 2000) or the Millennium Development Goals relating to gender in education in particular, and gender equality and empowerment in general (United Nations 2000).

Das Gupta *et al.* (1993), in a study prepared during the run-up to the implementation of the nationwide FSP in 1994, indicate that the most frequently mentioned advantage of educating girls was that they could get jobs. Although both men and women said this, almost 50 per cent of women cited it, compared with only about 30 per cent of men, men's responses tending to be spread over other categories such as 'educate her own children'. The second most frequently cited advantage overall was that education would help a girl to get a better husband. Sarker *et al.* (1995), in an evaluation of FSP pilot programmes, indicate that education for girls is mostly perceived as a domestic benefit, enabling them to get better husbands, to help their husbands, or to teach and look after their own children better. Similarly, Sweetser found that 'Typically, the first benefit of girls' education cited by villagers pertains to their future roles managing the home economy' (1999:17). As Haider notes, 'most of society's justifications for educating girls remains one of counting the benefits at large, while ignoring her individual rights and personal worth' (1995:121).

The 1993 Das Gupta study indicated that men in particular cite the cost of girls' education as a reason for not sending girls to school. All those interviewed for this study were worried that schooling endangers girls' morality and reputation, with mothers being particularly concerned that boys might harass their daughters on the way to and from school (Das Gupta, Islam, and Siddiq 1993). Sweetser's study shows older men focusing on the concern that education might lead to the undermining of traditional social and economic structures. Nor is everyone sure that education should or can help a girl to get a job. Sweetser reports one man's statement that it was pointless sending girls to secondary school because they would still have to bribe someone to get a job: 'what they really need, in his view, is a husband' (1999:18).

One issue which produces remarkably mixed reports is that of the impact of education on dowry, which can be seen as an indicator of the status and value of girls in society. Reduction in dowry is often cited as one of the benefits of girls' education (see Bellew and King 1993, for example). Several early FSP texts comment positively on the impact of education on dowry, although most cite no empirical evidence to support the claim (Thein, Kabir and Islam 1988; Mustafa *et al.* 1990; Das Gupta *et al.* 1993). More recent studies, such as Amin (1996), Jeffrey and Jeffrey (1998), and Arends-Kuenning and Amin (2001), link education to increased dowry demands. If this is the case, many parents may feel hesitant about sending their daughters to school beyond an age at which they can be 'married off' cheaply.

At the secondary level, apart from targeting girls' enrolment, many education programmes – the FSP being one – also have an objective of channelling girls into teaching. This is partly to ensure that girls have female role-models in schools, partly because teaching is seen as an 'appropriate' job for women, but also to meet the needs of the ever-expanding education system.

The study

The FSP 'case' was studied through interviews, questionnaires, observation, and a review of documentation. Most of the research for this paper was conducted in 2000; it was followed by work in Bangladesh which kept me in touch with the project, visits to donor and project staff, and a review of recent project documentation in 2004. The main fieldwork undertaken in Bangladesh consisted of 31 visits to schools and project offices, set up with the help of the Project Director of the GoB element of the project. To respect participants' privacy and to preserve confidentiality, the *thana* (small administrative area / district council), schools, and individuals are not named – or they have been given different names.

Forty-one interviews were conducted, with six secondary-school girls, four secondary-school boys, nine mothers, five fathers, nine head-teachers (some of whom also spoke as parents), and ten 'implementers' (project personnel, etc). A large proportion of those interviewed came from comparatively wealthy families, which is not representative of the country as a whole but is fairly representative of families with children in secondary schools in Bangladesh. Of the 24 parents and children interviewed, only five acknowledged that the stipend was the determining factor in school enrolment.

The questionnaires, administered to 456 respondents, indicated the degree to which a view expressed in an interview might be regarded as representative of a wider group. The questionnaire was given mainly to groups of students and teachers within the designated *thana*, because it was safe to assume that they were literate and therefore able to complete it. Questionnaires were completed by 233 girls, 166 boys, 15 female teachers, 31 male teachers, and five 'others' (for example, school-management committee members).

Limitations of the study include the fact that it was restricted to those in or connected with secondary schools; the case study covers only one *thana*, so findings are illustrative rather than generalisable; and all interviews were conducted in English (either directly or through an interpreter), which may have limited the articulation and detection of certain attitudes. The administration of written questionnaires was necessarily restricted to those who were literate; and the sensitivity of the subject may have inhibited some participants. The schools were in a *thana* only about 50 km from Dhaka, and the findings in this study are inevitably affected by the proximity to Dhaka.

Findings: the multiple meanings of girls' education

While collating questionnaire data, I was struck by the overall tendency of women and girls to use the 'extremes' of the attitudinal scale, while men and boys generally favoured the middle categories. Where girls/women had 'strong' opinions in 58 per cent of responses, only 46 per cent of responses from boys/men used these categories, and they were more likely to use the 'neutral' box (11 per cent male versus 6 per cent female). This strength of feeling was evident in the interviews, where women and girls gave answers with little or no hesitation; men and boys needed more time to formulate responses – and were occasionally unwilling or unable to answer. The difference in degree between male and female responses may well translate into different male and female behaviours, with girls/women acting in accordance with their strongly stated beliefs, and the behaviour of boys/men perhaps even contradicting stated opinions.

Perceptions of FSP and girls' education

Some interviewees see girls' education as strengthening traditional roles; others see it as leading to some sort of empowerment. Still others see it as a threat.

Of the nine mothers interviewed, four not only supported the project but also felt that it was right that it should be restricted to girls. One middle-class woman said:

> *I have a son, but I have no objection to boys not getting it – girls need it more. I think the government recognises that girls ... don't get to study as much as boys so they've done this to push them ahead. It's good that it's for girls only. The only negative thing I can think of about the FSP is that it would be bad if they got rid of it!*

However, this woman would send her children to school with or without the stipend, and she was obviously not familiar with financial hardship. Another woman, veiled but vocal and obviously not wealthy, was adamant:

> *No, it's not necessary for boys, they have enough advantages. Both my sons – they're now 20 and 25 – completed up to Class 4. My older daughter, she's 20 now, and married, had no school at all. But the last one is OK. She's lucky because she's the last one and we can get her educated. She's in Class 8 now, and we let her finish primary school because I knew she'd get the stipend in secondary school. My own life would have been much better if I'd been educated.*

The switch of pronouns here is revealing: 'we' let the girl finish primary school, but 'I' knew she would get the stipend. The 'I' almost certainly persuaded the 'we' that represents the husband, with whom she has to present a united front. The last sentence shows her wistful personal views of the value of education.

However, 'stipends for boys' is an issue, especially where there is poverty. A woman from a poor family said she thought it was a good thing that the FSP was for girls only, but – placing poor boys in the same marginalised area as girls in general – added that '*it would be OK if it was for very poor boys too*'. And one father with a large family, a low income, and one daughter receiving the stipend said:

> *I want the stipend for my sons. It's unfair that girls get it but boys don't. I agree that girls have definitely been less fortunate than boys in society, so maybe the programme has been introduced so girls can have a better future? But I've got five sons, and they need education.*

Fathers, most of whom had daughters benefiting from the FSP, were generally in favour of the programme – perhaps because it saved them having to decide whether to spend money on a daughter's education. However, the four boys interviewed felt that the programme was unfair to boys or '*not a very good idea*' – but the opinions expressed were mild.

The majority of girls strongly agreed with the questionnaire statement saying *'The FSP is beneficial to me'*, but a surprisingly high percentage of boys did too (40 per cent strongly agreed, with another 36 per cent ticking the 'agree' box). Interestingly, in the piloting stage of the questionnaire one project administrator questioned the validity of that statement in a questionnaire to be administered to boys as well as girls. He felt that no boy would be able to respond positively to it, because the FSP was clearly designed to benefit girls. Most of the boys interviewed felt that the FSP would benefit them by giving them an educated wife who would have a better chance of adding to the family income, and being a better mother to their children.

As to whether education will empower/liberate girls, there were marked differences between male and female responses. Girls/women optimistically felt that education was the answer to their problems. Boys/men also generally indicated that there was an element of liberation in girls' education, but the questionnaires did not show whether this was seen as a threat or not. The interviews were more enlightening.

One person in the 'implementers' category provided a good example of conflicting private and public views. The man ('Mostafa') was a loud advocate of girls' education, saying that educated women could be equal participants in the country's development, and his questionnaire presented model 'correct' responses. But his actions spoke even more loudly. When we visited Mostafa, we were given red-carpet treatment. While we were talking in his office, a woman moved among us, serving refreshments and making sure that our needs were met. At some stage, she was referred to as a mother of one of the schoolchildren. Only later were we informed that she was Mostafa's wife, a full-time teacher at the school, and that she had arisen at 5 am to cook in honour of our visit. After school, she took us to a neighbouring house to interview another woman, and we were then pressed into going to her own house for a meal. She did not sit down to eat with us, and when I suggested that she might, Mostafa spoke for her and said that it was 'her pleasure' to serve us. I tried several times to engage her in conversation, but each time, Mostafa responded for her. He had also arranged for a photographer to come and take pictures of his children with the visiting dignitaries (us). Mostafa was included in the photo; the woman/mother/ wife/teacher was not.

Like many other respondents, Mostafa is happy for women to be educated and undertake paid employment – as long as it does not erode his position within the traditional patriarchal structure. It seems that there is a general desire among men/boys for education to lead to employment – but not to empowerment. Both boys and girls tended to repeat the accepted view that girls' education makes them better wives and mothers, and benefits society as a whole. None spoke of individual benefits to the girls themselves. Only the mothers envisioned better things for their daughters. One, herself educated to the level of Higher School Certificate, said:

> *It's changing social status in the family. She's going to get a better job and because of that a better life, and better living conditions will follow. In the past it was only boys, but now it's also girls, and girls are a huge proportion of the population and girls and boys together add up, and that's going to develop economic and social status much more. Girls are already much more free because of this programme and they have new aspirations and hopes and they can probably discern a brighter future.*

Another, who had set up her own poultry-farming business and was earning an enviable US$ 42 a month (significantly more than her husband), said:

> *I can see the change already, especially a significant change in the neighbourhood, seeing so many women who were destined to be housewives, but got education and now have jobs. It's a revolution. After a girl is educated, why shouldn't she work for a better future? Why should anyone have anything negative to say about it? We all need to be independent. When they won't feed us, why not let each individual take care of themselves and make their own decisions?*

The 'they' in this last sentence presumably applies to patriarchy in general, and perhaps to her husband in particular.

If girls can get into the position where they can 'take care of themselves' (as this woman suggested), perhaps the need for dowry will disappear. Questionnaire responses conformed to the generally received wisdom that education reduces dowry demands (69 per cent agreed, noticeably girls/women). However, interviews produced more mixed views. Two of the boys were adamant that they did not expect a dowry if their wife-to-be was educated (*'it's illegal and it's bad'*). Two of the fathers also felt that dowry would not be necessary for an educated girl; another said *'it depends on individual families'*. But one bitterly reported:

> *I want to marry off my second daughter as soon as possible. She's just done her BA at college... I've paid all that for her education and now I have to find the dowry money. It will cost me not less than Tk 30,000–40,000 [about US$ 600]. The only reason I'm having to give the dowry is because she's educated, and she needs an educated husband. My eldest daughter wasn't educated, and I didn't have to give a dowry for her.*

Class-related issues may come into this. The man is an uneducated vegetable seller who has made exceptional sacrifices to provide education for his daughter. Prospective families willing to take on such a girl may ask more in dowry to compensate for her humble origins.

Most of the women/mothers felt that dowry demands would be lower for educated girls, but not all. Two did not, and they presented avoidance of marriage as a solution to the dowry problem:

> *Education for girls means you have to get a better-educated husband. That costs more… Having girls educated might help in the long run. It depends. By and large, there's probably a positive effect, because a girl who's educated can stand on her own two feet and look after herself. Marriage isn't as essential for her as it is for someone who's not educated.*

A second woman said:

> *I don't like dowry. I'm not planning it for my daughter and I won't ask for one for my son. Parents are still willing to pay for dowry for educated daughters, but what I'm saying is that girls, they can refuse it themselves, saying: 'No, we're educated, we can work on our own, we can survive on our own. There's no need to get us married now.'*

Further research is needed, but if it is shown that under certain circumstances education adds significantly to dowry costs, and the most commonly stated reason for not sending girls to school is financial, it may be that dowry costs should be factored into the standard direct costs and opportunity costs of educating girls. A stipend of about fifty cents a month is not much of a compensation for having to pay an increased dowry.

The purpose of girls' education

Girls' education was variously seen by respondents as a need, a right, or a luxury, as indicated by the perceived or stated purpose, the main purpose being 'employment'. It may be that women view education as a way of escaping tradition, whereas men (who tend to have more 'domestic' views of the purpose of girls' education) see it as a way of enhancing it. However, interviews with boys/men indicated that they were coming to terms with the idea of women working outside the home, although in particular households this may be a problem. Even if an educated girl/woman is allowed to work outside the home, paid employment opportunities for girls/women in rural areas are very limited, and attempts to promote income-generating activities for women have met with limited success – partly because of women's restricted access to markets.

Interviews showed that most people linked girls' education to employment, but for men/boys the stated reason was almost exclusively financial, whereas women/girls linked employment to such things as 'independence', 'confidence', and 'worth'. Views of what type of work is suitable for a woman were generally very stereotyped, based on an extension of women's traditional domestic roles, as the following 'public' interview example shows. A girl was asked what she wanted to do on leaving school:

> *Zakera: I want to have a job; I want to work – wherever there's a job. I'd like to work in a hospital.*
>
> *JR: What sort of job exactly?*
>
> *(Interruption from Iqbal, a high-status man present): A nurse, she wants to be a nurse.*
>
> *Zakera: (nods agreement)*

She might privately have higher aspirations, but publicly accepts being channelled into the lower-status option. An FSP promotional text presents a girl aspiring to be a doctor, but her motivation ('*I want to be a doctor to serve the sick...*') conforms to traditional 'feminine' attributes (World Bank 1993:3).

The majority of questionnaire respondents felt that secondary education for girls was good for society. However, although adult questionnaire respondents were unanimous in saying that education was a right, the children were less sure.

Education and cultural values

The official view – and that presented by FSP – is that education for girls generally enhances traditional cultural values (in preparing them to be better wives and mothers), and is for the national good. This is graphically depicted in a set of posters and calendars to promote girls' education (FSSAP / FEAP). Captions on the pictures present girls' education as contributing to the greater good; illiteracy is presented as a tragedy, with pictures of smiling school students and messages such as 'The sorrowful days are over' and 'Call the bird of happiness into this house of sorrow'.

The posters depict happy studious girls, almost all of whom modestly cover their bosoms with their schoolbooks. Girls' uniforms in Bangladesh have a stylised form of *dupatta*, a cloth that conceals the shape of the breasts. As if the *dupatta* were not enough, the books in the FEAP pictures even more effectively hide potentially disturbing signs of womanhood – and hence perhaps marriageability? In addition, all pictures are girls-only, even though most girls have no choice but to attend co-educational schools. Thus, the pictures show girls' education as posing little threat to cultural values. The only apparent cultural deviation is that many of the girls are making eye-contact with the camera, whereas adolescent girls are generally expected to keep their eyes modestly lowered. Perhaps because the books have obscured signs of sexuality, this eye-contact adds to the picture of youthful innocence: these girls do not yet know about sex; it is safe to let them out. Also revealing of the 'official' view of girls' education is the logo on FSP promotional materials. It depicts a girl firmly placed within a home, interacting with her book rather than with the outside world. There is nothing to threaten cultural practices here.

However, despite the official 'public' view, there is evidence of private misgivings about girls' education. This emerged in the questionnaires rather than the interviews, although only as a minority view. It could be that people are more willing to be honest in their responses to written questionnaires than in face-to-face interviews, or simply that the questionnaire sample was large enough to detect these misgivings.

For the questionnaire statements 'Educating girls will cause problems for the husbands', 'Adolescent girls should stay at home', and 'Secondary education is wasted on girls' there were distinct generational differences, with both girls and boys perhaps surprisingly showing more conservative views than the adults.

The statement 'Boys need secondary education more than girls' produced the widest spread of answers, with a quarter of respondents strongly disagreeing with the statement; other answers were spread over other categories. This is an indication that education may be viewed by some as a luxury for girls, but as a necessity for boys. A total of 16 per cent of respondents strongly agreed with the statement, the majority of these responses being from boys and male teachers. And as one father said: *'I suppose it's a good idea, girls getting education, but boys' need for education is bigger than girls'. They will be the breadwinners.'*

While the interviews produced little evidence of cultural bias against girls' education, it is worth noting that where it was evident, it was from boys/men, and most openly from boys. A couple of examples are given here, the first from the eldest of a family of three boys:

> *It's OK if she's educated to the same level as me, but I don't want her [i.e. his future wife] to work, I want her to stay at home. Most parents feel their daughters are going to get married when they grow up and they'll be housewives, so there's no need for them to get educated. It's a waste of money if they're going to spend all their time at home. But if they're educated, then maybe they can stand on their own feet, and can get jobs.*

Joynal seems rather confused. On the one hand he is saying that he wants an educated wife, but not for her to work; on the other hand, he says that the only point of education is to get a job. As he has no sisters, this is perhaps an issue that he has not yet had time or cause to consider fully. Another boy, Mokhles, simply asked: *'What's the point of getting girls educated when they're going to be married off as soon as possible?'* He has two brothers and one sister. The sister received no formal education (*'She was needed to help in the house and stuff like that'*), and was 'married off' at 16. Presumably his attitudes towards girls' education come from his family. But he too is confused about what he wants in a wife:

> *I want my wife to be educated to university level and good at all sorts of housework, and I would definitely like her to work outside the house to contribute to the family's income. But it's important that I am more educated than my wife.*

Mokhles expects a lot from his wife, but not equality. He was unable to say why he felt that he should have a higher level of education. Yet another boy felt that husbands should be older than their wives, thus providing more inbuilt inequality within the relationship. (The average age-gap between husbands and wives in Bangladesh is about seven years.)

It is difficult to know what these few muddled thoughts of adolescents mean. But if they are at all typical, they seem to be in conflict with Sweetser's 1999 findings of more conservative attitudes in older men. Or perhaps the boys have simply not learned to dissemble in the way that the men had? I suspect that the men whom I interviewed used 'money' as a coded argument against educating girls. With men, the cost of girls' education came up repeatedly, even though all but one were financially 'comfortable' and had no obvious problems in putting their sons through school. There is a detailed account (PROMOTE 2000) of a mother and a (woman) teacher trying to persuade a father to allow his daughter to stay in school. His sons were in Classes 8 and 10. His daughter was in Class 7, but he was arranging marriage for her because he was not willing to spend any more on her education. The argument is not about poverty, but about prejudice. Perhaps when men mention cost, they mean 'waste' (as in 'watering a neighbour's tree'), but they know this is no longer a publicly acceptable view. It could be that men use money as a convenient excuse, whereas women see it as less of a barrier. Perhaps the women know that if there is a will to educate daughters, there is usually a way. Unfortunately, the decision usually depends on the will of the husband/father.

The impact of expanded access to schooling

This case study revealed widespread approval of the FSP and the increase in girls' access to education. However, the study produced evidence that the impact of the expansion was not necessarily always good for girls, or that certain assumptions about girls' education were not necessarily true.

With regard to the quality of education, there is some evidence of negative impact. Many of the schools visited were seriously overcrowded, with classes of well over 100 students – a direct result of the FSP. In at least one co-educational but segregated school that I visited, boys' classes were divided into two sections, whereas the girls were squeezed into one section. The girls – who have a higher attendance rate than boys – were working in extremely cramped conditions. Thus, while the school benefits from the guaranteed fees paid for the girls, the girls are receiving a lower-quality education than the boys. In addition, the project is not linked to curricular change processes, so the schooling received has little relevance to the world outside, no direct links with employment or employers, and – apart from the stipend itself – no direct challenge to the gendered inequities that exist in Bangladesh.

Exam results indicate that there is still a significant gap between the achievements of boys and those of girls. In the 1998 SSC exams, girls in metropolitan areas achieved better results than boys for the first time. This caused a flurry of editorials and letters to the newspapers. There are indications that girls' achievements in 'good' rural schools are now almost matching those of boys, but that in the majority of rural schools not only do girls have a lower pass-rate, but far fewer girls are entered for the exam. Phase II of the FSP (Mahmud 2003) has addressed this to some extent by increasing the SSC allowance to cover the full fee, but as girls are still – for financial and 'security' reasons – denied the private tuition that is so necessary for passing the exam, this will probably not have much positive impact on results. It could even increase the gap, with more girls being entered for the exam but not given the academic support that they need in order to pass it.

To date, one of the criteria for continued receipt of the stipend is obtaining marks of 45 per cent or above in end-of-year examinations. For non-recipients, a pass mark of 33 per cent is sufficient to allow promotion to the next grade. This naturally works against the interest of girls from poorer families, who have less support in their schooling; but it has also led to many of the 'irregularities', with girls' grades being adjusted – for a variety of reasons – to ensure the continuation of stipends and fees. All strands of the FSP are currently considering lowering the requirement to 33 per cent, the main reason being to reduce the 'irregularities' (discussions with project personnel, 2004). While this could be seen as a more equitable measure for girls, it will probably result in more girls continuing to Class 10 without much hope of passing the SSC exam. Unless other measures are taken to support girls in their schooling, this might reinforce the idea that girls are simply not capable of academic success.

The final point relates to the need for women teachers to encourage girls' enrolment (Bellew and King 1993, World Bank 1997, Bellamy 2004). Many education initiatives are designed to increase the number of women teachers, partly for this reason. However, in the field study conducted in 2000 in which nine rural schools were visited, the most remote had no woman teacher (although the Head had made several requests for at least one – to teach Home Economics), but girls outnumbered boys 725 : 675. All schools visited had high girls' enrolment, regardless of how many women teachers they had. An estimated 55 per cent of rural schools have never had a woman teacher (Sanghbad 2000, newspaper article citing BANBEIS statistics). While there are many good reasons for encouraging women to enter the teaching profession, one might question the belief that the presence of women teachers is needed to encourage enrolment.

Conclusion

Overall, findings were positive, with widespread support for the FSP in particular, and the expansion of girls' education in general. The study showed that all groups saw the main purpose of education as enabling girls to take up paid employment. In the light of this, it is important to find out what employment opportunities there are for girls once they leave school. Given stated FSP project objectives of getting more girls into paid employment, it seems remarkable that there are no large-scale tracer studies to show how effective the project has been in meeting those objectives. If it is found that the chances of finding paid employment are too limited, the programme might lose its impetus and could even suffer a reversal. There is a strong need for the project to be linked to existing or future initiatives in employment opportunities and income generation, which must include a realistic appraisal of such opportunities in an essentially agrarian economy with limited scope for formal employment – for men or women.

As many of the interviews showed, most of the children in the sample would have been sent to school whether there was a stipend programme or not; only for a few was the stipend a determining factor. This finding strengthens arguments for the introduction of means-testing. Those families in which girls are sent to secondary school are those that have positive attitudes towards girls' education; more research is needed on the attitudes of those families from which girls do *not* attend school. In a country like Bangladesh, much non-enrolment can be attributed to poverty, but it may be that in some cases poverty is used as an excuse for not sending girls to school – when the real reason is based on traditional patriarchal values, and parents' reluctance to 'water a neighbour's tree'. Of particular interest is the effect of education on dowry demands. There is some evidence to show that increased dowry, linked to increased education, may be an inhibiting factor for some parents. It would be useful to establish the extent of this, and it may need to be factored into standard calculations of the cost of educating girls.

The attitudes of boys/younger men have been neglected in past studies relating to girls' education; but, as the patriarchs, husbands, and fathers of the future, their favourable views are vital for the continued expansion of education for girls. However, this study indicated that the views of the boys were less favourable than those of any other sub-group. Further research into the attitudes of this group could lead to better-targeted awareness programmes, and a long-term objective of making the husbands and fathers of the future more open to the possibilities offered by the education of girls.

Although the word 'empowerment' has crept into recent FSP documents, empowerment of women/girls is not an overt part of the programme. In this study, women/mothers were seen to be the strongest advocates of girls' education, but their own lack of empowerment restricts their role in decision making. A re-orientation of project objectives towards strengthening women's influence on family decisions would enhance the achievement of other project objectives (as well as enhancing the lives of the women). Such changes might best be achieved by linking with other programmes working in such areas as non-formal education, curriculum reform, and employment for empowerment, rather than a simple extension of traditional gendered roles. The FSP has a very strong momentum. By capitalising on that momentum and the widespread acceptance of the programme, the time seems right to build in modifications that actively promote the empowerment and equality of girls and women.

The parents in the case study are happy to send their daughters to school while someone else – in this case, the FSP – is 'watering the neighbour's tree'. But the project is not sustainable in its present form: proof of lasting change will be seen if the 'watering' continues even though funding stops.

Janet Raynor has worked as a teacher and education programme manager in Indonesia, South Africa, and Bangladesh. She has lived in Bangladesh for five years and worked on a range of education projects. She is currently completing her doctoral research at the Institute of Education, University of London.

Note

1   There are a number of names and acronyms for the various forms of the stipend programme. Here, I use 'FSP' as an umbrella term for all current and earlier versions of the programme.

References

Agence France Presse (2004) 'Bangladesh's micro-credit, girl-child education to be showcased in China', Agence France Presse
www.channelnewsasia.com/stories/afp_asiapacific/view/72634/1/.html, accessed 26.02.04

Ahmed, K. S. (2000) *Projection of Population, Environment and Costs to the State of Primary, Secondary and Higher Secondary Education in Bangladesh for the Period 2000–2020,* Dhaka: CPD-UNFPA Programme on Population and Sustainable Development

Ahmed, M. and M. Ahmed (2002) *Bangladesh Education Sector Overview*, Paper commissioned by the Japan Bank for International Cooperation, March 2002, www.jbic.go.jp/english/oec/environ/report/pdf/eban.pdf, 19.03.03

Amin, S. (1996) 'Female education and fertility in Bangladesh: the influences of marriage and the family' in R. Jeffery and A. M. Basu (eds.) *Girls' Schooling, Women's Autonomy and Fertility Change in South Asia*, New Delhi and Dewberry Park, CA: Sage Publications

Arends-Kuenning, M. and S. Amin (2001) 'Women's capabilities and the right to education in Bangladesh', *International Journal of Politics, Culture and Society*, 15: 125–42

BANBEIS (1998) *Bangladesh Educational Statistics, 1997*, Dhaka: BANBEIS / Ministry of Education

BANBEIS (1999) *Bangladesh Educational Statistics (at a glance)*, Dhaka: BANBEIS / MoE

BANBEIS (2001) *National Education Survey (post-primary)*, Dhaka: BANBEIS / MoE

BANBEIS (2002) *Statistical Profile on Education in Bangladesh*, Dhaka: Bangladesh Bureau of Educational Information and Statistics

BANBEIS (2003) *Pocketbook on Educational Statistics*, Dhaka: Bangladesh Bureau of Educational Information and Statistics, Government of Bangladesh

Bellamy, C. (2004) *The State of the World's Children 2004: Girls, Education and Development*, United Nations Children's Fund, www.unicef.org/sowc04/, January 2004, accessed 8.1.04

Bellew, R. T. and E. King (1993) 'Educating women: lessons from experience', in R. T. Bellew and E. King (eds.) *Women's Education in Developing Countries: Barriers, Benefits and Policies*, Washington: World Bank

Chanana, K. (1994) 'Social change or social reform: women, education and family in pre-independence India', in C. Mukhopadhyay and S. Seymour (eds.) *Women, Education and Family Structure in India*, Boulder: Westview Press

Chowdhury, A. M., R. K. Choudhury, and S. R. Nath (1999) *Education Watch 1999. Hope not complacency: state of primary education in Bangladesh*, Dhaka: UPL/Campaign for Popular Education (CAMPE)

CIA (2003) *The World Factbook: Bangladesh*, www.cia.gov/cia/publications/factbook/geos/bg.html, accessed June 2004

Daily Star (2003a, 24.6.03) 'FESP increases female enrolment at schools', Dhaka: *The Daily Star*, www.thedailystar.net/

Daily Star (2003b, 16.07.03) 'SSC success rate dips to 36.85pc', Dhaka: *The Daily Star*, www.thedailystar.net/

Daily Star (2004) 'From Hathatpara to Shanghai', Dhaka: *The Daily Star*, www.dailystarnews.com/

Daily Star (2005) '11 women killed a day: MMC study', www.thedailystar.net/2005/02/24/d50224060565.htm, accessed 24.02.05

Das Gupta, A., S. Islam, and M.S. Siddiq (1993) *Female Education Awareness Program of Female Secondary School Assistance Project - Baseline KABP survey: a report*, Dhaka: Associates for Communications Options, prepared for Academy of Educational Development

Esteve-Volart, B. (2003) 'Dowry in Rural Bangladesh: Participation as insurance against divorce' (preliminary draft), London School of Economics, http://econ.lse.ac.uk/phdc/0304/papers/bevotherpaper1.pdf, accessed April 2004

FESP (2004) *Number of Students Receiving Stipend*, Dhaka: Female Secondary Education Stipend Project: 3rd Phase, Government of Bangladesh

FSSAP (1999) *Semi-Annual Progress Report January – June 1999*, Dhaka: Directorate of Secondary and Higher Education / Ministry of Education

FSSAP (2004) *Annual Progress Report, January – December 2003*, Dhaka: Female Secondary Stipend Assistance Project – Phase II, Directorate of Secondary Education, Ministry of Education

FSSAP/FEAP, Promotional posters for the female stipend programme, Dhaka: World Bank, Female Secondary Stipend Assistance Programme

Government of Bangladesh (1996) *The Constitution of the People's Republic of Bangladesh (as modified up to 30th April 1996)*, Dhaka: reprinted by the British Council, www.bangladeshgov.org/pmo/constitution/consti2.htm#2A

Haider, R. (1995) *A Perspective in Development: Gender Focus*, Dhaka: University Press

Haq, M. u. and K. Haq (1998) *Human Development in South Asia: the education challenge*, Dhaka: University Press

Herz, B. (1991*) Letting Girls Learn: promising approaches in primary and secondary education,* World Bank

ICRW (2003) 'ICRW policy advisory on child marriage', International Centre for Research on Women, www.icrw.org/docs/childmarriage0803.pdf, accessed May 2004

Jahan, R. (1995a) *The Elusive Agenda: mainstreaming women in development,* London / Dhaka: Zed / UPL

Jahan, R. (1995b) 'Men in seclusion, women in public: Rokeya's dream and women's struggles in Bangladesh', in A. Basu (ed.*) The Challenge of Local Feminisms: women's movements in global perspective,* Boulder: Westview Press

Jalaluddin, A. and M.R. Chowdhury (eds.) (1997) *Getting Started: universalising quality primary education in Bangladesh*, Dhaka: University Press

Jeffery, P. and R. Jeffery (1998) 'Silver bullet or passing fancy? Girl's schooling and population policy', in C. Jackson and R. Pearson (eds.) *Feminist Visions of Development: gender analysis and policy,* London: Routledge

Kabir, S. M. (1996) 'An experience of religious extremism in Bangladesh', in World Health Organisation (ed.) *Reproductive Health Matters Fundamentalism, women's empowerment and reproductive rights*, London: WHO

Khan, S. R. (2001) *The Socio-legal Status of Bangali Women in Bangladesh: Implications for development*, Dhaka: University Press

Khandker, S. R. and H.A. Samad (1996) *Education Achievements and School Efficiency in Rural Bangladesh*, Washington, DC: World Bank

Koenig M. A. *et al.* (2003) 'Women's status and domestic violence in rural Bangladesh: individual- and community-level effects', *Demography*, 40:269–88

Mahmud, S. (2003) *Female Secondary Stipend Project in Bangladesh: a critical assessment.* Dhaka: Institute of Development Studies, portal.unesco.org/education/ev.php?URL_ID=25755, 03.02.04

Mannan, M. A. (2002) *Violence against Women: Marital violence in rural Bangladesh*, CPD-UNFPA Programme on Population and Sustainable Development, Paper 20, November 2002, 66, www.cpd-bangladesh.org/cunfpa20.htm, accessed 17.02.03

Momen, A. (1995) *Girls and our School Education: Question of gender equality and the position of women in our education*, Dhaka: Bangladesh Nari Progati Sangha

Mustafa, K. G., S.R. Howlader, J.H. Chowdhury, and M. Islam (1990) *Feasibility Study on Female Education Scholarship Program*, Dhaka: Associates for Community and Population research, sponsored by World Bank

New Nation (2004a, 26.05.04) 'Khaleda addresses Poverty Reduction Confce at Shanghai: Evolve new strategy to reduce rich-poor gap', Dhaka: *The New Nation* www.ittefaq.com/ittefaq_apps/javamail.jsp?subject=Khaleda%20addresses%20Poverty%

New Nation (2004b, 27.05.04) 'S Asia lessons figure at Shanghai confce', Dhaka: *The New Nation*, www.ittefaq.com/ittefaq_apps/javamail.jsp?subject=S%20Asia%20lessons%20figure%20at%

New Nation (2004c, 10.04.04) 'WB commends Bangladesh's economic, social progress', Dhaka: *The New Nation* www.ittefaq.com/ittefaq_apps/javamail.jsp?subject=WB%20commends%20Bangladesh%92s%

PROMOTE (2000, April 2000) 'Promote Model Teachers 2000', paper presented at the PROMOTE Gender Policy Dialogue National Seminar, Dhaka

Quisumbing, A. R. and J.A. Maluccio (2000) *Intrahousehold Allocation and Gender Relations: new empirical evidence from four developing countries*, Washington: IFPRI, Food Consumption and Nutrition Division, Discussion Paper 84 www.ifpri.org/divs/fcnd/dp/papers/fcnbr84.pdf, January 2003

Raynor, J. and R. A. Chowdhury (2004) *A National Assessment of Girls' Secondary Stipend Programmes in Bangladesh*, Dhaka: study commissioned by DfID, Bangladesh

Sanghbad (2000) 'PROMOTE female teachers in rural secondary schools', Dhaka: *Sanghbad*

Sarker, P. C., J.H. Chowdhury, and T. Tariq (1995) *Evaluation of BACE Secondary School Girls' Scholarship Project, Kaharole, Dinajpur*, Dhaka: Associates for Community and Population Research

Sattar, E. (1982) *Universal Primary Education in Bangladesh*, Dhaka: University Press

Sen, G. C. (2002, 18.06.02) 'Keynote Paper on Quality Education for Poverty Reduction in Bangladesh', presented at aWorkshop organised by the Ministry of Education, Dhaka

Sultan, M. (1994) 'Women's struggle against tradition in Bangladesh', *Convergence*, XXVII

Sweetser, A. T. (1999) *Lessons from the BRAC Non-formal Primary Education Programme*, Academy for Educational Development / ABEL Clearing House for Basic Education. www.dec.org/pdf_docs/PNACE308.pdf, March 2000

Thein, T.-M., M. Kabir, and M. Islam (1988) *Evaluation of the Female Education Scholarship Program supported by the Asia Foundation*, Dhaka: USAID, edited by Eleanore Boyce, Washington DC: USAID

Thornton, H., M.S. Haq, A. Huda, and U. Munsura (2005) *Pushing the Boundaries: Girls and secondary education in Bangladesh*, Dhaka: Social Development Direct

UNDP (2004) *Human Development Report 2004: Cultural liberty in today's diverse world*. New York: United Nations Development Programme
http://hdr.undp.org/reports/global/2004/pdf/hdr04_complete.pdf, 17.07.04

UNESCO Bangkok (2003) 'Adolescent Reproductive and Sexual Health, Bangladesh – Demographic characteristics of adolescents',
www.unescobkk.org/ips/arh-web/demographics/bangladesh2.cfm, accessed June 2004

United Nations (2000) UN Millennium Development Goals (MDG): United Nations.
www.un.org/millenniumgoals/, accessed 18.07.04

Unterhalter, E. (2000) 'Transnational visions of the 1990s: contrasting views of women, education and citizenship', in M. Arnot and J. Dillabough (eds.) *Citizenship, Gender and Education*, London: Routledge

Valad, P. T. (1995) 'The Female Secondary School Assistance Project in Bangladesh: enhancing women's opportunities for empowerment and development through stipends for secondary education', paper prepared for (World Bank) Education Week 1995

World Bank (1993) *Staff Appraisal: Report on Female Secondary School Assistance Project. Report No. 15496-IN / 11386-BD*, Washington DC: World Bank Population and Human Resources Division

World Bank (2003) *(Abadzi) Project Performance Assessment Report, Bangladesh Female Secondary School Assistance Project (Credit 2469)* (26226): World Bank
http://lnweb18.worldbank.org/oed/oeddoclib.nsf/DocUNIDViewForJavaSearch/8056C841585
8730385256D86006F44C0/$file/Bangladesh_PPAR_26226.pdf, 21.05.04

World Education Forum (2000) *The Dakar Framework for Action Education for All: meeting our collective commitments*, Paris: UNESCO

5 The challenge of educating girls in Kenya

Elimu Yetu Coalition

Although Kenya's education policy does not discriminate against girls and women, their participation is characterised by manifest disparities. There are serious regional disparities in primary enrolment, particularly in the Arid and Semi-Arid Lands, where pastoralism and nomadism predominate. There are also wide variations in drop-out rates between regions, and in the last ten years completion rates in Kenya have never exceeded 50 per cent. Low completion rates, especially for girls, mean that few pupils who do succeed in completing their schooling manage to penetrate the labour market.

The challenges that confront girls' education in Kenya include both in-school and out-of-school factors; they span the economic, cultural, social, regional, and policy realms. Since 2000, government and non-government agencies have tried to address these challenges, which are expressed in the interlinked problems of unequal access, poor rates of retention, and poor quality of education for girls. Their concerted efforts have in fact reduced the differential in girls' and boys' participation in basic education.

This chapter reports the findings of research conducted by the Elimu Yetu Coalition with the broad aim of reviewing the progress made in girls' education in Kenya, primarily in primary education, since the World Education Forum in Dakar in 2000.[1] It aimed to do this by identifying the problems and challenges facing girls in achieving equal and full participation in basic education, especially girls from marginal communities, hardship areas, and disadvantaged families/ backgrounds. The research also aimed to assess existing and on-going efforts by government and NGOs to map who is doing what in the field of girls' education, and what has and has not worked. A second set of objectives concerned documentation of best practice, aiming to provide information to inform Elimu Yetu's campaigning and other advocacy work for girls' education in order to achieve the Millennium Development Goals on gender parity and gender equality.

The first section of this chapter considers the factors that hinder girls' participation in education – both the out-of-school and in-school factors – in the three areas. It then examines the main interventions and programmes which the government of Kenya and a range of NGOs have been implementing to increase girls' participation. The third section considers the advocacy work that is being increasingly carried out to raise awareness of the importance of girls' education; it also considers the dynamics of policy and planning for the promotion of girls' education in Kenya.

The research methodology

The research was conducted in March 2003, using a variety of qualitative methods which included in-depth interviews with education officials, civil-society organisations, community leaders, and teachers. Interviews were conducted with out-of-school children, children newly enrolled through the government's Free Primary Education legislation, and girls 'rescued' from early marriages. Focus-group discussions were held with parents, community members/leaders, and pupils. In addition, a literature review of policy documents and research reports was carried out.

The interviews were conducted in two predominantly rural Districts – Tharaka and Kajiado – and in informal settlements in Nairobi. The information gathered in these areas was supplemented by interviews with NGOs working in a range of other rural and urban slum contexts. Kajiado and Tharaka are areas where the population is predominantly pastoralist, and the districts rural.

Kajiado district is one of the 17 districts in the Rift Valley Province. It covers an area of 21,105 km^2. The general topography of the district is characterised by plains and volcanic hills. The plains are dissected by several valleys. Children have to walk up and down the ridges in order to reach their schools. Cultural beliefs among the Maasai, who are the dominant ethnic group in the district, have affected children's education, and especially that of girls.

Tharaka district, carved out of the former Tharaka Nithi district in 1998, is one of the poorest districts in the country. The poverty level stands at 65 per cent in absolute terms. The average income for most people in the district per month is Ksh 500 (about US$ 6.50). The main factors that damage girls' educational progress in the district are female genital mutilation (FGM) and early marriages.

The informal settlements in Nairobi are characterised by poor living conditions, insecurity, environmental degradation, congestion, and unemployment. High heaps of garbage are common, there are few toilet facilities, and health-care facilities are absent – all of which creates the conditions for environmental diseases. Even basic schooling is not provided. Kibera, Kariobangi, and Mukuru are informal slums on the outskirts of Nairobi with high population densities. The occupants do not have legal tenure of the land, and schools are consequently not supported by the government.

Factors influencing girls' educational prospects

Across all the areas in the study, the out-of-school issues that influence girls' prospects of education can be classified as social and cultural practices (early marriage, FGM, and student pregnancies); the low social status of girls and women; poverty; and girls' and boys' unequal labour burdens. In-school factors include sexual harassment; teachers' low expectations of girls' performance; gender-stereotyped learning materials; high rates of repetition for girls; and inadequate sanitary facilities.

Out-of-school factors

Early marriage

The practice of early marriage was found to be most pronounced in Kajiado district, where girls are married at a young age (under 15 years) and often to older, wealthy men in order to fetch a good dowry, which in this region takes the form of cattle. (See Box 1.) In Nairobi, however, early marriage was not so pronounced, although it was found that girls becoming pregnant often dropped out of school and sought marriage.

Female genital mutilation (FGM) is another factor behind girls' premature withdrawal from school. FGM is widely practised among the Maasai communities (and others in Kenya). Once a girl has undergone it, she is considered an adult woman and ready for marriage. The age at which girls are circumcised has been declining, and their subsequent 'adult behaviour' includes sexual activity and a lack of interest in schooling. Medical complications resulting from FGM and pregnancy contribute to drop-out rates in some communities.

Low values attributed to girls and their education

In communities where 'traditional' practices such as FMG are widespread, both girls and boys interviewed felt that girls' education was not valued as highly as boys' education. Boys in particular emphasised the fact that girls were often kept at home, but parents insisted that they valued education for their sons and daughters equally. In the informal urban settlements, some parents expressed the belief that educating a girl simply enriches her husband's family, while educating a boy is seen as enriching his own family. Interviewees noted that too much education may prevent a girl from getting a suitable husband, and that educated girls may cause difficulties in marriage, which could lead to divorce.

The study also made clear the unequal gender division of labour in households. The work burden on girls at home was repeatedly cited as a negative factor affecting their education.

Box 1: Early marriage and schooling

I am from Engaroni Division of Kajiado District. I have three brothers and four sisters. Two of my siblings, one brother and one sister, have gone to school up to primary level. They are sponsored by our uncle, who is working in Nairobi.

I attended Engaroni primary school up to Class 2; then my father said he had no money to educate me. I was circumcised in 1996 and stayed at home the whole year. In 1997 I got married to an old friend of my father. He was my father's age; the old man (my husband) was around 40 years old. He paid dowry in terms of two cows and an unknown amount of money.

My mother told me of the arrangements, but I was too young to take any action. I was only 9 years old by then. Then one Saturday morning I went to the chief to report the matter. The chief came to my husband's home and demanded that I be taken back to my parents' home, but my in-laws made plans to take me somewhere else to hide from the chief.

When I heard about this plan, I ran away from my marriage and returned to my home. My father shouted at me and asked whether the chief had become my father. The following day my husband came and talked with my father. I was then ordered to go back with him, which I obeyed. After spending one night at my husband's home, I ran back home. My father asked me why I was back, but this time he did not send me back to my husband's home, because he feared the chief, who had threatened to jail him.

Therefore they allowed me to go back to school, but on condition that I would see my husband every weekend. I went to school for one week but refused to see my husband during the weekend, because it was shameful: other children would laugh at me, a married wife in school.

(14-year-old girl, Class 8, AIC Primary School)

One informant said, '*If there is a baby to be taken care of, it will be the girl to do so – at the expense of her education.*' Also, parents keep children – most often girls - at home on market days. Many girls are expected to take their younger siblings with them to school – a practice which many teachers do not encourage. '*But teachers also realise that forbidding girls to bring siblings increased the girls' drop-out rates, so they allowed them*' (interviewee, Aga Khan Foundation Nairobi).

In informal settlements in Nairobi, both boys and girls interviewed reported that girls were overburdened with housework, which included cooking, cleaning, washing, and taking care of the young ones. '*My sister is my mother's assistant. She even takes the baby to hospital. She also goes looking for water, where she might have to queue the whole day*' (pupil, Shadrack Kimalel School, Kibera, Nairobi).

In Kibera, where children attend private and community schools in the informal settlements, boys engage in hawking wares at weekends in order to earn money for school fees. They also seek casual labour during the holidays. Girls often work in saloons, and some resort to providing sex in exchange for money. Most girls who were interviewed lacked money to buy sanitary wear and consequently stayed away from school during their menstrual periods. Pornographic movies in the neighbourhood exposed girls to negative gender images. Drunkenness and drug abuse are daily activities in these settlements, and in Kibera drugs and beer are sold in the kiosks. Girls are exposed to this hostile environment on their way to and from school.

The number of HIV/AIDS orphans in Kenya is projected to be around 1.5 million in 2005 (MoH/NACC 2002). In the three areas surveyed for the study, informal settlements in Nairobi were hardest hit by the impact of HIV/AIDS. Here, many girls have assumed the extra responsibility of looking after their siblings, and child-headed families are on the increase. However, in Kajiado and Tharaka, HIV/AIDS cases are minimal. Both the government officials and teachers interviewed in these districts said they knew of few pupils who had dropped out of school in response to the impact of HIV/AIDS on their lives.

The case described in Box 2 illustrates effects of poverty on girls' education. Safety and security factors also play a key role in keeping girls out of school. Long

---

Box 2: Dropping out of school

I was born in 1989, and my mother is single. I was enrolled in Class 1 in 1995 in Majengo primary school [a private school], but my mother had a lot of problems, like raising money for food and rent. We were occasionally locked out by the landlord for not paying rent on time. So we moved to Mukuru informal settlement, and my mother managed to pay rent for some time. Initially, I found it difficult to cope, but later adjusted to the cramped and squalid living conditions in Mukuru.

When I was in Class 3, my mother had a baby and life became difficult. I began going to school without lunch, although our neighbour, called Baba Amos, would bring some food for us and give my mother some money. I learned later that he was my sister's father, and we eventually moved in with him.

My mother tried doing some business and she would travel up-country to buy cereals for sale. But one day in 1999 I returned home from school to learn that she had died in a road accident. There was no money for the funeral, and I have never seen her grave.

We still live with Baba Amos in one room. I wash clothes in people's homes to provide for my sister and I help Baba to sell *busaa*. I dropped out of school because there was no money for my fees, but recently I got a sponsor for my sister, so that she can go to school. When Free Primary Education was introduced, I wanted to go back to school, but Baba Amos became very angry. I don't think he has ever been to school, though he knows how to count money.

(Out-of-school girl, 14 years old, Mukuru Slum, Nairobi)

---

distances to schools from home expose girls to physical and sexual dangers and lead to drop-out. Distances are long in the Kajiado region (16 km–40 km), while in the urban areas commuting to school on public transport poses dangers to girls from harassment by drunks (Chege 1995).

Teenage pregnancy, a direct result of the security and poverty issues outlined above, strongly affects girls' ability to participate in education. According to the Kenya Domestic Household Survey, adolescent mothers constitute more than half (55 per cent) of adolescent girls. Although the Kenyan government has a policy of allowing the re-entry of girls to schools after giving birth, many girls and parents are not aware of it, and those who do return suffer from stigmatisation, ridicule, and abuse from both teachers and other pupils. However, it is the lack of child-care facilities that seems the main factor that keeps girls at home.

In-school factors

A clear finding to emerge from the study was that both teachers and male pupils harass girls. Teachers seek sexual favours from girls and are sometimes in competition with male pupils. Teachers were said to use girls to run errands, fetch water and cook for them.

Lack of female teachers emerged as a key in-school factor affecting girls' education. In Tharaka, a semi-arid district, female teachers are rare. Girls expressed the need for female teachers in schools so that they could confide in them and see them as role models. Most girls refused to discuss their problems with male teachers in the absence of female teachers. In Muslim communities, lack of single-sex schools may constitute a barrier to female education.

Late enrolment is another factor affecting girls' drop-out. Teachers force children who do not perform well to repeat a year, a practice which takes a higher toll on girls than boys because it widens the disparity between age and grade. Girls are exposed to ridicule, early sex, pregnancy, and eventual drop-out before completion.

Lack of guidance and counselling in schools accelerates the rate at which girls drop out. In interviews with pupils, girls revealed that they had not been prepared by either parents or teachers to deal with changes in their bodies. Some reported having been taught about menstruation by their home-science teacher, but this subject has now been removed from the syllabus.

Some teachers interviewed had a low opinion of girls' performance. They believed that science and technical subjects should be left for boys. Student interviewees reported that such teachers undermined and discouraged girls from learning.

In all three areas – Tharaka, Kajiado, and Nairobi – pupils reported having insufficient learning materials. In Tharaka, each textbook was shared between as many as five pupils. The situation was similar in Kajiado and Nairobi. In City Council schools in Nairobi, pupils are required to buy a desk on admission, and there are up to 115 pupils in each class. The situation was reported to be bad also in those non-State schools which had no NGO or church sponsorship. On top of paying 500 Kshs. a month, students have to provide their own books, pencils, uniform, and bags – despite the existence of the government's Free Primary Education programme.

Whereas some schools have adequate sanitary facilities, some are in very poor condition. In Tharaka, water was lacking in most of the schools. The pit latrines were almost full and in very poor condition, thus posing a danger to the pupils. In Kibera, some of the girls' toilets had no doors. The facilities were dirty and faced the front of the school. Girls felt embarrassed to use these toilets.

The study found drug and alcohol abuse to be a major problem in urban areas such as Nairobi. In Kibera both boys and girls were said to be involved in drug and alcohol abuse, and some girls reportedly assist their mothers in selling beer.

Interventions in girls' education

Although educational opportunities have indeed expanded for all children in Kenya, girls in marginal and urban poor areas still face many obstacles to education. Government and civil-society organisations recognise the need for gender equality and have responded in a range of different ways. The next section draws on the research data to present some of the key responses from government in terms of policy development and new legislation. It goes on to describe some of the practical responses from NGOs working with small-scale innovative projects to increase the participation of girls in education in Kenya.

Government strategies

The Ominde report (1964), produced by a commission that was set up immediately following independence, and all other education reports, such as Gachathi report (1976), Mackay report (1981), Kamunge report (1988), Master Plan on Education and Training (1998), and the Koech report (2000), all made reference to the need to accelerate improvements in the education of girls.[2] The Koech report, which proposed a new structure to the education system but was later shelved, also recognised the efforts already made by the government to improve girls' education, including affirmative action in the expansion of facilities to enable girls to study science and technical subjects, and a policy of allowing girls who drop out due to pregnancy to continue with education. These and other factors have yielded benefits, demonstrated by the increase of girls' participation in schooling (Republic of Kenya 2002).

Kenya's commitment to redressing problems concerning girls' education is evidenced through participation in international forums on gender and girls' education. The country is a signatory to nearly all international conventions on education and has ratified several international instruments relating to gender equality, thus joining the global community's commitment to redressing imbalances related to gender, learning, and underdevelopment. Progress has been made towards institutionalisation of the strategies but, as the previous section illustrates, there are still gaps to be closed and challenges to be met in terms of translating the policies into good practice.

Local efforts and strategies by the Kenya government to meet the goal of Education For All (EFA) at the primary level include the following.

- Operating multi-shift systems to ease congestion.

- Permitting a flexible timetable in areas where school competes with the economic and social activities of the community.

- Establishing a disaggregated system of unit costs for essential teaching/learning and other activities, as when the government introduced Free Primary Education (FPE), under which funds were allocated to specific school activities.

- Regularly monitoring and auditing primary-school performance.

- Operating re-entry policies for girls who leave school due to pregnancies, child labour, and other factors.

- Enacting (in 2001) the Children's Act, which recognises that education is the basic human right of every child. The Act combines into one law several pieces of legislation affecting children, including the Children and Young Persons Act, the Guardianship of Infants Act, and the Adoption Act. There is now a Children's Court, which is subordinate to the High Court of Kenya, with a presiding magistrate.

In January 2003 the newly elected government of Kenya introduced Free Primary Education and appointed the FPE Task Force to assist with the development of appropriate responses for implementing FPE. Although FPE opened doors to both boys and girls, regional disparities and cultural factors still affect girls' access, retention, and outcomes in marginal communities.

At the time when this research was conducted in 2003, the Kenyan government had a range of policies to promote girls' education, but they were not brought together to form one piece of legislation or plan. They are scattered across policy documents, such as the reports of different commissions and committees on education, development plans, and sessional papers. The Ministry of Education was at that time in the process of developing a Gender Education Policy Paper with aims that included the elimination of gender disparities in access, transition, retention, and performance in education. It includes measures designed to achieve the following.

- Address specific problems of access, retention, transition, and performance of the boy and girl child in the education system.

- Promote and support alternative systems of basic education, in collaboration with other stakeholders.

- Improve participation of children with disability, especially the girl child, in both special and vocational training.

- Ensure that literacy and post-literacy materials are gender-responsive and easily available to all learners (MOEST, draft 2003).

Some of the strategies to achieve these aims have already been put into action. For example, the government introduced a policy of expanding existing facilities in order to take care of the needs of disabled children; some of the schools visited in the course of the research had a unit for children with special needs. Units catering for children with hearing impairments or physical disabilities greatly improve the opportunities for girls, as it is mainly the girl child that suffers neglect. But the piecemeal nature of the changes and lack of a coherent legislative framework mean that Kenya has missed part of the MDG 3 target (eliminate gender disparities in primary and secondary education by 2005).

There is an on-going review of the Education Act to provide an adequate legal framework to improve management, co-ordination, and quality control in education and consolidation of the national action plan on EFA which will identify strategies for improving girls' education over the next ten years. There are also budget reviews and cost analysis, including tracking expenditure patterns in the education sector with a view to making the national budget gender-fair, and establishing an allocation for girls. However, these actions are being undertaken at a very slow pace, and at the time of going to press they are still awaiting finalisation. They are therefore key components of the Elimu Yetu Campaign for 2005 (see the following section).

NGO initiatives

This section presents some of the activities being undertaken by the NGO sector to improve education for girls.

Girls' re-entry programmes

In the recent past, the government introduced the Re-Entry Programme, which allows girls who have given birth to be re-admitted into schools. The Lutheran World Federation (LWF) established a project, funded by UNHCR, to cater for girls who had dropped out of the mainstream primary-education system and wished to return to school. The Western Kenya Girl Child Network chapter has helped teenage mothers to return to formal education after delivery.

Box 3: Re-entering primary school after giving birth

We are about 20 children in my family. My father has four wives, and my mother is the last wife. I am the fifth born in my mother's family of seven children. We are three daughters and four sons. They have all been to school. My elder siblings are educated up to Form 4, although one of my sisters, the one that I come after, only went up to Class 8.

I joined this school in 1991 in Nursery. Last year when I was in Standard 7, I got pregnant. I took a break in the month of October 2002 to go and give birth. I delivered a baby girl in January this year and then resumed school in May. I am currently in Class 8, but I will not sit for examinations, because I have missed many lessons.

Although it was a young single man who impregnated me, I did not want to get married to him and so I opted to come back to school. My parents suggested that I come back to school too, and I agreed. I am happy with my classmates and teachers, who treat me with respect. My mother takes care of the baby as I come to school. But I go home to breastfeed during lunchtime and after school. The baby does not affect my schooling at all. At home I have time to do my homework.

I am interested in learning even up to secondary level and beyond, but my parents cannot afford school fees for higher learning; that is why one of my sisters is at home. She helps Mother to take care of the baby.

(Girl, 16 years old, Moipei Primary School, Class 8)

Financing initiatives to support girls in education

It emerged from the study that poverty was one of the strongest factors affecting girls' education. To address the poverty issue, some civil-society organisations – for instance, the Basic Education Fund (BEF) – have encouraged school-management committees to be involved in income-generating activities. The Kenyan chapter of the Forum for African Women Educationalists (FAWEK), which partners BEF in Mbeere and Meru districts, provides seed money (initial financial assistance) to school managers, and the money is used to support gender-sensitisation clubs. Club members are encouraged to establish income-generating activities to sustain them. The money generated from the activities is used for meeting club needs. Club members are engaged in creative arts as a form of communicating about the rights of the girl child and the need to educate girls. They also generate income from such performances.

Another anti-poverty strategy is the financing of small businesses, a process funded by BEF and Oxfam GB to empower poor parents economically and give them an economic base from which they can pay for the education of girls. Oxfam GB works in partnership with Wema Center in Mombasa and Pendekezo Letu to provide educational and other basic needs for girls retrieved from the streets. Parents of these girls are given financial support for a period of three years to start income-generating activities.

In Kajiado, which is predominantly a pastoral area, chiefs try to reduce poverty by encouraging the community to supplement animal supervision with farming, thus earning extra money which can then be used for food and school fees for children. Dupoto E Maa is also working in this district to address the problem of poverty by encouraging head-teachers to register an association for lobbying the Ministry of Education. They are encouraged to act collectively to present the problems facing children in their schools, such as the need for school meals and lower fees for boarding schools.

ActionAid Kenya (AAK) established school resource bases in which levy-saving strategies are set up. Before the introduction of FPE, this fund helped poor households to pay school levies. But since the establishment of the new FPE programme, the fund is used to supply other school needs not met by the government. Under this project, AAK and the community each raise half the necessary funds; schools draw on the overall fund and develop budgets for purchasing teaching and learning materials and paying watchmen's salaries. The aim of the project is to encourage the schooling of girls from poor households. The project also encourages the spirit of working together.

In-school feeding programmes

A further intervention is the introduction of in-school feeding programmes. The Arid and Semi-Arid Areas have a particular problem with girls' access to schooling, because of the long distances between villages and schools. One of the primary reasons why girls in this position are not allowed to go to school is that they cannot afford to go back home for lunch. Special interventions have been implemented in some of these areas to improve enrolment, including an in-school feeding scheme in Kajiado, funded by the World Food Programme. However, at the time of writing this project was due to end in a few months, and already some of the schools visited under the study were no longer receiving food. In Kibera slum, Oxfam GB has a feeding programme for girls from poor backgrounds. In both situations, girls are prioritised because they are most likely to be withdrawn from school in cases of long distances and poverty.

Bursaries and sponsorship

Sponsorship is used as another intervention in girls' education. The GCN (Girl Child Network – a network bringing together all actors on girls' education in the country) and Christian Children Fund (CCF) sponsor girls from poor backgrounds. With the introduction of FPE, GCN turned its attention to sponsoring girls in secondary schools, while the CCF now buys uniforms, books, and other school needs for children from needy backgrounds. In an interview with pupils from Moipei and Oloosuyan primary schools in Kajiado, it was revealed that some of the participants were beneficiaries of the CCF.

The Young Muslim Association gives preference to girls in its bursary awards, while Oxfam GB supports a partner in Wajir which provides uniforms for school girls and builds separate toilets for girls in schools. Pupils of Mashimoni Squatters Primary School in Kibera reported that they receive clothes, uniforms, bags, and food from the Calvary Evangelistic group. This group offers breakfast, lunch, and supper to orphans. All sponsored children have their meals in the school.

Sinaga Center in Nairobi rescues children employed as domestic workers and sponsors bright pupils in the ABC (basic literacy) class to benefit from formal education in boarding schools. The centre has a withdrawal and counselling programme whereby girls are withdrawn from work as house girls. After counselling they are taught basic literacy before they are sponsored to join formal schooling. The Education Officer in Tharaka confirmed that the government has established bursary funds in the district in order to reduce the rates at which girls from poor backgrounds drop out of school.

Girls' clubs

The Girls' Education Movement (GEM) is an intervention implemented by Women Educational Researchers of Kenya (WERK) in order to improve the participation of girls in schooling. It is a movement led by young people, aiming to transform negative attitudes towards girls' education in Africa. A participatory movement, it is designed to give children and young girls maximum opportunity to develop and express their own ideas without adult interference. GEM emerged from a meeting of professionals in Kampala in 2000. WERK is working towards a partnership with UNHCR which will establish GEM clubs in primary schools and refugee camps. Three young Kenyan girls, who are members of WERK, participated in the workshop in Uganda. During this workshop they undertook a training course, and as a result they are training other girls in the country.

Flexible models of schooling

In promoting girls' education, ActionAid Kenya (AAK) arrived at an alternative approach to education, known as non-formal education (NFE), in Samburu, which is predominantly a pastoralist region. AAK conducts evening and after-work classes. Initially, the project targeted older children of both sexes, but it emerged that 65 per cent of the pupils were girls of school-going age who were left at home to milk and to take care of the weaker animals during times of drought, while boys took animals far from home in search of pasture.

In collaboration with the government, AAK has assisted in the establishment of out-of-school centres in Samburu next to the *manyattas* (the traditional houses of the Samburu). The Ministry of Education runs these centres, enrolling disadvantaged girls. Most teachers in these centres are formal professionals, employed by the government. They are motivated by incentives such as training courses in multi-grade teaching and exposure visits to other regions of Kenya.

The Mobile School Project in North Eastern province is another example of a successful intervention. The government has worked jointly with Oxfam GB to support mobile schools for the children of nomadic pastoralists in the province. Oxfam GB supports the Nomadic Primary Health Care and Mobile School in Wajir.

Head-teachers of schools participating in the research concurred that they engaged in several activities within their schools to promote girls' education. They include the following.

- Discouraging FGM and early marriage for girls.

- Inviting role models into school to address girls.

- Holding seminars with parents on girls' education.

- Providing guidance and counselling to girls.

- Giving awards to girls who perform well, to promote their morale and to encourage others.

Involving girls in income-generating clubs, such as the 4K clubs, with the aim of enabling them to earn money to meet their needs.

Promoting positive images of girls

Using positive role models has also proved an effective intervention to encourage out-of-school girls to attend school. The Girl Child Network operating in Coast Province, Kwale district, has introduced a programme similar to one run by the IIEP (Integrated Islamic Education Programme), whereby mentors act as role models to girls in schools. However, unlike the Aga Khan Foundation, which uses government teachers as mentors, GCN identifies role models through the provincial and district education officers. Formation of gender-sensitisation clubs in schools has further improved girls' participation in schooling. The Child

Welfare Society of Kenya and the Basic Education Fund, together with pupils in AIC girls' boarding school in Kajiado, also practise this approach. The clubs play a key role in creating awareness of the rights of the girl child. Some clubs, especially those sponsored by the Basic Education Fund in Mbeere, have enabled orphaned children – both boys and girls – to acquire education, by paying for their school needs. Through the Mbeere Club, members sensitise parents about the importance of girls' education.

Centres of excellence

Four chapters of FAWE (Forum for African Women Educationalists) in Kenya, Rwanda, Tanzania, and Senegal have been involved in another type of intervention: the establishment of centres of excellence. These model schools are designed to provide an environment conducive to high-quality learning and teaching. The schools demonstrate how accumulated information, knowledge, and experience can be used to formulate, implement, and monitor policies and practices that promote girls' education (*FAWE News*, April–June 2001).

Several Centres of Excellence have been established in Kajiado District, where parents, especially fathers, commonly marry off young girls to older men. All the civil-society organisations, government officials, community members, and leaders who participated in the Elimu Yetu study confided that they were engaged in rescuing girls from early marriages. The district has special schools which are used as 'rescue' centres, or centres of excellence. The first school to be used as a rescue centre has saved many girls from early marriage and at the time of writing has approximately 60 rescue cases. The schools emphasise holistic, high-quality education, achieved through use of regular in-service training of teachers. The teachers are trained in gender sensitivity, with emphasis on the creation of girl-friendly teaching environments, the use of counselling skills, and the up-dating of teaching methods. The school committee is trained in management skills, and the girls are trained to understand their rights. The school provides a girl-friendly teaching and learning environment, which produces girls who are empowered and full of confidence in themselves. FAWE has identified a gap between rescued girls and their parents and has now started reconciling girls with their parents, through consultations between chiefs and parents. Some girls now feel able to approach chiefs for assistance. In a focus-group discussion, three chiefs in Kajiado District commented: '*On the problem of early/forced marriages, we have one organisation that helps us: FAWE. When we hear of a girl getting married off, we retrieve her and enrol her at AIC Girls, a FAWE-sponsored school.*'

FAWE-Kenya takes a holistic approach to enhancing girls' education. Right from the inception of a project, it involves the community in all activities. Communities act as agents and are involved throughout the life of the project, providing locally available materials. FAWE uses research findings to identify areas of intervention. This research may be an initiative of its own, or it may be conducted by other organisations. After identifying the problem, FAWE researchers study it and propose suitable interventions. For example, the centres of excellence alluded to above were introduced as a result of the finding that girls are forced into marriage in exchange for cows. In response, rescue centres for such girls, such as AIC Girls' School which is described above, were established.

Teaching methodologies

The Aga Khan Foundation has initiated a programme in public schools that targets the improvement of teaching methodologies in primary schools. The programme focuses on re-adjusting methodologies to be gender-sensitive. Each teacher in these schools is allocated to a mentor. The Foundation has a technical team of five qualified persons who provide mentoring to the teachers and address monitoring, evaluation, documentation, and mobilisation. The mobilisation mentor deals with issues pertaining to school management. The Aga Khan Foundation has signed a Memorandum of Understanding with the Teachers' Service Commission to train their teachers as mentors. The training takes place at the Shanzu Teachers' College in Mombasa during school holidays.

Following the introduction of FPE, the Aga Khan Foundation had to refocus its approach to the school-improvement programme. The numbers of children in school rose and rose, yet teachers were not trained to deal with the large numbers, differing levels of ability, and widely varying ages of the pupils admitted during the introduction of FPE. As a consequence, schools started to lose some enrolled children: *'In one school, we lost 60 pupils within a month as the older pupils failed to cope with ridicule from younger ones. The most affected were big girls'* (interviewee, Aga Khan Foundation, Nairobi).

The Aga Khan Foundation initiates programmes as a response to community requests. For example, the organisation introduced the IIEP to the Muslim community in Kwale District, aiming to integrate academic learning with the values of the community. Prior to this, community members took their children to the mosque and *madrassa* classes, where education was limited to reciting the Quran. Girls in this community often married as young as ten years of age. On realising this, the Aga Khan Foundation devised an integrated curriculum, combining both Islamic and secular teachings, as a way of encouraging parents to delay their daughters' marriages and send their girls to school, since their religion was now part of the curriculum. To promote the retention and transition of girls to secondary level in schools in this area (Kwale), the Aga Khan Foundation trained most of the girls as teachers after primary or secondary schooling.

Advocacy and local sensitisation

Sensitisation on the rights of girls

Both the government and civil-society organisations are engaged in advocacy and sensitisation work to improve girls' access and retention. Several advocacy activities mounted by diverse interest groups can be singled out in this regard. For example, ActionAid Kenya (AAK) organises training on the Children's Act and harmful practices. In Narok District, AAK focuses its training on early marriages, to counter the cultural practice of marrying off young girls immediately after circumcision. During these training courses, local chiefs are mandated with responsibility for safeguarding the interests of the girl child. Surprisingly, most parents are not aware of children's rights: *'The communities were shocked to hear that they could go to jail for marrying off their daughters'* (interviewee, AAK Nairobi).

In Kajiado, Dupoto E Maa collaborates with the Anglican Church of Kenya (ACK) and the provincial administration to fight for the rights of the children. Forums are organised to address the education of the girl child in the rural areas. Such forums enlighten girls about their rights. As a result, many girls have rejected forced marriages and have been enrolled in schools. Box 4 typifies the testimony of girls saved from early/forced marriages by the provincial administration.

Box 4: Escape from forced marriage

It was in the year 2000 and I was 11 years old when a friend of my grandfather came to him, wanting to be given a girl. Grandfather notified my father about the request, and my father did not say a word. Among the Maasai, first-born children belong to the grandparents, and that is why my father did not object to he request. My grandfather then arranged to 'give me away'. My wedding was to be on Saturday, but, two days before, a friend of mine from school advised me to refuse the marriage. Then on the Thursday before the wedding I asked for permission to visit my maternal grandmother. I used the chance to come to school in Kajiado, where I was advised to go to the District Commissioner's office to report the case. The DC wrote down my story and took me back to school.

(Girl, 16 years old, AIC Kajiado Primary School)

The Basic Education Fund supports women's lobby groups, composed of professionals, throughout Kajiado district. The lobby groups campaign against retrogressive cultural practices such as FGM and early marriage. Government officials who are not from the Maasai community support this strategy. They argue that communities are more likely to listen to their own people. Lobbying has led to changes in the circumcision calendar. Circumcision used to be conducted at any time of the year, but after sensitisation the ceremony is now performed during the December school holidays, which are long enough for wounds to heal. It is culturally accepted practice for the female circumcision term to last three months, but this has been reduced to one month, to enable girls to go back to school. However, members of the lobby groups revealed that sensitisation in some regions of the district requires the involvement of men, since they are the decision makers within society. Professional women are sometimes dismissed as 'educated or town women' who do not uphold traditional culture.

Ntanira Na Mugambo, meaning 'circumcise with a word of mouth', is a community-based organisation (CBO) operating in Tharaka District. It was started in 1996 by a group of women on realising that FGM was widespread in the community and was the cause of early marriages and girls' high rates of school drop-out. The CBO focused on raising awareness about FGM by means of an adapted curriculum which covers harmful traditional practices, personal hygiene, boy/men/girl relationships, self-esteem, drug abuse, decision making, peer pressure, reproductive health, sexually transmitted infections, and HIV/AIDS. Through this programme many girls have been saved from FGM.

Organisation of forums at which girls can discuss their experiences has also been used as a strategy to improve their schooling. ActionAid Kenya organised a series of meetings in Western Kenya in 2003, at which girls had an opportunity to express their problems, among which were sexual harassment, rape and molestation, physical punishment in schools, domestic chores at home, and the requirement to work for teachers. The girls wrote letters to their Members of Parliament and the Ministry of Education, Science and Technology, appealing for changes to the gender policy. Currently, ActionAid Kenya is planning appropriate strategies to counter the problems mentioned. .

Mainstreaming gender across organisations

Civil-society organisations are working to ensure that their own practices are gender-sensitive. BEF led the development of a CARE Kenya gender-relations manual, used by managers, and a manual on gender equality in education for partners.

Advocacy for the implementation of national legislation

Although legislation exists which recognises the rights and responsibilities of government and schools, it is quite another issue to have these recognised and enforced. Many strong cultural and social norms perpetuate the practice of early marriage, and girls may not know of the legislation – or, even if they do, they may not be in a position to demand that their rights be recognised. NGOs and CBOs are working at the local and national levels to raise awareness and break down the barriers that hinder girls from achieving their right to an education.

The Women Educational Researchers of Kenya (WERK) work to bridge the gap between the re-entry policy for girl mothers and the continued stigma of being a school-age mother and securing child care. ANPPCAN has been involved in collective lobbying for girls' education with specific networks like GCN, and has promoted the importance of education of the girl child in the media. It was also involved in lobbying for the passing of the Children's Bill, when members sensitised parliamentarians on the importance of that legislation.

One of FAWE's strategic objectives is to influence policy formulation by working closely with the Ministry of Education. The government has also taken affirmative action on bursary allocation in response to FAWE's lobbying. Two million Kenyan shillings have been allocated for girls in every province, and this money is channelled through FAWEK. Another affirmative action under consideration by the government, thanks to FAWE's lobbying, is the admission of girls to university education: it is proposed that they should be accepted with slightly lower qualifications than boys.

The Kibera Slum Education Programme (KISEP), an umbrella group of three community-based organisations supported by Oxfam GB, has been lobbying and campaigning for government recognition of the Kibera informal settlement and the inhabitants' rights to education.

This section has provided an overview of some of the main initiatives on girls' education that have been taking place in Kenya. The challenges, however, are great, and government needs to push forward with its review of the Education Act and its policy paper for Gender and Education. The NGO sector, under the umbrella of the Elimu Yetu Coalition, is becoming a well co-ordinated and effective lobbying force to hold the government accountable to its commitments to EFA and the MDGs, as the next section illustrates.

Campaigning to influence policies and plans

The Elimu Yetu Coalition (EYC) was formed in 1999 as part of the efforts to make the Jomtien Declaration real and relevant for Kenyans, and to take part in related global campaigns for the attainment of good-quality basic education for all. EYC is a coalition of some 40 civil-society organisations, professional groupings, education/research institutions, and other practitioners in the education sector. The coalition is inspired by a vision of a literate society which values and practises democratic ideals and promotes cohesion in diversity. Its way of working towards achieving this vision is through campaigning for an education that is sustainable and responsive to the developmental and material needs of Kenyans. EYC believes that its mission is to influence and facilitate policy change and promote best practices that will ensure quality basic education for all that is free, relevant, and compulsory.

Box 5: Elimu Yetu's approach to campaigning and advocacy

- Engaging in critical awareness-raising to highlight problems facing the Kenyan education sector, to convince public opinion of the importance of education.

- Lobbying and working closely with the government, policy makers, development partners, and other educational institutions in various areas of education, to fulfil the commitment to provide basic education for all by 2015.

- Building a strong constituency, by strengthening the advocacy capacities of members and other key actors in education, with very clear goals and targets, to influence policy shift towards the attainment of EFA goals.

- Campaigning/advocating for, and where possible facilitating access to, education by special-interest groups such as girls and women, children and people with disabilities, and young people in difficult circumstances, especially those from marginal/disadvantaged communities.

- Championing the cause of education from a rights-based perspective, and mobilising resources to ensure its accessibility to all citizens in the most affordable way.

- Working with and through established networks and forums to achieve targeted goals in education.

- Conducting research on various aspects of education, with a view to providing empirical data to inform policy formulation and decision making.

The study on which this chapter is based is an example of the research that EYC has commissioned for the purpose of advocacy and lobbying. The research report was launched in 2003 by the Ministry of Education Science and Training (MOEST) and disseminated broadly to other stakeholders. It has provided background information to enable EYC to be an active member of the on-going Gender Education Policy Document review, and its findings are influencing the content of the policy. EYC is now working to establish key groups in Parliament, such as the 'Women Parliamentarians' Forum', which will debate and utilise this and other research to ensure that the Gender Education Policy Document achieves parliamentary approval and passes into law.

The EYC is also closely networked with key alliances and actors in Africa and elsewhere who are working for EFA and gender equality. EYC is a key contact and partner of ANCEFA (the African National Network for EFA) in Kenya, and the organisations are working jointly on a 'Global Call For Action Against Poverty'. EYC is also an active member of the Global Campaign for Education, with which it works on global issues relating to the attainment of EFA goals. A key campaigning opportunity for the EYC is its engagement with the Global Week of Action, which in 2005 adopted a strong focus on the importance of girls' education and campaigned for commitments from the government of Kenya to work towards gender parity and gender equality. Free Primary Education (FPE) was a big step forward for Kenya, but it is only a first step and much remains to be done to make free, good-quality education a reality for all boys and girls. EYC is one of the key partners of the Commonwealth Education Fund (CEF), a UK government fund which supports the strengthening of national coalitions, such as EYC, to build the capacity of its member organisations to engage with government on policy and practice change, and especially to work with government to achieve the MDGs, beginning with MDG 3.

Conclusion

The research that the Elimu Yetu Coalition commissioned illustrates how, despite a range of interventions and policy changes aimed at improving the education of girls, there are still many obstacles to further progress. It also demonstrates that these challenges need to be confronted and tackled by a wide range of stakeholders: government at all levels, civil society and its organisations, and the private sector. The research illustrates the need for persistent attention not only to the development of a national gender policy, but also to an action plan for its implementation. The Kenyan government has not yet submitted the long-awaited Gender Education Policy to Parliament, which is only a first step towards ensuring positive changes in girls' lives and girls' experience of education. This process needs to take place within the wider context of the review of the Education Act and the effective implementation of the provisions of the Children's Act, so that gender equality and girls' education are mainstreamed through these wider processes. Even though the government introduced Free Primary Education in early 2003, it is clear that affirmative action is needed to ensure that girls are not deterred from schooling by hidden costs and opportunity costs, and to ensure that the implementation of initiatives for girls' education is adequately budgeted, and that funding is available to ensure training in management and teaching to encourage more women into teaching. EYC and civil society have an important role to play in the development of strong strategies to ensure the implementation of such important education legislation. In 2004 a joint education survey was carried out by all actors in education – donors, civil-society organisations such as EYC, and the Ministry of Education, MOEST – to enrich the sector-wide approach and status of FPE in 2004. EYC is lobbying hard for the enactment of the Gender Education Policy.

Alongside these policy measures, the research indicates that government and civil society have much work to do together to continue to raise the awareness at community and local levels of the importance of education for girls, and for the imposition of harsher penalties for sexual abuse and harassment. The legislation on re-entry for girls who have dropped out of school because of pregnancy needs to be reinforced, and innovative programmes addressing the threat posed by HIV/AIDS must be supported.

For girls to attend school and achieve well in school, there is a need for adequate and appropriate physical facilities, and gender-sensitive learning materials and teaching practices. This chapter has documented some examples of good practice that are already being implemented by government and civil society. Good practices need to be documented and replicated in other areas, so that education is gender-equitable throughout the country and in all aspects of the system, rather than in patches.

The Elimu Yetu Coalition will continue to work with government at national, provincial, and local levels and to build a strong network of civil-society organisations to meet the challenge of educating girls in Kenya. Community sensitisation on cultural beliefs and practices will be critical in ensuring that parents send girls to school. There is a pressing need for female role models and representation at policy-making and managerial levels. Women in power need to take the bull by the horns and demand a strategy from the government that will ensure that every girl in Kenya gets a good-quality education.

Elimu Yetu Coalition, formed in 1999, comprises approximately 40 civil-society organisations, professional groupings, education/research institutions, and other practitioners in the education sector in Kenya. It is dedicated to the vision of a literate society that values and practises democratic ideals and promotes cohesion in diversity. The Coalition proposes to pursue a rights-based campaign towards achievement of Education For All, with a major emphasis on universal primary education that is free, relevant, and compulsory.

Notes

1   Elimu Yetu Coalition (2003) 'Gender and Education: The Challenge of Educating Girls in Kenya', Elimu Yetu Coalition and Oxfam GB.

2   www2.unesco.org/wef/countryreports/kenya/rapport_1.html

References

Chege (1995) 'Strategic gender needs: a challenge to education in Kenya', *Basic Education Forum*, 6

Human Rights Watch (2001) 'In the shadow of death: HIV/AIDS and children's rights in Kenya', *Human Rights Watch* 13/4(A)

Government of Kenya (1998) Master Plan on Education and Training, 1997–2010

Ministry of Education (2000) Report on the Commission of Inquiry into the Education System of Kenya (Koech Report), Ministry of Education and Training, Kenya

Ministry of Education and Training (2003) Gender Education Policy Paper (draft), Ministry of Education and Training, Kenya

Republic of Kenya (2002) National Report for the Special Session of the UN General Assembly on follow up to the World Summit for Children

6 Learning to improve education policy for pastoralists in Kenya

Ian Leggett

In Kenya, as in much of Africa, primary-education provision and participation expanded dramatically during the 1960s and 1970s. The number of primary schools doubled from approximately 5000 in 1965 to 10,000 in 1980; enrolment increased even more dramatically, from just over one million pupils in 1965 to nearly four million in 1980 (Eshiwani 1993). This expansion reflected policy changes which collectively represented major advances in Kenya's educational development and the strategic use of public expenditure in support of educational policy goals (Abagi and Olweya 1999; Makau 1995).

But the growth in provision and participation increasingly left behind the pastoral districts of Northern and Eastern Kenya (Nkinyangi 1982; Narman 1990). For although the policies that underpinned primary education expansion were responsive to the needs and interests of the majority, they proved to be inappropriate to the circumstances in Kenya's pastoral districts, and neglectful of the rights of children, especially girls, who lived there. The consequences are chronically low levels of educational participation among pastoralist communities, and marked disparities in provision and participation between pastoralist and other communities in Kenya.

This examination[1] of education policy focuses on primary-education provision and participation in Wajir District, North Eastern Province. It is in North Eastern Province that the lowest primary-school participation rates in Kenya are found. If education policy is to be an effective instrument of change, it will be in North Eastern Kenya that it is likely to be most rigorously tested. This study does not seek to dwell on the deficiencies and inequalities of the past – which are increasingly being acknowledged (Republic of Kenya/UNICEF 1999). For our purposes, learning to improve policy means identifying ways, based on a critical analysis of past policies and a consultative approach to pastoralist communities, in which education policy can be changed so as to enable Kenya to achieve the goal of Education For All. This goal is preferred to the more narrowly defined targets of the Millennium Development Goals.

The factors influencing provision and participation in Wajir are sometimes rooted directly in government policy and practice. Cost-sharing, for example, was the policy that underpinned the financing of primary education for the entire period of the first decade of Education For All. Although the effects of cost-sharing were profoundly negative and inequitable (Makau *et al.* 2000), that policy may yet prove to have been a relatively transient problem, one that could be directly overcome by the implementation of a new financing policy. A decisive step in this direction was taken in January 2003, when the government of Kenya implemented its pledge to provide free primary education.

Other factors, however, are more durable and complex, because they are rooted in cultural values, social norms, and economic systems. Unequal gender relations – reflected in the marked differences in access between girls and boys – illustrate the power and resilience of obstacles to increasing access to education that are rooted in beliefs and practice. For in Wajir, as in N.E. Province generally, there is only a limited acceptance of the notion that girls have an equal right to education, and this attitude leads to a persistent and widespread reluctance to send girls to school.

The pastoralist context

Pastoralism has long been the dominant feature of the regional economy, and it will remain so for the foreseeable future. The relationship between pastoralism and education is widely acknowledged to be problematic (Tahir 1991; Kratli 2000), leading some commentators (Alkali 1991) to assume that the continued pursuit of pastoralism is inconsistent with the provision of education. This way of thinking continues to exert a profound influence on governments and development agencies; its implication is that the attainment of education for all and gender equity in education provision is not possible among pastoralist communities. This line of argument underpins a policy approach which starts from the premise that pastoralists must settle down and stop being pastoralists. But it is a model that is fundamentally at odds with the demographic reality of Wajir and the other districts of N.E. Province, where more than 70 per cent of the population continue to live on, and move across, the rangelands. A different approach is needed, and this investigation into the factors that influence participation in education is intended to inform the policy choices that need to be made if Kenya is to make significant moves towards achieving education for all. Alternative models exist or can be developed. This investigation starts from the premise that a way needs to be found to reconcile the provision of education with the pursuit of pastoralism: an alternative approach which seeks to be responsive to pastoralists' needs and priorities, rather than seeking to transform pastoralism itself.

The World Declaration on Education For All (1990) drew attention to the need to remove educational disparities within countries. In addition to emphasising the importance of girls' education, the needs of particular groups – nomads are specifically mentioned – was highlighted (*ibid.*: Article 3). The World Declaration also encouraged 'learning through a variety of delivery systems' and the adoption of 'supplementary alternative programmes' (*ibid.*: Article 5). In the light of the World Declaration, the government of Kenya had the opportunity to revise its policies and practices to tackle chronic gender-based and geographical disparities.

My research in Wajir investigated the changes that have occurred in terms of provision and participation since 1990 and sought to identify the role of public policy in explaining those changes. If more far-reaching changes are to be achieved, this study argues that educational policy will need to go beyond the conventional responses of the past. The challenge is to address in a coherent and comprehensive way specific issues – poverty, gender bias, and mobility – which are identified as being the principal influences on participation.

Provision and participation: the national context

Geographical inequalities in school participation

Acting on a pre-Independence pledge to provide every child with a minimum of seven years' free education, successive governments harnessed popular support to expand primary education (Makau 1995). Communities provided labour or cash to construct or expand schools, and the State accepted responsibility for most of the recurrent costs. Such a division of responsibilities encouraged community initiatives to set up primary schools and became the expression of a public policy that led to significant and sustained growth in provision and enrolment (Eshiwani 1993).

This expansion, however, soon reflected significant geographical inequalities (Nkinyangi 1982). By 1977 just six districts in the whole country were enrolling less than 50 per cent of their estimated school-age population. All of them were pastoral districts: Marsabit, Samburu, Turkana, and the three districts (Mandera, Wajir, and Garissa) of North Eastern Province. Twenty years later, in 1998, almost nothing had changed, and the six lowest-achieving districts were the same, with the exception of Tana River, which replaced Turkana (Republic of Kenya/FAWE 2000). In Wajir District, 75 per cent of children still do not attend school. The gulf between enrolment in N.E. Province and the rest of the country (Table 1) remains enormous. The disparity in provision and participation between the pastoral areas of Kenya and the rest of the country represents the biggest obstacle that will need to be overcome if Kenya is to make significant progress towards achieving Education For All.

Table 1: Primary-school gross enrolment rates by sex and province, 1998

	Coast	Central	Eastern	Nairobi	Rift Valley	Western	Nyanza	North Eastern	Kenya
Boys	79.6	96.3	91.7	61.6	87.7	102.6	93.9	32.0	89.4
Girls	66.9	100.1	96.1	52.8	85.6	104.2	91.9	16.8	88.2
Total	73.3	98.2	93.8	56.9	86.7	103.4	92.9	24.8	88.8

Source: Republic of Kenya/Fawe (2000:9)

Gender inequalities in primary-school participation

In 1963 just over 300,000 girls were attending primary school in Kenya. Twenty years later, in 1983, there were well over two million. Perhaps even more impressive than the growth in the absolute numbers of girls attending primary school has been the growth in the proportion attending school. In 1963 girls represented just 34 per cent of the total number of students enrolled. That percentage increased steadily throughout the 1970s and 1980s, until by 1998 girls' participation had reached 49.4 per cent, leading the government to assert in its report to the World Education Forum (Republic of Kenya 1999) 'as a result of the general public awareness created on [sic] the importance of education for both boys and girls over the years, there has been parity between boys and girls at primary and secondary levels'.

National data may accurately reflect mainstream trends, but they are open to criticism when they inadvertently hide significant disparities at the margins. Contrary to the impression of equality that such figures give, profound levels of inequality are exposed when the data are disaggregated. In North Eastern Province, the female gross enrolment rate is half that of boys (see Table 1), and more than 80 per cent of girls do not attend primary school (Republic of Kenya/Fawe 2000).

High rates of non-participation may be tolerated, partly because they are more or less invisible at the national level, and partly because they can be explained by reference to 'traditional cultural values' (rather than shortcomings in policy and practice). That there is a deep-seated reluctance in many parts of Africa to provide girls with the opportunity to go to school is not in doubt. But by describing the problem principally in relation to cultural values, the temptation is merely to blame pastoralist communities for those disparities, and to absolve those charged with addressing those disparities from any responsibility for their perpetuation. Yet if the educational inequality of Kenya's pastoral districts is to be reduced, public policy is one tool that can help to transform social norms by introducing specific and sensitive initiatives (Stromquist 1997).

Provision and participation: the extent and limits of change

Provision

The first primary school in Wajir was built in 1948 (Turton 1974). The number grew only slowly over the next 30 years, and by 1979 Wajir District had just 18 schools with approximately 4000 pupils (Eshiwani 1993). By 1998, however, there were 62 primary schools in the district, with a total of 14,000 pupils (Republic of Kenya/FAWE 2000). The rate of growth during the 1990s stands in marked contrast to that of earlier decades. Between 1993 and 1998 the number of schools increased by 38 per cent, from 45 to 62. The rate of increase was the highest in the country over the period (*ibid.*) and contrasts sharply with trends in provision before the 1990s.

The unprecedented expansion in primary provision in the 1990s is, on the face of it, remarkable and prompts the question whether it was a response to policy changes in the wake of the Jomtien Declaration. Any expansion of provision clearly needs the support of the government, particularly with regard to the appointment and payment of staff. But this is not the same as attributing the expansion to the adoption of new policies. At best, what seems to have happened is that government responded positively to an increased demand for schools. There is no evidence to suggest that it re-directed resources to the pastoral districts in a determined effort to reduce disparities. Nor does the government appear to have taken any steps to develop new 'delivery systems', as encouraged by the World Declaration (1990), or to have used the opportunity of schools expansion to increase the number of girls-only schools as a culturally acceptable and gender-sensitive response. By doing little more than approving the construction of schools in settlements, the government was content to perpetuate a decades-old, demand-driven approach that simply expanded the provision of formal schools. It reflected a view that if pastoralists wanted their children to go to school, they would have to make the necessary adaptations. Despite the rhetoric of the Jomtien Declaration, no effort was made to change the way in which education was made available.

It is notable that almost all of the schools that have been built during the past decade are day schools. This form of provision marks something of a contrast with the past, when primary boarding schools were built in a deliberate attempt to provide opportunities for children – almost always boys, it should be noted – from nomadic backgrounds. This policy of boarding provision goes back to colonial times (Turton 1974), but was actively promoted by the government during the 1970s and early 1980s as a way of catering for the children of nomadic parents (Abdi 1999). By making a specific effort to provide education for children of pastoralist communities, policy was being used to address a key problem and to promote equitable educational development.

Commendable as such an initiative was in principle, it was a policy that has proved to be deeply flawed in practice. Drawing on research from other pastoral districts, Ponsi (1988) questioned whether boarding schools cater for the children for whom they were nominally set up to serve. More recently Abdi (2001) has demonstrated that boarding primary schools in North Eastern Province are severely under-utilised, while Obura (2002) suggests that, on grounds of cost and social acceptability, boarding schools are unlikely to make more than a marginal contribution to extending provision. Rather than simply condemning the policy as a failure (Nkinyangi 1981), one might use the unpopularity and inefficiencies of the boarding-schools approach to define the limits of mainstream responses and identify areas where less formal and more responsive approaches may be both necessary and more acceptable.

Enrolment

Table 1 on page 131 is a presentation of provincial gross enrolment rates for 1998 for the country. The rate for N.E. Province is very low, both absolutely and comparatively. Fewer than one third of boys attend primary school. Four out of five girls do not go to school. These statistics are remarkable for a country in which, since Independence, the demand for education has in general exceeded the places available, and increases in participation were achieved simply by increasing provision. Relevant and appropriate as such a strategy may have been for most parts of Kenya, there is a growing acceptance that it has not been effective in making basic education accessible to 'vulnerable groups' (Republic of Kenya/ UNICEF 1999). Nor has it been effective in reducing disparities between the pastoral districts and the rest of the country (Abdi 1999; Obura 2002). To continue to rely on the same strategy as a way of reducing disparities in the future is almost certainly doomed to failure. What is needed are policies that go beyond the boundaries of current practice and complement existing provision by adopting innovative, targeted, and specific measures to promote participation and to increase girls' participation in particular.

Retention

In keeping children at school so that they complete the full cycle of primary education, Kenya has performed much less effectively than in providing access in the first place. In a detailed analysis of the period between 1981 and 1998 Makau (2000: 35) concludes that 'the completion rate remained below 50% of the intake in Standard 1'. There is an absence of such longitudinal data for Wajir District, but Makau's conclusion is supported by an analysis of the 1991–98 cohort.

Table 2: Primary-school completion rate for 1991–98 cohort: a comparison of Wajir District data and national data

	Std. 1 enrolment			Std. 8 enrolment			% completing		
	M	F	Total	M	F	Total	M	F	Total
National (in 000`s)	476	447	924	221	215	436	46	48	47
Wajir	956	588	1544	518	242	760	54	41	49

Sources: Makau (2000: 35) for national data; Oxfam (1999:10) for district data

While the overall level of completion for both boys and girls is low, it is notable that retention in Wajir District is slightly higher than nationally. The very wide gap between Wajir and much of the rest of the country in terms of enrolment is not repeated, suggesting that those parents in Wajir who send their children to school are as interested in keeping them there, and able to do so, as parents elsewhere in the country. There is however one major difference between the national and district data – and that difference is based on gender. Nationally, girls are more likely than boys to stay at school; but in Wajir, girls are more likely to leave school early.

Factors influencing participation

Urbanisation, sedentarisation, and mobility

Wajir is the largest district in N.E. Province and one of the most sparsely populated in Kenya. In 1979 its population was approximately 140,000, of whom 13,000, less than 10 per cent, lived in Wajir town (Republic of Kenya/Oxfam 1996). Twenty years later, the population of the district was estimated to be 325,000 and that of Wajir town 50,000.[2] Other urban centres have developed; their combined populations are approximately 25,000. With a total urban population of not less than 75,000, the demography of Wajir District has changed markedly in just 20 years, with at least 25 per cent of the population now being town-dwellers. This change in population distribution has had a direct impact on the demand for primary education, and on the potential for access to school. The increase in the number and size of towns and settlements is closely related to the growth in the number of schools which has been such a distinctive feature of the 1990s.

Table 3 demonstrates the relationship between participation and urbanisation. In 2000, two thirds of the children enrolled in primary schools in Wajir district lived in Central and Habaswein educational divisions.[3] Though not exclusively urban, these divisions include the two largest urban concentrations.

Table 3: Wajir District primary enrolment by gender and division, 2000

Division	Boys	Girls	Total	% Girls
Bute	1191	530	1721	31
Centra	4582	2683	7265	37
Habaswein	2078	957	3035	32
Griftu	1443	679	2122	32
Tarbaj	895	474	1369	35
Total	10189	5323	15512	34

Source: District Education Office, Wajir

On the question of who goes to school, urbanisation seems to exert a positive influence on girls' access, although the evidence here is more equivocal. Within Central Division, which includes Wajir town, there is a notable narrowing of the differential between boys' and girls' enrolment. On the other hand, Habaswein has the second-lowest proportion of girls in school, suggesting that there are tensions between what might be called the 'pro-school' influence of urbanisation and 'the anti-school' influence of gender bias.

The relationship between settlements in pastoral areas and the provision of education has been a contentious policy issue. The crux of the debate is whether education facilities (and other economic and social facilities, such as water supplies and health centres) are used to attract pastoralists as part of an overall, if not explicit, policy of sedentarisation. There is no doubt that such objectives have informed policy and practice in countries as diverse as Iran and Nigeria. From this perspective, the provision of education was not so much a right of citizenship but a way of weakening and transforming pastoralism, part of a strategy to modernise it and convert pastoralists into farmers, labourers, or watchmen (Kratli 2000).

An alternative approach seeks to understand pastoralist responses to educational policy and provision within a broader context of economic and social change (Dyer and Choksi 1997) and of pastoralists' adaptation to changing circumstances (Frantz 1990). From this perspective, education may be adopted as a way to diversify the pastoralist economy, even if it involves the settlement of some family members on a temporary or permanent basis.

The place that education occupies within a long-term pastoralist livelihood strategy will vary between households and from place to place. In Wajir, and in N.E. Province generally, individual decisions are shaped by a context in which pastoralism is under pressure because of population growth, insecurity, limitations on herd movements (RoK/Oxfam 1996), and a market system that is both inadequate and distorted (O'Leary and Wakesa 2000). In these circumstances the possible benefits of education become more attractive, even to those still within the pastoral sector. Having an education may not yet be as prestigious as 'having herds' (Dahl and Hjort 1976); but both are increasingly recognised as being important as it becomes harder to survive by pastoral means alone (Salzman and Galaty 1990).

In judging how best to strengthen the household economy in the medium-to-long term, parents increasingly appear to divide the family labour force. Some children are sent to school, while others are kept at home to look after the animals and/or to be responsible for looking after the house. 'The role of the town employee has become part of the division of labour' (Kratli 2000: 41), providing a source of income which is not subject to the same vulnerabilities as herding. In return, family members who remain on the range will look after the animals of those in town. In effect, investing in education for some children represents a livelihoods-diversification strategy (Republic of Kenya/Oxfam 1996) which is designed to strengthen the household economy within the context of a continuing engagement – as a family – with pastoralism.

In considering the expansion of primary-school provision in Wajir in the previous decade, this study suggests that the relationship between formal education and pastoralism has not been wholly antagonistic, nor has it been part of a dominant strategy designed to settle and transform pastoralists. There has been a significant growth in the urban population – but poverty, not public policy, is widely acknowledged to be the most powerful driving force behind that growth. Those who move to towns are, by and large, pastoralism's 'forgotten people' (Broch-Due 1999), driven to the point of destitution and possessing few alternatives. For such people settlement is not a threat to an otherwise viable pastoralist existence: it is a refuge to which they have moved in the hope that it will offer them a better future. And education, many of them believe, may open the door to employment opportunities that will help to secure that better future. From this perspective, education is not so much 'instrumental to sedentarisation' (Kratli 2000: 9), an inducement with which to attract pastoralists into towns, as it is a tool by which families can re-build their livelihoods and social networks.[4]

While education policy may not be primarily responsible for enrolment trends over the past decade or so, a fundamental policy goal – that attendance at primary school should be made compulsory – is challenged by these conclusions. Decisions about the education of pastoralist children, girls and boys, are based on their parents' judgement of what is in the best interests of the family. Contrary to an approach that is based solely on the rights of individuals, these judgements are made by weighing up the wishes and abilities of individuals on one hand against the collective interests of the family as a whole on the other. These parental decisions inevitably reflect the socio-cultural context in which they are taken – and in Wajir that means two things. First, it means placing an emphasis on strengthening the capacity of the family to preserve and build up its herds, social networks, and other economic safety nets. Second, and specifically in the context of gender relations, it reflects the importance that is attached to protecting what is perceived to be the honour and reputation of girls and to preparing them for their future roles as wives and mothers. The outcome is that some children – usually boys – will attend school for as long as is practicable. Others – some boys, but most girls – will remain at home to look after the animals and other members of the family who need to be cared for, and to do domestic duties.

These observations on parental decisions about access to schooling challenge the assumption that the population of Wajir can be neatly divided into families who have access to education and, on the other hand, those who are excluded or display a 'negative' attitude towards school. In reality the situation is more complex, and within any given family there are likely to be some children who are, or have been, attending school and others who are not. The extent of this relative engagement with education is reflected in the fact that only 30 per cent of the parents interviewed for this study had sent all of their school-aged children to school for at least part of the primary cycle. The others had decided to keep at least some of their children at home.

If Education For All is to be made meaningful, it surely requires policy makers to take steps – as they were encouraged to do by the Jomtien Declaration – to make available 'alternative programmes' and a 'variety of delivery systems'. When provision means, in effect, attendance at a school in a settlement, it is inevitable that many parents who are practising pastoralists may choose not to exercise the right of their children to education. Expansion of just one form of provision effectively excludes pastoralist children and is consistent with neither the spirit nor the letter of the commitments made in Thailand and Senegal.

Abdi (2002) highlights the need for flexibility in the way in which education is made available. But in Kenya efforts to provide pastoralist children with an education on terms that are consistent with their lifestyle have been confined to small-scale, innovative projects that are often run by community groups, funded by external NGOs. These projects reflect the absence of government policy – not its expression. In essence, they are recent attempts to fill a policy vacuum.

The Mobile School project in Wajir (Hussein 1999) is an example of a small-scale initiative to develop practicable alternatives to mainstream education. It is modelled on the indigenous and widespread Koranic schools, or *dugsi*, which are specifically adapted to provide teaching in the context of mobility. The teacher lives and moves as part of a herding group and provides instruction at times that are consistent with herding and labour responsibilities. This model is based on a fundamentally different premise from that which has informed formal 'schooling', in that it accepts the primary responsibility of children, both girls and boys, to look after the family's herd. Enrolment figures for the project indicate both a quick take-up of the programme and an approximate equivalence between girls and boys. Irrespective of a number of shortcomings in the implementation of the project (identified by Hussein, *op. cit.*), it provides evidence to suggest that there is a latent demand for education among pastoralists. It suggests, too, that non-formal types of provision may be particularly effective in addressing deeply rooted gender inequalities, by offering a way to reduce obstacles to girls' access.

This possibility is supported by the experiences of the Alternative Basic Education in Karamoja initiative in Uganda (Odada and Olega 1999). What is especially notable about this project is that many more girls than boys enrolled in the learner centres. This fact may be explained by reference to the division of labour between girls and boys in Karamojong society – where homesteads are much more fixed, cultivation is more common, and girls spend less time on the rangelands. But its significance is that it provides compelling evidence that rapid progress can be made to increase girls' participation in contexts where female enrolment has been chronically low. Mobile schools and similar innovative projects have tended to be justified on the grounds of making education more accessible to pastoralists as a group, rather than in terms of a gendered analysis of accessibility. Yet both the Wajir Mobile School project and the Karamoja programme suggest that 'supplementary alternative programmes' can be especially effective in terms of increasing girls' participation. To that extent, such initiatives may not only be of general benefit in terms of increasing enrolment, but may also be a good example of a gender-sensitive approach with enhanced benefits for girls.

Gender inequality

Gender inequality, rooted in individual and social bias against girls, operates in association with other factors. Three were mentioned time and again in this study in Wajir and are remarkably consistent with analysis based on research in other pastoral districts of Kenya (Makau *et al.* 2000). The three factors were poverty, gender bias, and the mobility of pastoralist families.

Given that attendance at school for almost all of the past 25 years has required payment of school fees and a variety of other charges and levies, the depth and extent of poverty means that few households can afford to educate all their children. Choices have to be made, and dominant values mean that parents are less likely to send their daughters to school.

Another explanation that is invariably offered to explain why girls are not in school is the contribution that they make to the running of the household. In a social context in which girls have been ascribed the role of providing domestic labour and child care, the contribution of girls to the household economy is often deemed to be too valuable to lose. The stage of economic development in Kenya is such that households depend on children's labour as a contribution to the production and consumption needs of the household. Unlike productive labour, which is a shared responsibility, domestic labour continues to be characterised by a sharp gender-based division, with men and boys making a minor contribution. From a very early age, girls are socialised into roles in which they prepare and cook food, collect water, and look after the young and the sick. The dependency of the household on girls' labour thus represents an opportunity cost of their attendance at school (Colclough *et al.* 2000). This cost lowers the enrolment of girls in school or, at the least, contributes to weaker performance and earlier drop-out.

Nevertheless, the argument that domestic labour responsibilities are a critical obstacle that prevents girls from attending or completing primary school in Wajir is not entirely persuasive. Girls who live in the district's towns and settlements are living within an urban or semi-pastoral context, rather than one typical of the rangelands, and their domestic duties are likely to be similar to those of girls in other parts of Kenya. In such circumstances the 'domestic labour' argument does not explain the gap between girls' enrolment in most of the country, with a national female gross enrolment rate (GER) of 88 per cent, and that in Wajir and N.E. Province, with a female GER of less than 20 per cent. The contribution of girls to herding, rather than to domestic labour, is likely to explain some of the difference, but the implication is that there is something else, another factor, that is critical.

That factor is summed up by the term 'status', a term designed to capture the ambiguous but powerful nature of gender inequality. It is the subordinate status of girls and women that explains why, to paraphrase the head-teacher of Wajir Girls Primary School, 'in all aspects of education, girls are left behind'. The notion that girls have a right to education, a right that is equal to that of boys, is not consistent with prevailing values and beliefs in Wajir or more widely among pastoralist communities in Kenya (Makau 2000) and elsewhere in Africa (Niles 1989; Csapo 1981; Wynd 1999). Schooling is thus either irrelevant or, in a context in which the separation of girls from boys is desirable as soon as a girl shows signs of maturity, a risk which leads parents to remove their daughters from school before she 'is spoilt' or 'develops immoral habits'.

While change will not happen until individuals modify their opinions and behaviour, public policy has an important role to play in stimulating and rewarding change. It is patently clear that the policies of the past have failed to convince parents, and society at large, of the advantages of educating girls. Unless public policy is used in a more targeted and effective way to influence attitudes and norms of behaviour, the extent to which girls are excluded from access to basic education is unlikely to be significantly reduced in the foreseeable future. The inescapable conclusion is that initiatives designed to increase the participation of girls, rather than to increase participation generally, are needed if Kenya is to achieve gender parity in education provision in pastoralist communities.

During the 1990s there was a notable absence of such initiatives. The most significant measure that has been taken in Wajir in recent years goes back to the 1980s, i.e. even before the Jomtien Declaration. It was then that the decision was taken to build a primary school specifically for girls in Wajir town. It remains the sole girls-only primary school in the entire district. Opened as a way of reducing the dangers of road travel for girls, rather than as a deliberate attempt to increase access, the school has proved to be an outstanding success. The Girls Primary School increased its enrolment from 122 girls at its inception in 1988 to 469 in 2000. But this success has never been replicated. It is an example that demonstrates that public policy, by providing the kind of school most likely to be acceptable to the community at large and enjoyable for the girls who attend, can positively influence change. That nothing else like it has been provided is a measure of the failure of public policy that allows a pronounced gender inequality to persist unchallenged.

Poverty and the financing of education

There has been a long tradition of cost-sharing in education in Kenya, epitomised by the phenomenon of *harambee* (or self-help) schools. During the 1970s the nominal commitment to providing free primary education sat uncomfortably with the practice of *harambee* collections, but in 1988 this contradiction was resolved when cost-sharing was formally made the basis of education financing. If access to education is conditional on the payment of fees of various kinds, it ceases to be a right, an entitlement of citizenship, but becomes instead a commodity that is available only to those with the money to buy it. And in a country as poor as Kenya, a policy that made parents responsible for maintaining the nation's primary education infrastructure as well as meeting the costs of school attendance was bound to lead to 'falling enrolments and failing schools' (Republic of Kenya/UNICEF 1999). Adopted two years before the Jomtien Declaration, cost-sharing was designed to address problems with the management of the national economy. It was not adopted as a policy designed to help Kenya to achieve education for all.

The vast majority of people interviewed during this study described cost-sharing, in all its manifestations, as the biggest single problem that limited children's participation in education. Teachers and parents alike argued that the removal of all fees and all charges would be essential if participation were to be significantly increased. There can be little doubt that the depth and extent of these feelings was a key factor in persuading the new government that its first policy initiative in education in 2003 should be the abolition of primary-school fees. It is important to acknowledge that the abolition of cost-sharing represents a fundamental policy shift on the part of the government. For the first time since the Jomtien Declaration was passed, Kenya has put in place a financing policy that addresses one of the most acute obstacles to the achievement of Education For All. It is equally important to bear in mind, however, that this policy change is national in scope and may prove to be of relatively tangential significance to the broader issues of pastoralists' participation in education.

Kenya's educational history shows that the abolition of fees has an immediate and positive impact on participation. Analysing enrolment data for the 1970s, when fees were formally abolished for a short while, Sibabi-Nyukuri (1989) demonstrates that increases in enrolment may be temporary, especially if fees are, in effect, re-introduced under another name. It is a little early to make judgements on the impact in pastoralist districts of the abolition of school fees and other levies in January 2003. Preliminary research (Sifuna 2003:7) concludes that in pastoralist districts throughout the country 'the free primary education programme seems to have (led to) a remarkable increase on overall enrolments'. There are, however, significant variations between districts, and in Wajir the increase was much lower than in all other sampled districts.

What is even more striking is the differential impact on the basis of gender. The enrolment of boys has increased far more dramatically than that of girls. In every district, without exception, the increase in enrolment of girls is lower than that of boys; and in Wajir a 19 per cent increase in boys' enrolment in 2003 should be compared with a 6 per cent increase for girls. If this trend continues, the outcome will be to increase the disparity in educational participation on the grounds of gender. It is a consequence that is directly at odds with the commitment to attain gender parity. This is not an argument for reversing or diluting the new financing policy; but it is a compelling argument to complement the policy of providing free primary education by introducing additional and specific policies which address the other obstacles to increasing access to education in pastoralist societies.

This study has argued that three factors are the principal cause of low rates of participation. These are poverty, gender bias, and the mobility of pastoralist families. The removal of school fees addresses the first of these obstacles and is a big step in the right direction. But, in isolation, it is an insufficient response. It will not achieve maximum impact unless it is part of a comprehensive and imaginative set of initiatives. What are needed now are similarly bold policy initiatives that will address the other two problems. This means re-thinking provision in order to make education available to boys and girls who live on the rangelands, far away from any school. And it means recognising the depth and breadth of gender bias and finding ways to dilute its potency.

Policies for effective change

The principal official reports generated during the first decade of Education For All (Republic of Kenya 1997; Republic of Kenya 1998; Republic of Kenya/UNICEF 1999) have little to offer in terms of policy changes specifically formulated for Kenya's pastoral communities, let alone to girls in those communities. The inevitable conclusion is that it is insufficiently recognised that these areas have distinct and chronic problems, over and above those faced by the sector as a whole. Treating the pastoral districts of Kenya and its peoples as if they were the same as the rest of the country is not an effective way of addressing decades-old disparities. Policy and practice changes are essential – and need to be targeted and consistent with a vision based on responsiveness, diversity, and innovation.

The Jomtien Declaration provided an opportunity to reflect on the shortcomings of previous practice and to support initiatives that are compatible with pastoral livelihood strategies and priorities. This study found little evidence to suggest that the opportunity had been grasped. Wajir, and most of the pastoral districts of Kenya, are as firmly fixed at the bottom of the table of primary participation as they were before Jomtien and Dakar. Although there has been a significant growth in provision in Wajir (compared with the past), it is a growth that reflects changes in population distribution and settlement patterns, not more imaginative ways of providing access to learning. Doing nothing more than building schools in settlements represents the continuation of a policy that has failed to acknowledge the diversity of cultural and physical contexts to which education has to adapt if it is to be accessible and meaningful.

If the inadequacies of current policies are to be effectively overcome, the particular needs of the pastoral districts – and of girls within them – will need to be accorded more visibility and significance. The recent publication of a draft policy on Gender and Education (Republic of Kenya 2003) suggests that there is a growing recognition that gender parity in education – in terms of performance as well as enrolment – will not be attained unless specific objectives are set and strategies defined. Like the new policy on financing, the production of a gender policy is a step in the right direction. But given that it is in Kenya's pastoralist districts that the most glaring gender-based educational disparities in the country are to be found, the failure of this draft policy to highlight the particular needs of pastoralist girls is more than disappointing. Unless this omission is corrected, the gender and education policy is in danger of reinforcing their 'invisibility' and of being irrelevant to those who suffer the most profound levels of discrimination.

In addition to the need for a more pastoralist-aware gender strategy, there is an increasing demand for a national and comprehensive strategy for pastoralist education. Its substantive elements have begun to be debated (Karani 2002). A critical element – and one that distinguishes this debate from earlier attempts to provide education to pastoralists in Kenya – is that new modes of provision must be designed. For too long 'strategies have been biased towards supporting the expansion of conventional schooling, with few results' (Obura 2002: 6). It is a form of provision that is neither practicable nor cost-effective for mobile communities in areas where population density is very low. It needs to be supplemented by a range of alternatives that are responsive to the lifestyles of pastoralists. As we have seen, evidence from projects such as Alternative Basic Education in Karamoja (ABEK) suggests that the development of non-formal types of provision is not only effective in changing attitudes towards education but also effective in terms of learning (Hestad and Focas Licht, 2002).

The development of an education system that integrates both formal and non-formal provision will necessitate not merely expansion of provision – the underlying concept that has dominated thinking in the past – but a measure of education reform. Such an approach is consistent with the thinking that informed the Jomtien Declaration. The outstanding success of the Escuela Nueva in Colombia (Colbert and Arboleda 1990; Torres 1992) – admittedly conceived in quite different circumstances – may be a source of inspiration, though not necessarily a model to be imitated.[5]

One of the lessons to be learned from the Escuela Nueva programme is the value of having a dedicated unit within the central ministry. Perhaps reflecting the fact that the relationship between pastoralism and education has been fraught with problems for decades, there is currently no institution in Kenya specifically responsible for addressing those problems or for developing a policy to do so.

A second lesson to be learned is that the use of non-formal methods should not be undertaken in the expectation that it will provide education 'on the cheap'. Given that such an approach would be introducing new ideas and practices in Kenya, and given that it will be operating in areas of weak infrastructure and low population densities, there will inevitably be high investment and on-going costs. Similarly, non-formal education has too often been under-valued, offering a limited and second-rate service to those who have fallen through the net of formal education. If non-formal education is to be established as an essential element of an integrated education strategy, those perceptions will need to be challenged. And one way to do so is to ensure that the quality of non-formal education is not an inferior imitation of 'the real thing'. At the least this will mean working to the principle that non-formal education should be expected to provide good-quality learning outcomes in its own right, and not merely to function as a gateway to the formal sector. Transition to the formal sector should be possible as part of an integrated system. But it should not be seen as a failure – either of the system or of individuals in it – if this does not happen, provided that other and arguably more relevant learning outcomes are achieved.

Conclusion

The relationship between education and pastoralism has been problematic for a long time. But this study did not confirm the common belief that pastoralism is inherently inconsistent with participation in education and is, by extension, an obstacle to education for all. There is a wide variety of reasons why pastoralists have not engaged with the education system in the past. Some are economic and financial; others are culturally defined or the product of historical experience. But as pastoralism adapts to new pressures, as well as to new opportunities, this study suggests that that it is untrue that pastoralists have a distrustful and negative attitude to education.

Instead of being adverse or irrelevant to the production system, education can have a complementary relationship to pastoralism. This complementarity reveals itself in the way that the household labour force is increasingly being divided so that some children are sent to school as a way of improving the well-being of the family in the short and long terms. It reveals itself too in the way that poor pastoralists, especially those who have been forced into the peri-urban quarters of Wajir's towns, will try to use education as a way of re-building assets and social capital.

Limited participation in education is a consequence not only of pastoralism but also of the education system itself. And in contrast to the flexibility of pastoralism, the education system has shown a marked lack of adaptation. Few concessions have been made to adapt the form and content, the procedures and practices of primary education to make it more compatible with the particular circumstances of pastoral communities. Current policy represents a 'take-it-or leave-it' approach to education, with communities having to adapt to the needs and demands of the education system, rather than planners working to make the system responsive to diverse contexts.

Despite the rhetoric of the Jomtien Declaration, little has changed in terms of Kenya's education policy in the past decade or more. The introduction of a new financing policy for primary education in 2003 may mark the beginning of a period when policy will be used more constructively. But if significant progress is to be made in the decade leading up to 2015, the Kenyan government will have to move decisively to overcome the remaining obstacles to participation. This will mean devising a policy framework that specifically recognises the extent of the bias against educating girls in North Eastern Province and other pastoralist districts, and supporting initiatives designed to increase access by changing dominant attitudes and behaviour.

But it is not only at the community level that change is needed. Just as important, policy makers need to listen to the concerns and opinions of pastoralists so as to develop policies and practices that will make education accessible to nomadic people. In ways that it has never done before, the education system in Kenya needs to learn to adapt. For too long the onus has been on pastoralists to adapt their way of life as the price for gaining access to education. It is a price that most pastoralists have not been prepared to pay. If pastoralists' right to education is to be fully realised, the education system will have to become more responsive and innovative.

Ian Leggett, formerly Regional Manager of the Oxfam GB East Africa programme, has a particular interest in development in pastoralist areas. He is currently Director of People & Planet, a student-led campaigning organisation working on global poverty, environmental, and human-rights issues.

Notes

1   This paper is based primarily on research conducted in 2001 as part of an MA course at the Institute of Education, University of London, reported in my dissertation 'Continuity and Change in Primary Education in the Pastoral Districts of Kenya: a Study of Wajir'. That work was supplemented in 2002 by a further visit to advise Oxfam GB on the development of its education programme for pastoralists and by participation in a workshop to stimulate policy debate.

2   Interview with Oxfam staff, Wajir, May 2001.

3   There are five educational divisions in the district, but 13 administrative divisions.

4   Interviews with Hashim Musa and Omar Jibril Hussein.

5   The origins and objectives of the Escuela Nueva programme are rooted in educational inequalities in Colombia. They reflected a creative tension between quantitative expansion and qualitative reform. They incorporated a belief that relevance and quality had to be addressed at the same time as considering how to increase access. This debate was applied to areas, similar to the rangelands of Kenya, in which population density was low and schooling did not easily fit with prevailing livelihoods and lifestyles.

References

Abagi, O. and J. Olweya (1999) 'Educational Reform in Kenya for the Next Decade: Implementing Policies for Adjustment and Revitalisation', Institute of Policy Analysis and Research. Nairobi

Abdi, A.H. (1999) 'Education in Pastoralist Communities of Kenya', Nairobi: Oxfam GB

Abdi, A.H. (2001) 'Access to Education and Community Participation', presentation to a stakeholder workshop on education, March 2001

Abdi, A.H. (2002) 'Basic Education Provision to Pastoralist Communities', paper presented to a National Workshop on Education for Pastoralists and Nomadic Communities, May 2002

Alkali, H. (1991) 'The challenges of educating pastoral nomads in Nigeria: limitations and options', in *Education and Pastoralism in Nigeria*, ed. G. Tahir, Zaria: Ahmadu Bello University Press

Broch-Due, V. (1999) 'Remembered cattle, forgotten people: the morality of exchange and the exclusion of the Turkana poor', in *The Poor are not Us: Poverty and Pastoralism*, eds. D. M. Anderson and V. Broch-Due, Oxford: James Currey

Colbert, V. and J. Arboleda (1990) *Universalisation of Primary Education in Colombia: The New School Programme*, Paris: UNESCO/WFP/UNICEF

Colclough, C., P. Rose, and M. Tembon (2000) 'Gender inequalities in primary schooling: the roles of poverty and adverse cultural practice', *International Journal of Educational Development* 20: 5 –27

Csapo, M. (1981) 'Religious, social and economic factors hindering the education of girls in Northern Nigeria', *Comparative Education* 17/3: 311–19

Dahl, G. and A. Hjort (1976) *Having Herds*, Stockholm Studies in Social Anthropology, University of Stockholm

Dyer, C. and A. Choksi (1997) 'The demand for education among the Rabaris of Kutch, West India', *Nomadic Peoples* (NS) 1/ 2: 77–97

Eshiwani, G. S. (1993) *Education in Kenya since Independence*, Nairobi: East Africa Publishers

Frantz, C. (1990) 'West African pastoralism: transformation and resilience', in P.C. Salzman and J.G. Galaty (eds.) 1990, *Nomads in a Changing World*: Naples, Instituto Universitario Orientale, Series Minor XXXIII

Hestad, I. and M. Focas Licht (2002) 'Lessons: Basic Education in Rural Africa', Oslo: Save the Children

Hussein, A.A. (1999) 'Hanuniye Mobile School Evaluation Report', Nomadic Primary Health Care Project, Wajir

Karani, F.A. (2002) 'Provision of Basic Education to Nomadic Pastoralists in Kenya', Nairobi: Ministry of Education, Science and Technology

Kratli, S. (2000) 'Education Provision to Nomadic Pastoralists: A Literature Review', draft version, Brighton: Institute of Development Studies

Makau, B. (1995) 'Dynamics of partnership in the provision of general education in Kenya', in J.. Semboja and O. Therkildsen (eds.) *Service Provision under Stress in East Africa*, Copenhagen/London: Centre for Development Research/James Currey

Makau, B. with M. Kariuki, A. Obondoh, and G. Syong'oh (2000) 'Harnessing Policy and Planning for Attainment of Education for All in Kenya', Research Report prepared for ActionAid (Kenya), Nairobi: ActionAid

Narman, A. (1990) 'Pastoral peoples and the provision of educational facilities: a case study from Kenya', *Nomadic Peoples* 25–27: 108–21

Niles, F. S. (1989) 'Parental attitudes toward female education in northern Nigeria', *The Journal of Social Psychology* 129/1: 13–20

Nkinyangi, J. A. (1981) 'Education for nomadic pastoralists: development planning by trial and error', in J. Galaty, D. Aronson, and P. Salzman (eds.) *The Future of Pastoral Peoples*, Ottawa, International Development Research Centre

Nkinyangi, J.A. (1982) 'Access to primary education in Kenya: the contradictions of public policy', *Comparative Education Review* 26/2: 199–217

Obura, A.P. (2002) 'Case for the Establishment of A National Commission for the Education of Pastoralist and Nomadic Communities: A Concept Paper', submitted to the Kenya Country Working Group on Non-Formal Education. Ministry of Education, Science and Technology, Nairobi

Odada, M. and H.D. Olega (1999) 'Alternative Basic Education for Karamoja', review report prepared for Redd Barna, Uganda, Kampala: Redd Barna

O'Leary, M.F. and E. M. Wakesa (2000) 'Wajir Pastoralist Development Project; Phase Two, End Project Review', report to DFID, East Africa, Nairobi: Department for International Development

Oxfam GB (1999) 'Education Accessibility in Wajir District: A Case Study', Kenya: Oxfam GB

Ponsi, F.T. (1988) *Sex- and Birth-order: Selective underenrolment in the primary schools of Kenya's arid and semi-arid districts and the 'kepyiong' phenomenon*, Working Paper 462, Institute for Development Studies, University of Nairobi

Republic of Kenya (1997) Master Plan on Education and Training 1997 – 2010, draft version, August 1997, Nairobi: Ministry of Education

Republic of Kenya (1998) National Primary Education Baseline Report (draft version), Nairobi: Ministry of Education and Human Resource Development

Republic of Kenya (1999) Education for All: Assessment of Progress: Kenya Country Report, draft version, August 1999, Nairobi: Ministry of Education

Republic of Kenya (2003) Draft Policy on Gender and Education, Nairobi: Ministry of Education, Science and Technology

Republic of Kenya/ FAWE (2000) Education Statistical Booklet 1990–98, Nairobi: Ministry of Education, Science and Technology/ Forum for African Women Educationalists

Republic of Kenya/Oxfam (1996) 'Pastoralists under Pressure: the effects of the growth in water sources and settlements on nomadic pastoralism in Wajir District', Department of Livestock Production/Oxfam, Wajir

Republic of Kenya/UNICEF (1999) Comprehensive Education Sector Analysis Report 1994, Nairobi: Ministry of Education and Human Resources/UNICEF

Salzman, P.C. and J. G. Galaty (1990) 'Nomads in a changing world: issues and problems', in *Nomads in a Changing World*, eds. P.C. Salzman and J. G. Galaty, Naples: Instituto Universitario Orientale, Series Minor XXXIII

Sibabi-Nyukuri, M. (1989) 'Facts and Figures of Education in 25 years of "Uhuru", Kenya', Nairobi: Bureau of Educational Research, Kenyatta University

Sifuna, D.N. (2003) 'The Pastoralist Communities and Free Primary Education in Kenya: A Preliminary Survey', Nairobi: ActionAid Kenya

Stromquist, N. P. (1997) 'Gender sensitive educational strategies and their implementation', *International Journal of Educational Development* 17/2: 205–14

Tahir, G. (1991) *Education and Pastoralism in Nigeria*, Zaria: Ahmadu Bello University Press

Torres, R.M. (1992) 'Alternatives in formal education: Colombia`s Escuela Nueva Programme', *Prospects* 22/4: 512–20

Turton, E. R. (1974) 'The introduction and development of educational facilities for the Somali in Kenya', *History of Education Quarterly* 14: 347–65

World Declaration on Education For All (1990) in *Beyond Jomtien: Implementing Primary Education for All*, eds. A. Little, W. Hoppers and R. Gardner, London: Macmillan

Wynd, S. (1999)' Education, schooling and fertility in Niger', in *Gender, Education and Development: Beyond Access to Empowerment*, eds. C. Heward and S. Bunwaree, London: Zed

7 When access is not enough: educational exclusion of rural girls in Peru

Patricia Ames

This chapter examines a study conducted in the late1990s to investigate the causes and dimensions of educational exclusion of rural girls in Andean areas of Peru. It considers the continuing problem of access to schooling for particular social groups. With reference to those who do attend school, it considers the ways in which gender inequities persist, and the multiple factors that work against girls' completion of primary education.[1]

During the 1990s, most Latin American countries achieved almost universal enrolment, showing an average net primary enrolment ratio of 96.6 per cent. Although many countries have achieved gender parity, in Brazil, Guatemala, Antilles, and Saint Lucia fewer girls have access than boys, and 56 per cent of the children who are out of school in the region are girls (EFA 2004).

Peru follows this regional trend. Statistics for 2000 show a gross enrolment ratio of 96.9 per cent in primary education and 85.9 per cent in secondary education (Guadalupe *et al.* 2002). Gender parity has been achieved in primary education, but fewer girls than boys are enrolled in secondary education (Gender Parity Index: 0.93[2]), a feature that contrasts with the general characteristics of the region (Guadalupe *et al.* 2002; EFA 2004).

Despite these achievements, the problem of inequity has not been solved. Twelve per cent of the adult population are illiterate, but this figure comprises 17.6 per cent of women, in contrast with 6 per cent of men.[3] This pattern is amplified when the differences between urban and rural areas are considered: 36 per cent of women in rural areas are illiterate,[4] and their average number of years of schooling is 3.7, in contrast with the statistics for rural men (5.1 years), urban women (8.3), and urban men (9.2).[5]

These features are partly remnants of a past situation when fewer women had access to education than men. But among the younger population (15–24 years old), 56 per cent of those without schooling or incomplete primary education are women,[6] and 13.5 per cent of rural girls between 5 and 17 years old do not have access to school (Montero and Tovar 1999). Thus, despite relatively high levels of enrolment, some segments of the female population still suffer from educational exclusion.

This chapter takes a close look at four Andean villages where more boys than girls attend school, and where more girls than boys have dropped out. For those attending, more boys than girls were promoted beyond Grade 6 exams, which are the final exams of primary school. The results of this study in rural Andean areas showed that there were multiple factors influencing girls' schooling, but that overall there was a fragile relationship between students and the school, due to the precarious economic conditions in which the students live. Differential social and cultural expectations of girls and boys had a bearing on their school attendance, and certain school practices strengthened rather than counteracted drop-out and school failure among girls.

Research sites and methodology

The study was conducted in four Andean villages over one school year, with a follow-up visit in the subsequent academic year. Two villages (Las Chulpas and Abracancha) are in the Department of Cusco in the Southern Andes, where the population is mostly Quechua-speaking; and two villages (Las Lomas and San Juan[7]) are in the Department of Cajamarca in the northern Andes, with a Spanish-speaking population.[8] The selection of villages reflected different situations which might affect girls' schooling. These included not only language but also productive activities, ecological location, and pattern of settlement, as well as size, location, and type of school.

Abracancha is a small village at 4000 metres above sea level, with a single-teacher school offering the first three grades (of a total of six) of primary schooling. This Quechua-speaking population subsists through the cultivation of potatoes and some cereals, and the raising of llamas and alpacas. There is no electricity or water supply to the households, which follow a semi-dispersed pattern of settlement. Las Chulpas, located in another province of the Department of Cusco, also lacks electricity and running water; but the pattern of settlement is more concentrated. However, the settlement has two sectors, one closer to the school than the other. This village is slightly bigger than Abracancha and has a bigger school, which has two teachers covering the complete six grades of primary education, plus a pre-school run by another teacher. The villagers raise sheep and cultivate cereals.

San Juan is the smallest community in the sample, with only 22 families and a single-teacher school, covering primary grades 1–4. Las Lomas, by contrast, is a bigger village, with 132 households and a primary school with five teachers. Only one teacher has two grades in the same classroom, and the others work in mono-grade classrooms (that is, one teacher to each grade). Las Lomas is not located far from San Juan – some two hours by foot – but it is not so high, and so the agricultural production is more varied. Neither community has electricity, but clean water is available at outdoor stand-pipes and, unlike Abracancha and Las Chulpas, each household has a latrine. The four villages have a very restricted public transport service, but San Juan is the most isolated, since no cars reach the village. A summary of the main features of each village is presented in Table 1.

Table 1: General information about selected villages

	Las Chulpas	Abracancha	Las Lomas	San Juan
The school				
# Teachers	2	1	5	1
# Students	70	40	132	22
# Grades	1 to 6	1 to 3	1 to 6	1 to 4
The village				
Location	Cuzco	Cuzco	Cajamarca	Cajamarca
Altitude (m. above sea level)	3700	4000	2350	3800
# Families	57	68	265	68
Pattern of settlement	Semi-concentrated	Dispersed	Dispersed	Concentrated
Language	Quechua	Quechua	Spanish	Spanish
Main productive activities	Agriculture (cereals and sheep)	Agriculture (potatoes and sheep)	Agriculture (corn)	Agriculture (potatoes and cereals)
Water supply	From a stream	From the river	In the house yard	In the house yard
Electricity	No	No	No	No
Toilets	No	No	Yes	Yes

The research team consisted of a general co-ordinator (Carmen Montero), a research co-ordinator (Patricia Oliart), and a fieldwork co-ordinator (Patricia Ames). There were also three regional research assistants (Fritz Villasante, Willy Lezama, and José Luis Arteaga).

The regional research assistants made four visits during the school year to each of the villages. As a fieldwork co-ordinator, I visited the four villages on at least three of the four visits to carry out the research activities. The same set of research instruments was applied in all schools. On the first visit, we carried out a census of the whole population, noting whether school-age children were attending school or not. We also registered all children enrolled at school at the beginning of the year and investigated the reasons why some children did not attend school. We asked teachers about patterns of attendance among girls, and we identified those with poor attendance rates. During the second visit, we approached those girls not attending school and those attending infrequently and conducted interviews with them and their families. We also carried out classroom observation at schools, focusing on trying to determine whether the school could be possibly promoting exclusion. We conducted interviews with teachers and observed their interactions with the children and their families in and out of school. The third visit, after the main school holiday and the harvest, aimed to evaluate the impact of agricultural work on children's attendance. We continued classroom observations and conducted interviews with students and with young women who had dropped out of school in second or third grade. We also continued monitoring girls with good attendance and their families. The fourth visit, at the end of school year, allowed another look at the school register to check promotion, repetition, and drop-out of students attending that year. At the beginning of the following school year we did a final visit and checked enrolment and attendance again. Through these detailed sets of observation and data collection, we identified those students who attended regularly, those who attended irregularly, those who dropped out, and those who did not graduate to the next grade at the end of the school year, and we inquired about the reasons for this behaviour.

Daily life, work, and poverty: the fragile relation with the school

The poverty that affects rural areas in Peru is widely documented. Extreme poverty[9] is concentrated in rural areas: 76 of every 100 people in extreme poverty in Peru live in rural areas, and 49 live in Andean rural areas (Montero *et al.* 2001). Conditions of poverty in rural villages require that all members of the household contribute to economic survival, assuming tasks and duties that sometimes compete with the time demanded by the school. Looking at national features (see Table 2), it seems that this competition does not have such a strong influence on the attendance of the age group between 6 and 11, but it does in the age group of 12 to 16, particularly among girls in rural areas.

Table 2: School attendance ratios – percentage of age groups in school

Age group	Total	Male	Female	Urban	Rural
3–5	68	67	69	74.3	59.6
6–11	97.6	97.8	97.4	98.6	96.2
12–16	83.4	85.9	80.9	86.5	78.3

Source: ENAHO 2001-IV

During the studies in the Andean villages, we observed in detail the daily routine of girls at different ages. Children were usually involved progressively in domestic and productive work from an early age (5 or 6 years old). Between the ages of 6 and 11, girls were mostly involved in domestic activities such as fetching water, collecting firewood for cooking, cutting grass to feed domestic animals, cleaning the house and the dishes, washing clothes, shopping, taking care of animals and grazing them, taking care of younger siblings, and helping to cook. However, they also helped in agricultural activities away from the house, such as hoeing, planting seeds, distributing fertiliser, and harvesting, collecting, selecting, and storing agricultural products.

Although at a young age the tasks assigned to boys and girls were very similar, they were differentiated according to gender as they grew older, until they resembled the expected roles assigned to men and women in their society. Girls tended to assume most of the domestic work, with some agricultural work, while boys increased their participation in agricultural activities. Between the ages of 11 and 15 years, in addition to their domestic tasks girls also engaged in spinning and knitting and sewing – making not only their own clothes but those of other family members. They also cooked for the family, helped in sowing and harvesting, and took major responsibility for grazing the animals. As their tasks grew in complexity and intensity, they demanded more time (see Box 1). In the light of these responsibilities, the fall in the school-attendance ratio for this age group is understandable (see Table 2 opposite).

Box 1: Life in Las Chulpas

Winter mornings are cold in Las Chulpas, situated at 3700 metres above sea level. Teachers usually start the lessons one hour late because of the cold. However, boys and girls such as ten-year-old Anita wake up every morning at 5 a.m. She helps around the home, carrying water, feeding animals, taking care of her younger sister, Luzmila, who is six, or the baby Marlith, who is one, and doing some cooking with her mother. Her parents have to leave early for the fields, or *chacras*. They have no sheep, but in families that do own sheep, the mother or an older sister leads the flock to the grazing area. They can be seen each day, winding through the paths crossing the wheat fields surrounding the community. School children such as Anita and her sister will stay behind in the village to attend school, while the youngest children go with their mothers. In the afternoon, after school, the children go to the *chacras* to help their parents, bringing them some lunch and gathering some natural fuel on their way back home. Girls also wash clothes, clean the house, or take care of younger siblings. Around 5 p.m. the flock is herded back to the village, and the women and girls cook the dinner. Everyone goes to bed early, because there is no electricity in Las Chulpas; with the sunset everything becomes quiet and calm.

As every family member has to contribute to family survival, we found that having one parent out of work due to illness or even death was one of the causes of drop-out for girls. In such cases, girls assume more duties in their families and cannot continue attending school. The situation might be temporary or permanent, but even when temporary it constitutes an interruption in regular schooling, and some girls do not return to school after dropping out for a year or two. In Las Chulpas, for example, 14-year-old Santusa took responsibility for domestic duties when her mother was sick, and she thereby lost one school year. But Bernardina (16 years) and her brother Pablo (17 years) in Abracancha, who lost their father, abandoned primary school before completing grade 6 and became totally absorbed into adult activities in their household.

We found also that the poorer families (with infertile lands or few resources) in each community could not afford to send their children to school, because they were needed for work. That was the case of 18-year-old Leocadia, who, along with her siblings, did not attend school because of her family's poverty. Families with only one parent found schooling difficult to afford, because the remaining parent needed more help with work to provide enough food to maintain the family. Furthermore, the hidden costs of schooling (such as uniforms, notebooks, and educational materials) also influenced the prospects of children in poorer families. The age of a girl, her position in the family, and the number of siblings available to help with domestic and agricultural tasks also influenced the school attendance. A girl is less likely to attend school if she is the oldest sibling, or if she is approaching adolescence and her siblings are too young to help with the work demanded by the family.

Another study in the southern Andes (Uccelli 1999) found that some families with scarce resources will focus on the schooling of one selected child. Usually, a child is chosen because of his or her ability at school, rather than a simple preference for sending boys. Nevertheless, Uccelli found that school failure – that is, failing end-of-year exams and having to repeat the whole year again – was less tolerated by parents for their daughters than for their sons. School registers indicated that more boys than girls had repeated grades several times. Girls who repeat therefore are more likely to be withdrawn. We also noted that the ability to read and write and to speak Spanish, although valued for both girls and boys, was considered as especially important for boys, who will become the head of their family in the future and will require the skill. For example, as heads of families men participate in the communal assembly and may have a position on the Assembly Board, where they will need to read and write and manage a range of legal papers, as well as speak Spanish to the extent of being able to negotiate with local and regional authorities. Men also take charge of managing official documents and papers concerning their families' land, acquiring identity papers, and so on. In addition, men are more likely to migrate temporarily to the city for seasonal work, where they will need Spanish language and literacy skills. This gives boys an advantage over girls – although opportunities are more equal today than they have been historically.

In general there is a correlation between the structure of the family, its resources, and the nature of children's attendance at school. However, in Las Chulpas, a group of out-of-school girls belonged to wealthier families who owned large flocks of sheep. The girls attending school were from poorer families who had no animals. One girl from a poorer family said: *'If I had sheep, I would not attend school'*, thus indicating the restrictions that one kind of family asset place on girls' attendance at school.

Rural Andean children work not only because of economic need, but also because of cultural and social needs. Indeed, it is through participation in agricultural and domestic activities that children learn the skills and abilities to become economically active adults. Participation in these activities gives children a sense of achievement and learning that is often more elusive at school, as the next section discusses. Some of the girls interviewed had themselves chosen to drop out of school so that they could find employment or take a greater part in domestic activities, albeit against the will of their parents. They did so because they felt that they were learning more at home than at school, and they believed that this learning would be more useful for their future lives. Opting out was particularly evident among girls in the 12–16 age group who, as adolescents, were developing new interests. In many cases girls decided to leave school without consulting their parents, although in a number of cases it was the parents who took this decision.

Beginning secondary education was a considerable challenge for girls. Secondary education is not available in the villages, and so the children had to walk for several hours or live in the town where the school is located. Most girls therefore do not attend secondary education, because of the costs of accommodation, transport, and food that most families cannot afford. Besides, it was not considered appropriate for girls to live far from home or to walk alone on the long journey to school. These issues are also pertinent to primary-school attendance in cases where the school is not close to girls' homes (see Box 2). In two of the study villages, their dispersed pattern of settlement meant that many of the children had a long walk to school. The young children were most affected. (Table 2 shows lower attendance in this age group, in part because of this factor.[10]) In two villages, schools offered primary education for the first four years only. To complete primary schooling, students have to walk to a neighbouring village, but girls are less likely to do this, so their primary education is incomplete.

> **Box 2: Distance and availability as barriers to girls' education**
>
> Abracancha is high in the mountains, and snow peaks are clearly seen from almost every angle in the village. The weather is cold and dry, and only potatoes can be cultivated at this altitude. This used to be a very dispersed settlement, because of each family's need for pastures for their flocks of llamas and alpacas. Nowadays some families have moved closer to the small, single-teacher school, but for other families their children from the age of four and five years have a walk of 30, 40, or even 75 minutes to reach the school. Attendance at the pre-school dwindles each day as the term progresses.
>
> Distance is one reason why some children start their schooling late, because parents prefer to wait until they consider that a child is strong enough to do the walking. But for the children who do attend school, many do not complete their primary education. The one-teacher school in Abracancha offers only the first three grades, and to continue schooling children must go to Lares, the district capital, one hour by car from the village. But there is only one bus per day to Lares, so children must stay there the whole week to study. Only a few children do this – and of these few are girls.
>
> The situation is similar in San Juan in the northern Andes. There is no pre-school, because there is no teacher, and the primary school offers only grades 1–4. To study further, children have to walk some two hours to the school in Las Lomas. Secondary education is not available at Las Lomas and is thus an even more remote possibility for the girls of San Juan – even for those of Las Lomas.
>
> Marleni, a young girl from San Juan, was studying fourth grade for the second time in 1997 because there was no opportunity for her to attend the fifth grade in Las Lomas school, due to the distance involved.

When access is not enough: the school experience

At the four schools studied there were many obstacles to girls' attendance; but for those who overcame these obstacles and succeeded in attending school, the quality of education offered in rural schools was very low. Over the course of the school day little time was dedicated to learning; indeed, on average the time spent on learning hardly surpassed two hours (see Box 3). Instead, the school hours were swallowed up in late starting, early closing, long breaks, and activities focused on maintaining order in the classroom and administrative tasks. Added to this were national and local holidays and teachers' absence to collect their salaries and for administrative purposes.[11]

In all four schools, most lessons are dedicated to 'the basics', that is mathematics and Spanish language, with a very small amount of time allocated to social and natural sciences. Although a national training programme began in 1996 to train teachers in new methods and active pedagogy, its impact was still very limited during the research period. Teaching and learning approaches were characterised

---

Box 3: The school day

The school day in Las Chulpas starts late – around 9 a.m. – with an opening ceremony which can take between 10 and 45 minutes. Students stand in rows while the teacher makes announcements, asks or designates 'volunteers' to come to the front to sing, tell a tale, or share an event. There are two primary-school teachers in Las Chulpas; one who teaches grades 1 and 2 in one classroom, and one who teaches grades 3–6 in another classroom. There is also a pre-school teacher. When the school is 'in', there are clusters of sandals (*ojotas* – made from old car tyres) in front of each classroom door, because children are asked to remove them before they enter the buildings, to keep them clean. (The son of the pre-school teacher, however, is allowed to keep his on, and they are not *ojotas* but trainers.) There is a break at around 10 a.m. that lasts one hour, when the children play and have breakfast, cooked by mothers and/or older girls. In Abracancha, where there is no school breakfast, children bring some food (toasted corn, potatoes, cheese) and sit in small groups, sharing what they have brought. After the break children return to classrooms and stay until 1 p.m., after which they return home.[12]

---

by drill, memorising by rote, and repetition, making learning a rather boring and mechanical task. This is a feature that characterises teaching in the vast majority of rural schools (Ames 2001; 2004).

Teachers' approaches to teaching and learning were limited, not only because of low levels of training but also because they had few educational resources or teaching aids. When we started our research, educational materials for teaching and learning were few and outdated. One year later, textbooks, workbooks, and materials for mathematics started to arrive at the schools as part of a national programme to provide schools with libraries in an attempt to improve this situation. But in some schools these materials remained unused. Teachers were afraid that materials would become damaged or lost if children used them, or that they were too difficult for them to understand. In Las Chulpas, for example, the teachers stored the textbooks and used them occasionally to prepare a lesson; but they did not allow their regular use by children. This reluctance on the part of teachers was related to their lack of familiarity with these materials and their lack of training in how to use them (see also Ames 2001).

The language used at school in the two Quechua communities was Spanish, although few children started school with any command of it. Teachers used Quechua to communicate with their students, but most of the lessons were given in Spanish. However, not all the teachers were Quechua-speaking, and at least one had to learn Quechua from her students in order to communicate with them. In any case, the methodology of second-language acquisition had not been part of these teachers' training, and they used both languages without a clear strategy to enhance the learning of Spanish, while insisting that children speak in this language.

In general, the professional training of teachers seemed inadequate for successful teaching and learning. The quality of their own learning was poor. Their training had not equipped them for working in multi-grade classrooms: on the contrary, teacher training and in-service initial training for untrained teachers ('professionalisation') is based on the assumption that teachers work in 'complete' schools, that is schools with one teacher for each of the six grades, and, moreover, that they work in 'ideal' contexts where access and resources are not a key challenge. It is not surprising, then, that teachers approached their multi-grade classes as if they were two or three distinct mono-grade classes with invisible walls between the clusters of children and desks. They set different lessons for each grade group, or at best grouped two grades together for the same lesson.

This lack of training for the conditions in which they had to work produced constant dissatisfaction and frustration. In interviews the teachers, who do not originate from the villages where they teach, complained that the poverty of the schools and the village environments made their jobs difficult. They had no professional support, and moreover were separated from their families, who remained in the towns while they stayed in the village during the school week. Their sense of dissatisfaction, their alienation from the students and villagers, and the material poverty of their environments negatively affected their motivation. This situation is not unique to the cases studied, but has been reported in national surveys and other studies among rural teachers (Montero *et al.* 2001, Tovar 1989). The head teacher of the school in Las Chulpas commented:

> *I would like to work in an urban area, because I have been trained to work with children, to teach. Sometimes I feel bad, because, at the beginning, for example, I came with desires to work because I was practising with Spanish-speaking students; thus everything I planned I achieved, but here it is not so, sometimes the very fact you have to speak to them in Quechua means they fail in literacy. Therefore I don't feel satisfied with it. I would like that my students learn quickly, wouldn't I? And see the product of my work also in them. But you don't see it, and this is not the only place, I mean, I am not the only one that feels that way. There are many teachers in rural areas that want to work, but with these children they disappoint us… I don't feel well working here, it is different, it is another reality.*

This teacher expresses not only her dissatisfaction working in a rural area, but her low expectations of her students. She perceives rural, indigenous children as less capable than their urban, Spanish-speaking peers. Teachers' low expectations are also common in other rural schools and they extend to rural parents, who are seen as less able to support their children's education (see for example Ames, 1999a, 2004).

Another feature of school practices that adversely affected students' participation was physical punishment. In Las Lomas, corporal punishment by the male teacher at the school was reported as one of the main causes for the drop-out of a group of students in grade 5. In Abracancha, a small whip hung on the wall next to teacher's desk as a visual reminder that misbehaviour would be punished; it was used sometimes during our observations. Order and obedience are highly prized by teachers, and a silent classroom is regarded as a sign of good control on the part of the teacher. This order and control were also enforced through threats, and mockery and humiliation of children (see also Ames 1999a; Aikman 2003). Children's self-esteem becomes damaged by such techniques, as Vasquez and Martinez (1996:74) point out:

> ... *expressions of inconvenience, gestures indicating that one is losing too much time with a child, telling him he [sic] is saying silly things or does not understood, contribute to inhibit him and lead him to build a self image centred on his inabilities.*[13]

Indeed, children often lose faith in their own capacity to learn, in response to the continuous criticism of their mistakes and lack of feedback on their achievements. This is expressed in a common phrase among children to explain their failure: '*mi cabeza no da*' (my head is not good enough).

These characteristics of schooling and teaching and learning in the study villages appeared to affect girls and boys equally, but there are other aspects of school life that affected girls particularly. Teachers' expectations of their students' ability are low for rural children in general, and even lower for rural girls. Although in formal interviews teachers recognised the importance of education for both girls and boys, in informal discussion they expressed the strong opinion that rural girls will not complete their basic education because of the constraints of poverty and their families' ignorance of the value of education. At best the teachers hoped that they might complete primary schooling before marrying and becoming overwhelmed in caring for a family. Therefore teachers did not see the value of investing their energies in stimulating girls' learning or helping them to achieve their full potential.

Teachers emphasise, reproduce, and naturalise the domestic role of women among their students. Some teachers ask girls to perform domestic duties for them, such as washing their clothes or cleaning their dishes (in Abracancha and Las Chulpas respectively). A teacher in Las Chulpas brought her baby to the school and sometimes asked one girl to care for the baby while she was teaching: thus the girl missed part of the lesson. Girls are sometimes in charge of preparing the food for breakfast, bringing the firewood and the water, and then doing the cooking, which represents time away from the classroom. (In some schools, mothers do this job.)

Teachers did not often interfere in conflicts between children – even inside the classroom and the playground – and thus left unprotected those more vulnerable to abuse, such as younger children and girls. Indeed, it was observed that boys usually tease girls, for instance by stealing their bags for fun, occupying most of the playground space, and laughing about girls' mistakes in the classroom, thus creating an embarrassing situation for girls. Although some teasing is seen as play, some entails real aggression towards girls, and they feel humiliated, embarrassed, and uncomfortable.

However, the schools were not a wholly negative place for girls. Girls commented that they liked many aspects of their school, such as the opportunities to meet other girls, and the chance to play together and have fun, especially when their domestic tasks did not allow them other space and time to do this. They enjoyed learning to read and write, to draw, and to speak Spanish if they did not already do so, and learning mathematics in order to calculate and engage in the town market with their families. They reported that they enjoyed being in the company of others and learning things to improve their lives. They also created their own strategies to minimise uncomfortable situations. For example, a group of girls who regularly attended Las Chulpas school sat together in the front of the classroom, as far from the boys as possible, thus constituting a cohesive group to defend themselves against the boys' teasing. When two new girls later joined this multi-grade class, they were not initially part of the group and they became the butt of teasing from the boys. Girls kept a low profile and were quiet as part of a strategy for reducing the risk of being punished by the teacher.

The picture that the study revealed of girls' schooling experience from the four communities was not therefore all negative, and girls were not passive victims of the system. However, girls may feel that the cost of schooling is too high, and that drop-out is a logical choice. This may be because of violence, aggression, or physical punishment, and/or because the education on offer – meaningless exercises and a focus on knowledge and realities far removed from their lives, concerns, and interests – has little to offer of value for them. Girls drop out when they have other, more valued, spaces for learning and work in the context of their own households.

Reflections

As Oliart (2004) points out, many actions can be taken to counteract rural girls' problems of access and attendance at school. For example, an adult from the community might accompany girls if they have a long walk to school. This may reassure parents and girls, and improve attendance. Economic aid in the form of bursaries for poorer families to enable them to send their girls to school has been tried in countries such as Mexico (*Oportunidades* programme) and Brazil (*Bolsa Escola* programme). These programmes provide monetary compensation to families (and in the case of *Bolsa Escola* usually to mothers) for the economic value of the girls' work lost through school attendance.[14] The provision of school breakfasts in rural schools is an incentive for poorer families to send their children to school on a more regular basis. Recently, some initiatives in Peru such as the projects *Nuevos Horizontes* (New Horizons/ CARE–USAID) and *Abriendo puertas para la educación de las niñas rurales* (Opening Doors for the Education of Rural Girls/UNICEF–USAID) have achieved agreements with parents and communities to guarantee the enrolment of all girls of school age, in an attempt to avoid children enrolling late and then dropping out because they feel too old to be at primary school. These projects have also worked intensively, not only at local level but also at regional and national levels, to raise awareness of the problems and disadvantages faced by rural girls.

Although not specifically directed at girls, a general effort to improve the quality of education in recent years may help to make the school more attractive and effective for girls. In the past, some NGO-supported bilingual projects in the Andes, particularly the Bilingual Project in Puno (PEBI–Puno), have reported that the overall interventions have helped to improve learning among girls in general and among boys who have less exposure to Spanish (see Ames 1999a; Rockwell *et al.* 1989). In the past decade, some efforts at the national level to introduce active pedagogy and acknowledge diversity in the curriculum have also helped to meet the educational needs of rural girls. Nevertheless, as many of these projects and efforts have not paid particular attention to the situations of rural girls, many indicators such as drop-out, promotion, and completion rates still show a gap between girls and boys (see Ames 1999b). Therefore, although the improvement in the quality of the education at rural schools will benefit both girls and boys, particular actions are still required to meet rural girls' specific problems.

Indeed, as this study of four Andean villages shows, there are issues over and above the quality of schooling that affect girls' exclusion. Neither the school nor the community is a gender-neutral institution or agent. They both produce and reproduce through their practice a structure of opportunities marked by gender inequalities. Consciously or unconsciously, and reinforced by economic constraints, girls' exclusion and drop-out from school have reinforced rural women's subordinate status. In rural communities and at home, literacy, schooling, and the ability to use the Spanish language are socially valued forms of knowledge which determine the place of the person in the group, his or her status, and the social recognition that can be obtained from them (Ames 2004, 2002). Women who lack this knowledge and the ability to use it are often relegated to subordinate positions in relation to the men from their own families and social group. In our interviews with adult women who had little or no schooling, we found that their lack of qualifications had a negative impact on their status inside and outside their families and communities. This resulted in making them dependent on male decisions and men's ability to act on a range of issues. Most of these women belong to a generation for whom girls' education was not considered necessary. In most of the homes that we visited, the expansion of the school system and the discourse of Education For All have strengthened the demand for schooling for both girls and boys, and have changed the perception that education for girls is unnecessary. However, we also found that despite a more equal discourse among parents, in practice girls' schooling is more fragile and fragmented than schooling for boys. This is reflected not only in the situations described and analysed in this study, but also in the features of drop-out, promotion, and attendance that each community presents.

Although our research did not pay particular attention to textbooks (since they were rarely used), research has shown that textbooks and school lessons suffer from gender bias. Through examples that attribute domestic roles to women and girls, and productive roles to men and boys, or through the absence of female characters in history, science, and the arts, school textbooks and lessons continue to reinforce gender prejudices concerning female and male roles (Anderson 1986; Espinoza 2004).

Another point of concern relates to changes in marital preferences. In a study in the southern Andes, Oliart (2003) found that a growing proportion of young men with education migrate temporarily out of the community. When they return to the community, they tend to prefer more educated women for wives, and girls with less education are at risk of single motherhood.

The schools included in this study face many challenges ahead if they are going to offer gender equity in education. It is true that many teachers have started to change the practices that have a negative impact on girls' attendance. In Las Lomas, for example, as a result of a local teacher-training programme led by UNICEF, female teachers stopped using physical punishment when they became aware of its possible effects on drop-out rates. In Las Chulpas, the head teacher attended the national training programme (PLANCAD) aimed at promoting active pedagogy. In a visit to the village two years after the end of the study, we found that she had started to try out new methodological strategies, such as group work and written tasks to produce more attractive and significant learning situations for her students, with positive results. In both cases, in-service training helped teachers to identify problems and solutions to improve their classroom practice. This illustrates that teachers are willing to change and improve when they are helped to recognise their prejudicial gendered practices, and when they receive support, training, and resources to enable them to overcome the problems that they face and the isolation that they have felt. However, there is still a need not only to provide such support and training on a more regular basis, but also to tackle more subtle problems, such as low expectations and prejudices about rural children and girls in particular. Some small-scale projects have been started which propose educational interventions with the aim of improving the quality of schooling, but with the specific target also of improving the situations of rural girls in particular, thus working with parents, teachers, and communities to sustain girls' schooling (see for example the projects *Warmi Warmakunapa Yachaynin* – Girls' Knowledge – and *Musuq Yachay* – New Learning, and methodological innovations for pre-school and primary school with an emphasis on girls, initiated by CARE/USAID, and the Project for Gender Equity in the Education of Rural Girls in Quispicanchis, by Fe y Alegría 44/ IPEDEPH).

Thus, a range of factors must be taken into account to improve girls' education: from the school teachers in the classrooms to the educational system that trains and supports their teaching, to the design and distribution of textbooks, pedagogic strategies, and other resources. The economic condition of rural societies also needs attention. A deeper reflection on the gender-biased preconceptions of all agents involved in the education effort is needed by educators, parents, and policy makers. A closer examination of how these preconceptions reinforce male domination and exclude girls and women is urgently required if the goal of equality is going to be truly achieved.

Patricia Ames, PhD in Anthropology of Education, University of London, is a researcher and lecturer at the Faculty of Education at the Universidad Peruana Cayetano Heredia, and a member of the Institute of Peruvian Studies. Her writings have examined various issues in rural education such as gender equity, multi-grade schooling, literacy, use of textbooks, and political socialisation of children.

Notes

1. The project on which this article is based was funded by the Royal Embassy of the Netherlands. It was carried out at the Instituto de Estudios Peruanos IEP under the general co-ordination of Carmen Montero and the research co-ordination of Patricia Oliart. I owe a debt to them for their guidance, and to all the girls of the 'rural girls' educational exclusion project', for allowing me to be part of their lives.

2. This measure is used by UNESCO in its annual Education For All Global Monitoring Reports. It is the ratio of female-to-male value of a given indicator. A GPI of 1 indicates parity between sexes; a GPI that varies between 0 and 1 means a disparity in favour of boys; a GPI greater than 1 indicates a disparity in favour of girls. However, a country can have a GPI of 1, indicating complete equality between boys and girls, but still have low rates of access, retention, and achievement for girls and boys.

3. ENAHO Encuesta Nacional de Hogares/National Home Survey, 2001.

4. ENAHO Encuesta Nacional de Hogares/National Home Survey, 1996.

5. ENAHO Encuesta Nacional de Hogares/National Home Survey, 1997.

6   ENNIV: Encuesta Nacional de Niveles de Vida /National Survey on standards of living, 1997.

7   The names of the villages have been changed to preserve confidentiality.

8   I continued to visit Las Chulpas for two subsequent years, doing research into other aspects of school life. When appropriate, I draw on information from these visits.

9   Defined as below the minimum of nutritional intake required to ensure human survival.

10   Another factor affecting low attendance in this age group is the availability of pre-school education in many rural villages.

11   Some time after our research indicated these features, the Ministry of Education published the fact that rural schools get an average of 250 school hours per year, in contrast with the 600 hours that urban schools get, and far less than the 1000 hours stated by official norms (Ministerio de Educación 2002).

12   In Las Lomas and San Juan the school day is different, because children attend in the mornings from 9 to 12, and in the afternoons from 2 to 4. They also get school breakfast at mid-morning.

13   My translation.

14   See www.oportunidades.gob.mx/ and www.mec.gov.br/secrie/default.asp.These programmes are aimed at children in poverty, including girls. In the case of Mexico, the programme tries to focus on girls, especially in the first year of secondary education, when they are more likely to drop out or avoid enrolment.

References

Aikman, Sheila (2003) *La educación indígena en Sudamérica: Interculturalidad y bilinguismo en Madre de Dios*, Lima: Instituto de Estudios Peruanos

Ames, P. (1999a) 'El poder en el aula: un estudio en escuelas rurales andinas' in M. Tanaka (comp) *El poder visto desde abajo: educación, democracia y ciudadanía en espacios locales*, Lima: Instituto de Estudios Peruanos

Ames, P. (1999b) *Mejorando la escuela rural, tres décadas de experiencias educativas en el campo*, Documento de trabajo No. 96, Lima: Instituto de Estudios Peruanos

Ames, P. (2001) *¿Libros para todos? Maestros y textos escolares en el Perú rural*, Consorcio de Investigaciones Económicas y Sociales, Lima: Instituto de Estudios Peruanos

Ames, P. (2002) *Para ser iguales, para ser distintos. Educación, escritura y poder en el Perú*, Lima: Instituto de Estudios Peruanos

Ames, P. (2004) 'Multigrade Schools in Context: Literacy in the Community, the Home and the School in the Peruvian Amazon', PhD dissertation, University of London

Anderson, J. (1986) 'Imágenes de la familia en los textos y vida escolares', *Revista Peruana de Ciencias Sociales,* Vol. 1, No. 1, Lima: FOMCIENCIAS

EFA (2004) 'Regional overview: Latin America and the Caribbean', in EFA Global Monitoring Report 2003/4 (www.efa.unesco.cl/ept_esp/todo.htm)

Espinoza, G. (2004) 'Género y curriculum: Resultados preliminares de investigación', presentation at GRADE Research seminar series, Lima, April

Guadalupe, C. *et al.* (2002) *La educación peruana a inicios del nuevo siglo,* Documento de trabajo No. 12, Lima: Ministerio de Educación

Ministerio de Educación (2002) *Educación para al democracia. Lineamientos de política educativa 2001-2006,* Lima: Ministerio de Educación

Montero, C. and T. Tovar (1999) *Agenda abierta para la educación de las niñas rurales,* Lima: CARE-Perú, IEP, Foro educativo

Montero, C., P. Oliart, P. Ames, Z. Cabrera, and F. Uccelli (2001) *La escuela rural: estudio para identificar modalidades y prioridades de intervención,* Documento de trabajo No. 2, Lima: MECEP – Ministerio de Educación

Oliart, P. (2003) 'Género, sexualidad y adolescencia en la provincia de Quispicanchis', Informe de consultoría (unpublished)

Oliart, P. (2004) '¿Para qué estudiar?: La problemática educativa de niñas y mujeres en áreas rurales del Perú' in I. Schira (ed.) *Género, etnicidad y educación en América Latina,* Madrid: Ediciones Morata

Rockwell, E. *et al.* (1989) *Educación bilingüe y realidad escolar: un estudio en escuelas primarias andinas,* Lima: Programa de Educación Bilingüe de Puno

Tovar, T. (1989) 'Ser maestro. Condiciones de trabajo docente en el Perú', Lima: DESCO, UNESCO (OREALC)

Uccelli, F. (1999) 'Democracia en el sur andino: posibilidades y esfuerzos de las familias campesinas para educar a sus hijos', en Tanaka (comp) *El poder visto desde abajo,* Lima: Instituto de Estudios Peruanos

Vasquez B., A. Martínez, and I. Martínez (1996) *La socialización en la escuela: una perspectiva etnográfica,* Barcelona: Paidós

8 Crossing boundaries and stepping out of *purdah* in India

Mora Oommen

This chapter describes and begins to analyse how the nation-wide Total Literacy Campaign (TLC) in India set in motion a process of empowerment that opened up space for women to cross social and geographical boundaries. I have based this chapter on research conducted for a larger study which sought to examine the link between literacy skills and empowerment in the lives of the women participants in the TLC. During fieldwork for this study, in response to my inquiries about how empowerment had manifested itself in the lives of women, I frequently heard the phrase '*Women are now stepping out of purdah.*' This chapter explores the meaning of this response. I came to understand that to speak of women's empowerment required an understanding of the roles played by women, and the challenges that they had to overcome.

In May 1988, the government of India launched the Total Literacy Campaign (TLC) under the National Literacy Mission (NLM), with the aim of imparting functional literacy to people in the age group of 15–35 years (GoI 1988). The TLC model was extraordinary, in that it took responsibility for increasing national literacy out of the central government's hands and made local government administrators responsible for its implementation, with the involvement of community organisations. This partnership allowed for local ownership and unprecedented voluntary participation.

Literacy was imparted through innovative approaches, involving entire populations in a process that was area-specific and time-bound. The TLC mobilised and trained 10 million people throughout India as voluntary trainers to impart literacy skills in basic reading, writing, and numeracy to approximately 68 million individuals (BGVS nd). Volunteers were trained in a pedagogy known as **Improved Pace and Content of Learning (IPCL)** to achieve the objective of imparting these skills in 200 hours (BGVS 1993). Three multi-grade primers containing exercises and tests were supplemented with locally developed material (such as short stories, plays, and songs) to increase the appeal to the participants. In addition, topics in the primers included functional information on agriculture, economics, livelihood, health, and local history. Separate classes in groups of 10–15 men and women were held close to the homes of the participants. Particular emphasis was given to increasing the involvement of women. This resulted in many evaluation studies highlighting the very high levels of women's participation in these adult education programmes (Singh 2000; Sundararaman 1996).

In July 2002, ten years after the official end of the TLC, I conducted an ethnographic study in a cluster of villages (identified as a *gram panchayat*) located in Begusarai District in Bihar. The civil-society partner that conducted the literacy campaign, and my host and guide in this district, was the Bharat Gyan Vigyan Samiti (BGVS).[1] The study is based on data gathered through interviews and participant observations conducted in July 2002 in Shantipur[2] *gram panchayat*. The ethnographic style of the study was facilitated by my fluency in Hindi, but the insights of the study draw as much on my perspective gained from growing up in urban India as on my observations in Begusarai.

Of the people who were involved in the literacy campaign in Begusarai, 80 per cent were women (BGVS–Begusarai official records). In a State that has strong cultural norms limiting women's independence and rights, the work of the BGVS was unprecedented: it set in motion a dynamic process of redefining women's role in society. As became apparent to me during my research, women played three main roles in the campaign: as organisers (recruited as co-ordinators and leaders to encourage other women to participate); as volunteers (trained to teach or carry out other tasks in the organisation); and as learners (the recipients of the literacy training). This study examines what 'stepping out of *purdah*' meant to the women in each of these groups.

After spending time in the community, I understood that the literacy campaign, although seeking to impart literacy skills, had a much richer story to tell about the changes in women's lives. Understanding the empowerment of women went beyond merely determining how formerly non-literate women were using their newly acquired reading and writing skills in their daily lives. Reviewing the changes in the lives of women who participated in the TLC as organisers and volunteers indicated that although they came from different starting points and had different levels of access to material, social, and human resources, the campaign opened important spaces for all of to make the most of these resources.

For more than ten years, women's literacy has been an important proxy indicator for measuring women's empowerment (King and Hill 1993; Patel S 1996; Rockhill 1993; Robinson-Pant 2000; Rowlands 1997, 1999; Athreya and Chunkath 1996). The concept of women's empowerment first began to take shape in 1985, at the United Nations Women's Conference in Nairobi, through the Development Alternative for Women in the New Era (DAWN). This resulted in an examination of women's empowerment in a patriarchal system that instituted sexual division of labour and controlled women's sexuality (Sen and Grown 1987). However, to quote Batliwala (1993), the means of measuring empowerment remains 'fuzzy'. By the end of the 1990s, a number of writers had agreed that empowerment is a process (Stromquist 1997; Kabeer 1999; Ramachandran 1999; Rowlands 1997, 1999; Oxaal and Baden 1997), although there remain differences about how to identify and measure tangible changes that result in empowerment.

Stromquist looked at the process of gaining literacy and concluded that it is more important than the eventual use or knowledge of coding and decoding letters and numbers. She stressed the 'unintended outcome' of empowerment from literacy (Stromquist 1997:29). Writers such as Boserup (1970), Kabeer (1994), and Park (1996) argue that literacy should not be an end in itself, but should be linked to the functional part of development projects, especially those affecting income generation, so that women can have access to financial resources. The link between the process of acquiring literacy skills and gaining empowerment since the 1990s has clearly remained an important issue for scholars and practitioners. However, in this literature I did not find any analysis of the literacy process which takes into account not only the move from illiteracy to literacy for the women learners, but also the changes for women who were organisers and volunteers. In the context of such programmes as the TLC, developed on a mass basis, I have found it critical to assess the campaign process, which suggests a process of empowerment for women participating in different roles. An attempt to understand the roles that different women played, the types of struggle that they faced, and the measures employed by them to overcome barriers is an important part of understanding the process of empowerment that can result from a literacy campaign. Begusarai's experience is significant because it can provide insight into the process that enabled women to cross boundaries which previously had limited their participation in the public realm.

Total Literacy Campaign in Begusarai District

In Begusarai District, Bihar, the TLC was organised and administered from 1994 to 1996 by the Bharat Gyan Vigyan Samithi (BGVS) in partnership with the government. Begusarai was the first district in the State of Bihar where the BGVS completed the TLC phase. Begusarai has remained actively involved in activities related to the Post-Literacy Phase (with activities that include publishing a local newspaper for neo-literates, and setting up libraries, women's self-help groups, and supplementary classes to increase school enrolment). During the time of my visiting, BGVS had begun the Continuing Education phase, intended to sustain the gains of the campaigns by re-introducing literacy classes and supporting women's participation in local government.

Covering an area of 1918 square kilometres, Begusarai is one of the 37 administrative districts in the northern Indian State of Bihar. It is divided into 17 blocks, 247 *gram panchayats*, and 1100 inhabited villages (CMS 1999). BGVS–Begusarai works in all 17 blocks of this district. According to the 2001 census, the population of Begusarai is 1.2 million men and 1.1 million women, of whom 87.6 per cent profess Hinduism and 12.3 per cent Islam. The predominant language is Hindi, spoken by 89.6 per cent (GoB 1991a). Statistics on transportation, education, and health-care facilities show that Begusarai is quite well provided, but a more detailed study shows that there are wide economic and social disparities between the urban and rural populations. For example, while 14.5 per cent of the total population is from the Scheduled [low] Caste (SC), 94 per cent of the rural population belongs to the SC (GoB 1991b). Most public amenities, such as running water, schools, electricity supplies, and health centres are concentrated in the urban areas.

Literacy levels in Begusarai district in 1991 were 49 per cent for men and 24 per cent for women; in 2001, these figures increased to 60 per cent and 36 per cent respectively (GoB 1991a, GoB 2002). These figures are still much lower than the 2001 national average of 75.9 per cent and 65.4 per cent. Analysis of the literacy rate among SC women in rural areas reveals that in 1991 only 5.54 per cent of this population was literate. As Figure 1 shows, in rural settings, where the poor, landless, SC women are the most marginalised social group, the opportunity to gain skills such as literacy has been denied to them. Thus, we see that the national literacy level of 65.4 per cent masks the much lower rate for rural, SC women, who suffer discrimination because of location, caste, and gender. Hence, the literacy campaign clearly needed to focus on the women in rural areas.

According to the 1991 census, there were more than 400,000 illiterate people in 1100 villages in Begusarai district. The BGVS estimated that it would require more than 40,000 volunteers to carry out the literacy campaign. On 20 November 1994, BGVS conducted an extensive survey throughout the district, involving an innovative mass-based mobilising methodology called *kalajatha* (cultural carnivals). The survey was well co-ordinated throughout the district and created energy and motivation to catalyse the campaign. Through this survey, 246,000 women and 188,000 men were registered for classes. As classes for women and men had to be organised separately at the local level, an estimated 16,400 women (one teacher: 15 learners) needed to be recruited as volunteers and trained to teach.

Classes began in the district in January 1995 and were followed by intensive teaching, monitoring, re-training, and re-motivating sessions. A communications structure was set up to connect volunteer trainers (VTs) with master trainers (MTs) and key resource persons (KRPs). The MTs and KRPs were hired to be full-time co-ordinating organisers, working across the district. Volunteer trainers were predominantly high-school students trained to organise and hold literacy classes in their villages. In June 1996, a *Mahapariksha Abhiyan* (final exam campaign)

Figure 1: Literacy rates among Schedule Caste women in Begusari District in 1991

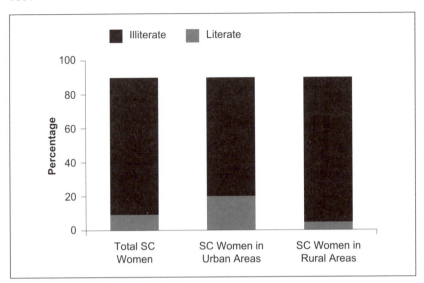

Source: GOB, 1991.

completed the teaching phase of the TLC. The results of the test showed that of the 330,000 enrolled learners who took the exam, 88 per cent completed Primer I; 61 per cent, Primer II, and 56.1 per cent, Primer III. This translated into 52 per cent of the learners becoming literate according to NLM norms (Rampal and Manimala 2002:100). Even after this intensive, large-scale literacy campaign ended, BGVS continued to engage the participants in programmes related to education, health, and livelihood issues.

Women's role as campaign organisers

Women participated in the campaign as organisers, volunteers, and learners. Organisers were women in leadership positions in BGVS at the block and district level. On the whole, men dominated the leadership of the organisation, and few women were present at this leadership level. Most women organisers joined the campaign as Master Trainers (MTs), then moved up to senior co-ordinating positions and membership of the District Task Force (an executive team which co-ordinated all the activities in the district). Organisers, who were given the responsibility to arrange and manage events and activities for women, were generally 25–35 years of age when they joined BGVS. Almost all had college degrees (Bachelor's level) and some had a graduate degree (Master's level). They came from upper-caste, land-owning families which had high social standing.

Many were married and had had children while they were still teenagers. Typically such a woman lived in her husband's village with other members of his family (the Hindi term for this is *sasural*). In field work for this study, meetings and interviews were held with four of the twenty organisers in the district.

Women as campaign volunteers

Volunteers were young women who had completed at least eight years of formal schooling, although some had high-school or college-level qualifications. They joined the campaign in two waves. More than 15,000 women were active volunteers during the TLC period (1994–1996) when they were 12–18 years old. Volunteers generally joined the organisation as *kalajatha* performers, Volunteer Trainers, and Master Trainers. The second wave of volunteers joined after the TLC phase (1998 onwards). The second-wave volunteers were very young when the literacy classes started, and they watched TLC activities in the district as they grew up. Volunteers from both waves took up positions in the Post-Literacy programmes run by BGVS. Some were given specific responsibilities; for example, running the children's supplementary schools called *Vikalp Shiksha Kendra* Centres, the *Panchayat* Libraries, and women's self-help savings groups, called *Sambals*. The organisation also supported the candidacy of many volunteers for roles in government programmes: nomination to serve on the Village Education Committees, responsibility for running the *Anganwadi* Centres (day-care centres for very young children), and election to positions such as Ward Commissioners and *Mukhiya* (village representative) in the July 2001 *Panchayat* elections. When the BGVS initiated or expanded a project, the volunteers were usually the group that was mobilised, given training, and eventually assigned to carry out the task. Volunteers were diverse in age and economic and caste backgrounds, but very few belonged to the Scheduled Caste. Volunteers received little or no remuneration for their work. Most were unmarried when the campaign started, and they lived with their parents in their natal village (termed *maikai* in Hindi). But, in time, many came under family pressure to get married, which reduced their participation in BGVS activities. During the field study, meetings were held with 80 volunteers, and in-depth interviews were conducted with ten.

Women learners

A majority of women learners were from the lower castes. They were landless or had small land-holdings and limited financial resources. Many had never had access to formal schooling, and contact with the TLC was their first opportunity to learn to read and write. The TLC targeted a diverse age group, between 15 and 35 years of age. The external evaluation of the Begusarai TLC, conducted in 1999, pointed out that the majority of learners who achieved literacy were in the 15–24 age group (CMS 1999). I interviewed many of the learners who had acquired literacy skills during the campaign and had remained in touch with the BGVS, through initiatives like the savings groups. But unlike the organisers and volunteers, learners did not occupy formal positions in the organisational structure. They were encouraged to participate in BGVS programmes like the libraries and *Sambals*. Most of the learners were married and lived with their in-laws. During the field work, I met with approximately thirty learners and held in-depth interviews with eight.

Crossing boundaries: stepping out of *purdah*

Before the literacy campaign in Shantipur, tradition limited the extent of women's interaction outside their homes. The Hindi term used by most people for this physical, social, political, and economic seclusion is *purdah pratha*. This practice most commonly manifests itself with women covering their heads with the edge of their traditional garment: a sari. The *purdah* acts as a physical restriction on women's mobility by defining their proper space as being within the boundaries of the home, where they are protected from contact with men who are not members of their family (Parker 1995). It creates a sexually segregated world, which identifies men with the public/social sphere and women with the private/domestic sphere (Kabeer 1985). The power of the *purdah* lies in the way in which it defines the interaction that women can have with the outside world. Patricia Jeffery, in her book on women living in *purdah* in India, defines this practice as follows:

> *For Muslims, purdah in the sense of complete veiling seems to operate after puberty in relation to all men, except very close kin. In north India, for Hindus, purdah in this sense is largely a question of veiling only after marriage and in relation to the husband's older male kin. Hindu women do not veil themselves in the place where they were born and where their own kin live, unless their husband or one of his male relatives is present.*
> (Jeffery 1979:3)

In this chapter I have used the term *purdah* as a demonstration of boundaries that limit women's participation in the public realm. Stepping out of *purdah* is not limited to women who question this tradition, but reflects changes in more subtle, tacit forms of boundaries formed around women. When the literacy campaign began, the BGVS women had to overcome the obstacle of *purdah* so that women could be recruited locally to teach and motivate others. The BGVS considered it essential that the literacy programme should reach out to both men and women so it made a concerted effort to provide women with space outside their homes in which to participate in the scheme. As some studies have already acknowledged:

Large-scale social mobilisation that is elicited by literacy campaigns obtains a 'social sanction' for women's participation in literacy programmes. Various patriarchal considerations that hinder their participation become at least temporarily inoperative as women come out of their homes and take part in the literacy campaign with great enthusiasm.
(Patel and Dighe, 1997:5)

The experience of the organisers

This form of suspension of *purdah* was evident in Shantipur, but was experienced differently by organisers, volunteers, and learners. The organisers spoke of *purdah* as a constraint on their mobility and on their ability to choose the kind of life that they would like to lead. Being educated, economically well-off, and enjoying a respectable standing in society, they had access to resources (material, social, and human), but strictly defined gender roles limited the extent to which they could exercise these resources. The BGVS, through the literacy campaign, opened spaces for those upper-caste women to begin a process of change. They achieved tangible benefits in terms of social recognition, rather than monetary gains. Deepa, one of the first women to join the organisation, recalls her initial interaction:

I was the only woman in my area who had completed my BA. So people were informed that my father-in-law has a daughter-in-law who is educated and he is the person to talk to. So people came to speak to my father-in-law and said that a meeting will be taking place in the village and if he would allow me to come for the meeting because I was educated … My father-in-law is interested in such matters. He said, 'Okay, she will do this work'. So I went to the meeting (and) in the meeting I didn't even know how to stand up and speak my name! … I covered my head and stood there. Then they told me about the kind of work that has to be done, that there is a huge offence against women, women are being burnt because they have not brought in enough dowry … All this began to touch my heart slowly. What they are saying is completely right, but in our village there is so much purdah …If I say yes to them maybe I will be able to do some work to solve their problems.
(Deepa, interviewed on 25 July 2002)

In this account, Deepa points out how she both possessed and was aware of the resources that she had: her BA qualification and her family's high standing in the village. She also was aware of current limitations on her life: her family had control over her interactions in the public realm. There were certain social practices that she was required to adhere to, and these were defined by her family's social standing. She acknowledged that '*they are saying things that are completely right*', but she also knew that she possessed the potential to make a change (*'if I say yes'*). The process of emerging from the constraints imposed by her family for the sake of other women was a process of empowerment. For her, BGVS provided the platform from which she was able to step out, with the resources that she already possessed.

Other organisers, like Deepa, often stressed the geographical boundaries that they had to cross, which in turn motivated other women to step out of their houses. Shakti said:

> ... *Then I joined the BGVS. Until I was working at the Panchayat level there was no problem. I used to work all day and then in the evening I used to come home. As I started to work at higher levels in the organisation, it became more difficult. For example, I returned yesterday after an eight-day trip. When I started to stay out of the house for more days, two days, four days, obviously the problems increased. Nobody's husband would like his wife to stay outside the house for so many days. But then I would sit down and try to explain to him, what kind of work I was doing. If I did not do this work, then what would happen to all the other women?*
> (Shakti, interviewed on 17 July 2002)

She broke out of the *purdah* by stepping out of the house and extending her work beyond the borders of her village, block, district, and State. Shakti's view was that she needed to push the social and geographical boundaries for all women. She needed to create the opportunities for other women by being the first to come out.

Stepping out of *purdah* for organisers like Deepa and Shakti meant that they drew on resources such as their education and high socio-economic status in a new space opened up by the literacy campaign. So for the organisers, overcoming geographical boundaries and travelling independently was a key form of empowerment.

The experience of the volunteers

When I spoke to the volunteers, a majority of them stated that the significant change in the lives of women was that they were out of *purdah*. Interestingly, they did not necessarily identify *purdah* as a barrier that *they* needed to overcome. Volunteering as teachers/trainers in the campaign was accepted as an extension of their schoolwork. Volunteers talked about the Literacy Campaign with a feeling of excitement. They clearly had fond memories of activities that gave them recognition and responsibility in the public sphere. As long as the work was confined to the local level of the village, it was seen as acceptable for young women to participate. As Savita, a volunteer, said:

I was told, any women living near you between the ages of 14 and 40 you should bring them to your centre and teach them. In the training we were told that it is likely that they will ask for things like oil, or say that we do not have time. So how will you explain things to them, we were given such training.
(Savita, interviewed on 17 July 2002)

The skills that they learned in school were relevant and useful in the campaign, and the volunteers were seen as vital participants in the programme by the BGVS leadership. Most volunteers referred to the fun and excitement of being included as part of a social change. They saw imparting literacy skills as a simple task, as an extension of their schoolwork:

We did not find teaching difficult at all. We held their hands and showed them how to write letters, patiently. Like this: ma, ka, na …
(Participant in focus-group discussion on 22 July 2002)

Many volunteers were not married at the time of the campaign. As they were living in their natal homes, they had fewer constraints on their mobility. In this society there were fewer restrictions on the lives of women at home than on the lives of married women living in their *sasural*.

During my stay in Shantipur, one of the young women who had been an active volunteer for the past five years got married and, as is customary, had returned to stay with her family for a few months. This practice signified her last few days at home before her final move to her *sasural*, after which she could no longer make claims on her natal family. As we began to talk, other BGVS volunteers teased her, saying that now she was married she had become quiet and demure, unlike her previous assertive, activist self. I asked her once if she thought she would continue her work when she went to live with her in-laws. Her eyes immediately looked down, and she said quietly that this would depend on her husband's family. Although she had asked her parents to find her a husband who would be open to her working outside the house, she did not think that his family would allow her to do this.

My interactions with the volunteers suggested that *purdah* was not a barrier that they had to confront directly. This result may perhaps be attributed to the successful struggles of the older women in the community, who created protected environments in which the younger women could step out. Another reason presented was that many of their activities were limited to areas close to their homes and did not require too much interaction beyond the protective circle of the community. But it suggests that the real test of volunteers' scope to move beyond *purdah* will not come until each one of them begins to leave her village, or starts to question social norms.

The experience of the learners

'Coming out of *purdah*' had a more direct, literal meaning for the learners. The social and physical limitations placed on them by gender and caste were very overt. Strict geographical boundaries in villages physically separated the areas inhabited by members of the lower caste from those of higher-caste women (or men). For women of a lower caste to step out of their homes and go to upper-caste areas to learn or participate in BGVS activities was itself a crossing of a major social and geographical boundary. As observed by other researchers who have studied literacy classes in north India, Patkar (1995) notes: 'There are striking disparities between scheduled and non-scheduled caste female participation rates in the North, where the caste barriers on women's entry into the public sphere appear to be rigidly enforced' (Patkar 1995: 403).

Such behaviour was emphasised when I spoke to many learners. Cheshta said:

> One day my mother-in-law asked where I was going and when I told her I was going to study, I got a huge beating from her. She asked me how I could step outside the house and go to someone else's place. So we used to secretly go for the classes at 12 noon when my parents-in-law would go to work in the fields. We would hide the slate in our box and never let them see it.
> (Chesta, interviewed on 20 July 2002)

Chesta revealed how she was prevented from going to 'someone else's place'. Her mother-in-law was stopping her from leaving her side of the village to go to the other side; in this way she was reminding her not only of the step that she was taking into an unknown person's house, but also of the boundaries that she was crossing by stepping out of her community into the space of upper-class families. Even though literacy classes were being conducted throughout the district, making it seem like an accepted community activity, the limitations on individual women's scope to make the very public step of coming out of their homes to acquire a skill carried grave risks. Although the physical distance covered by them may have been small, the social distance that they bridged was significant.

Participating in the literacy classes was not a simple matter for learners. They would often have to brave repeated hecklings on their way to classes. Vidya described this:

> People used to say a lot. They said, 'From your childhood you have not learned anything and now at this age you are going to learn? How do you think you will learn?' ... Even listening to them, we used to go.
> (Vidya, interviewed on 21 July 2002)

Thus coming out of *purdah* for her meant publicly admitting her lack of literacy skills and participating in a group to learn them. In one of the group conversations, Kalpana referred to herself bitterly as a fool (*moork* in Hindi) prior to the literacy campaign:

> *I was a fool … Then one of the VTs, she came to my house and said that such an activity has started where we teach people to read and write. If you remain a* moork *then how will you know what is happening? It is better if you learn to read and write. It was on her insistence that I went.*
> (Kalpana, interviewed on 21 July 2002)

Kalpana equates her illiteracy to being foolish, and associates being literate with gaining skills that would maker her a better person. The VT reinforced this self-impression. The boundaries that the learners had to cross were more rigid and overt than those crossed by organisers and volunteers. As my research revealed, the learners were the most marginalised of the women in Shantipur. Participating in the literacy campaign required stepping out of their homes, which required crossing socio-geographic boundaries of caste, class, and gender. In addition, it also meant publicly coming out and admitting the lack of literacy skills, and facing the risk of humiliation. Therefore, coming out of *purdah* for the learners was a risky endeavour, leaving them most susceptible to criticism.

Conclusion

This chapter has described the context of an unprecedented effort to increase literacy levels in a region that had one of the lowest literacy rates in India. The process of involving large numbers of people locally to administer and conduct the literacy classes required a high level of women's participation. The TLC in Begusarai offered women unprecedented space to 'come out of *purdah*'. But different women played different roles in the campaign, and coming out of *purdah* had different starting points and implications for each of the groups of women. The organisers in some ways took the first step out of *purdah* as the vanguard for other women in the society, by breaking traditional limits on their participation in the public sphere. It is important to note that the high social standing of their families, and their high levels of education, made things easier for them. The volunteers perhaps will be the measure of how far the *purdah* tradition has been overcome. As they develop from adolescence to womanhood and move away from their native region to participate in social change and progress, the extent to which the volunteers will be able to maintain the momentum built up during the TLC will need to be assessed. The learners perhaps took the largest personal risk, because they were most vulnerable when stepping out to a space created by upper-caste, educated women. Their own commitment to learning to read and write had to overcome societal restrictions on their physical, social, and economic activities. The process used in the TLC in Begusarai went beyond simply imparting literacy.

It clearly questioned a number of social norms constraining women's participating in public life. This glimpse into a decade of development in the lives of a group of women indicates the sensitivity required to understand an overarching term like 'women's empowerment' in all its complexity, rejoicing in the crossing of boundaries imposed by caste, gender, age, economy, and geography, but also cautioning the reader about the fragility of these efforts.

Mora Oommen worked with Indian education NGOs in the late 1990s. Most recently she has worked as a consultant on programme and resource development with innovative social initiatives, such as the Youth Employment Summit (YES) Campaign and World Computer Exchange, Inc. The research for this chapter was conducted as part of her work for her MA at the Institute of Education, London University.

Notes

1   BGVS is a nationwide non-government organisation, with chapters formed at the District Level. During the TLC, they worked across India in partnership with the government to shape, develop, and implement the campaign. The organisation remains in existence to this day, working on a variety of social issues related to basic literacy, children's education, health education, women's empowerment, and other livelihood issues.

2   The names of this *Panchayat* and the participants have been changed, to preserve confidentiality.

References

Athreya, V. B. and S.R. Chunkath (1996) *Literacy and Empowerment*, New Delhi: Sage

Batliwala, S. (1993) *Empowerment of Women in South Asia: Concepts and Practices*, New Delhi: FAO-FFHC/AD

BGVS (1993) *Total Literacy Campaign: A Guide Book*, New Delhi: BGVS

BGVS (nd), Bharat Gyan Vigyan Samiti, official website, www.bgvs.org/html/intro.htm

Boserup, E. (1970) *Woman's Role in Economic Development*, New York: St. Martin's Press

Bown, L. (1990) *Preparing the Future: Women, Literacy and Development*, London: ActionAid

CMS (1999) *A Report: External Evaluation of Total Literacy Campaign in Begusarai*, July 1999, New Delhi: Centre for Media Studies

GoB (1991a) Census Report 1991, Census Planning and Development Department: Directorate of Statistics

GoB (1991b) *A Portrait of Population: Bihar*, New Delhi: Directorate of Census Operation

GoB (2002) Official State website, http://bihar.nic.in/Governance/Districts/Begusarai.htm

GoI (1988) Government of India, *National Literacy Mission*, New Delhi: Ministry of Human Resource Development

Jeffery, P. (1979) *Frogs in a Well: Indian Women in Purdah*, London: Zed

Kabeer, N. (1985) 'Do women gain from high fertility?' in H. Afshar (ed.) *Women, Work, and Ideology in the Third World*, London: Tavistock

Kabeer, N. (1994) *Reversed Realities: Gender Hierarchies in Development Thought*, London: Verso

Kabeer, N. (1999) 'Resources, agency, achievements: reflections on the measurement of women's empowerment', *Development and Change* 30: 435–64

King, E.M., M. A. Hill, and World Bank (1993) *Women's Education in Developing Countries: Barriers, Benefits, and Policies*, Baltimore/London: Johns Hopkins University Press for the World Bank

Lind and Johnston (1990) *Adult Literacy in the Third World: A Review of Objectives and Strategies*, Stockholm: Swedish International Development Authority

Literacy Online www.literacyonline.org/products/ili/pdf/ilprocrp.pdf (accessed 9/02)

Oxaal and Baden (1997) 'Gender and Empowerment: Definitions, Approaches and Implications for Policy' (Report 40), Briefing prepared for Swedish International Development Cooperation Agency (SIDA) on line at www.ids.ac.uk/bridge/reports_gend_con_meth.htm

Park, R. (1996) 'The Role of Literacy Training in NGOs' Efforts to Improve the Self-Sufficiency of Rural Indian Women', paper presented at World Conference on Literacy, held in March 1996 in Philadelphia

Patel, I. and A. Dighe (1997) 'Gender Issues in Literacy Education', Introduction to the Working Paper Series (WPS), Anand: Institute of Rural Management on line at www.panasia.org.sg/nird/clic/rrd1101/htm

Patel, S. (1996) 'From a seed to a tree: building community organisation in India's cities' in S. Walters and L. Manicom, *Gender in Popular Education*, South Africa: CACE

Patkar, A. (1995) 'Socio-economic status and female literacy in India', *International Journal of Educational Development*,15:4: 401–9

Ramachandran, V. (1999) 'Adult education: a tale of empowerment denied', *Economic and Political Weekly*, 10–16 April (877–0)

Ramachandran, V. (2000) 'Literacy, development, and empowerment: conceptual issues' in R. Wazir (ed.) *Gap in Basic Education: NGOs as Change Agents*, London: Sage

Ramdas, L. (1990) 'Gender issues and literacy: an analysis', *Convergence*, 23/4: 37–47

Rampal, A. and Manimala (eds.) (2002) *Naav Vikas Lay Sabjan Padbai: Saksharta Abhiyan per Sanjha Shodh*, New Delhi: Books for Change and Mousoorie: NLRC

Robinson-Pant, A. (2000) *Why Eat Green Cucumbers at the Time of Dying?: Women's Literacy and Development in Nepal*, Hamburg: UNESCO Institute for Education

Rockhill, K. (1993) 'Gender, language and the politics of literacy', in B. Street (ed.) *Cross-cultural Approaches to Literacy*, Cambridge: Cambridge University Press

Rowlands, J. (1999) 'Empowerment examined' in D. Rowan-Campbell (ed.) *Development With Women*, Oxford: Oxfam GB

Sen, G. and C. Grown (1987) *Development, Crises and Alternative Visions: Third World Women's Perspective*, London: Earthscan

Singh, A. (2000) 'Education for All: The Year 2000 Assessment Report: India, The EFA 2000 Assessment', UNESCO on line at: www2.unesco.org/wef/countryreports/home.html

Stromquist, N. (1997) *Literacy for Citizenship: Gender and Grassroots Dynamics in Brazil*, New York: SUNY

Stromquist, N. (1999) 'Gender and literacy development' in D. Wagner, R. Venezky, and B. Street (eds.) *Literacy: an International Handbook*, Oxford: Westview Press

Sundararaman, S. (1996) 'Literacy campaigns: lessons for women's movement', *Economic and Political Weekly*, 18 May (1193–7)

9 Pastoralist schools in Mali: gendered roles and curriculum realities

Salina Sanou and Sheila Aikman

This chapter is based on on-going work with pastoralist schools in the Gao region of north-east Mali, funded by Oxfam GB. It examines strategies for improving gender equality in education through the work of *animatrices* – female community mobilisers – who support girls' access to education and foster their participation through complementary developments designed to make the curriculum more gender-equitable.

We argue that the work of the *animatrices* has been successful in increasing the access and retention of children, and especially of girls, in school. However, recent evaluations suggest that the *animatrices* do not challenge conventional assumptions about roles for women and girls and may even have increased women's workload. We consider ways in which the *animatrice* model can be supported to become more challenging and transformative, as part of a wider strategy for gender equality involving, among other things, curriculum change. In the wider context of decentralisation and education reform, *animatrices* can work simultaneously with other initiatives for opening up democratic spaces and gender equality. As this is work in progress, the chapter draws primarily on unpublished reviews and evaluations and interviews with key NGO staff.

Background

Mali is one of five West African countries where Oxfam GB has been implementing a pilot programme entitled 'Promoting Gender-Equitable Basic Education in West Africa'. Although Mali has had some of the worst figures in the world for education, current statistics demonstrate encouraging results as far as access is concerned, with a rise in the Gross Enrolment Rate (GER) in the first cycle of basic education from 32 per cent in 1992 to 67 per cent in 2003 (Ministry of Education 2003), and recent statistics indicating 70.5 per cent for 2003–4 (Ministry of Education 2005). However, the gender gap is still very wide, with girls' primary enrolment estimated at 59.9 per cent and boys' at 81.3 per cent (*ibid.*).

The Gao region is an area of semi-desert, inhabited by nomadic and semi-nomadic pastoralists (including Touareg, Songhai, Bella, and Arab peoples). The communities move with their herds of sheep and camels in search of pasture in the region, which is beset by drought. At the time of writing (mid-2005), they are experiencing severe food shortages in the aftermath of the widespread destruction of crops and pasture by locusts in 2004. The region is disadvantaged in terms of communications, infrastructure, and basic services. Its political marginalisation was one of the factors that prompted the Touareg rebellion of the early 1990s. Since Mali's independence in 1960, there have been attempts to provide some education for pastoralist children, starting with a policy whereby government officers forcibly took one child (usually a boy) from each family to attend boarding school. More recently some children received primary education at mobile schools, but the government found this initiative too costly and difficult to sustain. The current Oxfam programme is supporting government schools in communities where there has been no prior provision, and in contexts where parents face very real problems in sending their sons and daughters to school.

In the pastoral communities of Gao in northern Mali, girls' school attendance is as low as 30 per cent, and non-completion rates for primary education are very high. A range of factors hinder girls' attendance, including practices such as early marriage; girls' excessive work load; an assumption that girls and women are inferior to men in intellect; and widespread economic poverty. A review conducted in 2002 (Terry 2002), and subsequent interviews with teachers, students, and parents have identified two sets of barriers to girls' education in the pastoralist communities of northern Mali (and northern Niger). The first set applies to both boys and girls, while the second applies to girls (see Table 1).

Terry notes that where demand for girls' education is already low, poor provision tends to have a more negative impact on girls than on boys. Members of Parents' Associations and mothers often expressed the view that girls are weaker and more vulnerable than boys and are thus in need of protection. Girls and boys often have to walk 4–8 kilometres to and from school, which may militate against girls' attendance. Moreover, where feeding arrangements at school are inadequate or non-existent, parents who think that girls need to be especially well fed in order to mature may be deterred from sending their daughters to school (Terry 2002: 10). When girls and boys have to walk long distances, and the school day is itself long – from 7.30 a.m. to 5 p.m., with a break during the hottest part of the day, when temperatures can reach 45 degrees Celsius – attending school is onerous, and girls have limited time left to assist their mothers in domestic tasks.

It was within this context that Oxfam GB, together with its three local NGO partners,[1] initiated an education programme in 2000 with the aim of promoting gender-equitable basic education for pastoralists in remote and marginalised areas of Gao (Sanou 2001). The nomadic and semi-nomadic lifestyle of the peoples of the north makes providing education and health services and ensuring

Table 1: Barriers to education in Mali

Factors applying to both boys and girls	Factors applying to girls
Distance from home to school.	Vulnerability during long walks to school.
Pastoralists' need to move with their herds in search of water and pasture, which compounds the problem of distance.	Parents' wishes for daughters to marry early (as young as eight years old).
Lack of clean water at schools: a major problem in many schools.	Fear that girls will become pregnant if they go to school: a dishonour that may reduce their chances of getting married.
Difficulty in feeding children at school, compounded by general food insecurity in these communities.	The higher a girl's level of education, the higher the dowry that the husband's family have to pay.
Communities' pessimism, based on past experience, about their children's chances of attaining primary-school certificates.	The belief that keeping girls at home and feeding them up will lead to earlier maturity and marriageability.
Traditional religious beliefs that children who go to school will grow up to be 'heathens'.	The gendered division of labour, which makes girls and women responsible for tasks such as collecting water and pounding millet, in an area where water is in short supply.
High poverty levels among pastoralist communities in the Sahel, due to factors such as drought, desertification, and the legacy of conflict.	The idea that girls are vulnerable and intellectually inferior and need to be sheltered at home.
The political marginalisation of pastoralist communities, compared with the sedentary population.	Resistance to girls' education on the part of some local religious leaders.

the quality and relevance of such services a big challenge, because schooling is developed according to a model designed for permanent, static communities.

Gender equity in education is an issue much broader than the question of opportunities for girls in pastoral communities, as a recent case study of education services in Mali indicates (Public World 2004). This study notes that, with the exception of some women's NGOs, no one working to achieve greater access to school for girls was challenging existing gender inequalities in the school system or wider society – or, indeed, questioning whether increased access to schooling for girls could or should have any impact on the traditional role of Malian women as first and foremost good wives and mothers. The Oxfam GB programme has responded to the challenge of achieving gender equality and quality education for girls (and boys) by developing a flexible innovative approach which aims to increase significantly the number of girls who go to school and stay in school, and to ensure that they acquire relevant and sustainable basic skills in mathematics, literacy, and key aspects of health and nutrition. Through some basic training in health and hygiene and HIV/AIDS awareness for members of Women's Associations and Parents' Associations, it also aims to improve child mortality rates and family health in the communities.

By encouraging positive attitudes to school attendance for girls, while discouraging practices that infringe the rights of girls and jeopardise their well-being, the programme aims to change beliefs and ideas about schooling for girls, using a rights-based approach. Oxfam's strategic aim is to ensure that all children living in poverty will achieve their right to a good-quality basic education which is gender-equitable (Roche and Roseveare 2001, Oxfam GB 2004).

Before presenting a detailed examination of this programme and its work with *animatrices* and national curriculum reform, we tell the real story of a young Touareg girl, Fatimata, which illustrates some of issues that constrain girls' participation in schooling – constraints that Oxfam and its partners are attempting to address.

The story of Fatimata

Fatimata lives in Bourem town, in Bourem district in the Gao Region.[2] Bourem is about 96 km from Gao town, in an area inhabited by nomadic and semi-nomadic Touareg, Songhoi, and Arabs. It is a poor district, with very little rainfall, hence long droughts and poor harvests. The people eke out a living from keeping livestock (cattle, camels, goats, and sheep) and subsistence farming, mainly rice cultivation with traditional and vulnerable irrigation systems. The district was severely affected by the Touareg rebellion of the early 1990s, which forced many young men to become migrant labourers in neighbouring Libya, Gabon, Ghana, and Côte d'Ivoire. Consequently, migrant labour is an important source of income in the district, and the larger the remittances the more successful is each household/family.

The population of Bourem is conservative and predominantly non-literate. Women occupy a subordinate place in society, with little or no autonomy in decisions regarding certain aspects of their lives, such as choice of partner or age of marriage.

Sidiki, a 30-year-old Touareg and migrant labourer working in Ghana, decided that it was time to get married. He returned to his home town of Bourem to marry his first cousin Aisseta, who was 15 years old and attending secondary school in the town of Gao. He paid a handsome dowry and gave lavish gifts to Titi, Aisseta's mother. Realising what was planned for her, and not wanting to marry, Aisseta fled from her home in the middle of the marriage preparations. Afraid of the scandal that Aisseta's flight might cause her family, the elderly Titi decided instead to give Fatimata, her 11-year-old daughter, to Sidiki. Fatimata, a jovial, bright pupil in Standard 2 in Bourem Primary School, was not happy about this, but she was accustomed to doing her mother's bidding.

Fatimata had an aunt, Djeneba, who lived some distance from the family and worked as an *animatrice* in one of the Oxfam-supported schools. Djeneba came to visit Titi, and her visit coincided with Fatimata's marriage preparations. On hearing of the intention to marry off the 11-year-old, Djeneba threatened to have Sidiki and Fatimata's father imprisoned. She quickly mobilised members of the local women's association, and together they went to see the headmaster of Fatimata's school and the school inspector to try to prevent this marriage. Djeneba had herself been a victim of an early forced marriage 20 years previously and she did not want the same fate to befall her niece.

Sidiki, seeing the trouble that this marriage was going to cause, and seized by fear, announced to the family that he would allow Fatimata to continue her education. But he did not renounce the marriage altogether. Titi reluctantly accepted this turn of events, but complained that '*the best school for a woman is getting married and having children*'. Fatimata was able to continue her studies in Bourem Primary School, and her aunt Djeneba continues to keep a close watch over her.

Fatimata's story[3] is typical of the situation in which many schoolgirls find themselves, although not all are able to continue their education. It is not known how many girls have been forced into early marriage, nor how many have been able to escape. How long will Sidiki wait for Fatimata while she continues her education – or will he try to prise her away? Experiences like that of Fatimata provided the motivation for Oxfam and its partners to work with parents and the wider community to promote acceptance of girls' right to education, and to raise issues of gender equality. This led to the development of the '*animatrice* model' of working, an approach based on understanding the reasons why girls do not participate in formal schooling, and the expectations of the parents and the girl themselves. From this understanding, *animatrices* talk with and listen to parents and students and work together to find ways of encouraging parents to send their daughters to school.

This approach aims to link pastoralist women and girls and their schools with wider concerns and demands for girls' education. For example, the schools and *animatrices* were involved in activities during the Global Week of Action in April 2003, which provided the opportunity for developing broader understandings of the importance of girls' education. The activities of the Global Week of Action also brought an awareness that other communities in Mali were asking for better access and quality of education for their daughters. And not only in Mali but across West Africa and around the globe: parents, communities, and NGOs were demanding that their governments provide basic education for girls. This involvement raised many questions about why girls were not attending school, and eventually it led to the annulment of the marriages of three schoolgirls by their parents in Menaka district. The three girls were re-integrated into the school system and were allowed to continue their education.

The *animatrice* model

In order to develop models of schooling which meet the lifestyle needs of nomadic and semi-nomadic pastoralist peoples, Oxfam and its partners decided to work with *animatrices* (female community mobilisers). An *animatrice* is appointed to each school to work with parents, telling them about the importance and value of schooling for both girls and boys. They monitor girls' attendance, and they work with the teacher to ensure safe and girl-friendly school environments, so parents are more likely to allow their daughters to make the long daily walk to school or stay in the school itself during their families' long treks in search of pasture. When girls drop out of school, the *animatrices* follow up with families to find out the reasons and try to encourage the girls to return.

The *animatrices* are local women, most of whom, but not all, have completed Grade 6 of primary education. Most of them have previously been social workers or community mobilisers for health projects, cereal banks, micro-credit schemes, or other projects. The programme has given them some training in community mobilisation and, most recently, in gender awareness. One of the first successes of the programme was to find and contract *animatrices* for the schools in a region where women's education rates are very low, and few have the skills or capacity to perform this role. This success was in large part due to the commitment and expertise of the local partner organisations, which have been working with these communities for many years, themselves pastoralists and engaged with the communities in a range of interrelated activities and programmes, including livelihood support, food-security planning, and conflict reduction.[4] With a minimum of training, the *animatrices* have quickly created strong links between school and parents and communities.

The *animatrices* lobby for changes in attitudes towards girls' abilities and their right to attend school, both in the community, with parents and community members, and in the school, with teachers and head teachers. As relatively well-educated women in paid employment, promoting schooling, the *animatrices* serve as positive role models for local girls (Sanou 2003). Another important dimension of their work is with the Parents' Associations. In the recently decentralised Malian education system, Parents' Associations provide a great deal of support to the School Management Committees which run the schools. The *animatrices* carry out training with members of the Parents' Associations to develop their capacity to take on this role. Their work includes supporting literacy and numeracy classes, organised for parents and for the women's associations which are engaged in small-scale income-generation activities.

Challenges

A peer review of the Mali Education Programme, conducted in 2003 by Plan International, confirmed that there have been important changes in the communities' attitudes to girls' education, and the changes can be attributed to the work of the *animatrices*. The review drew attention to a greater awareness of girls' right to attend school and the fact that, contrary to widely held beliefs, girls and women are not less intellectually able than boys and men (Alainchar 2003). Recent discussions with mothers and young women indicated that they highly value the literacy and numeracy training, and the opportunity to socialise and discuss issues important to them. They also stressed that their daughters were learning valuable skills at school which they could later put to use for generating their own sources of income.

Constant dialogue between the *animatrices* and the members of the communities has also influenced attitudes and had an impact on early marriage practices. One *animatrice* told of how an old man and 20 young girls walked for miles, determined to find a school which they could attend. She reported also that in the district of Menaka three girls have completed primary school. They are the first girls in their community to do so, encouraged not to drop out by the sensitisation work of the *animatrice*. *Animatrices* have also managed to reintegrate five girls into the school system after they were forced into marriage by their parents (Oxfam GB 2003). Anecdotal evidence suggests that the average age of marriage is rising from 10–12 years old to 14–16 years of age.

Despite their obvious successes, *animatrices* are also confronted with challenges, including tensions with school directors (all men), who feel that the *animatrices* are encroaching on their own rightful responsibilities, such as the supervision of supplies for the school canteen (Terry 2002: 13). Similarly, parent–teacher associations are predominantly male, and some *animatrices* have reported difficulties in working with them; even where women are members, they do not participate to the same degree as the men (*ibid.*: 16). *Animatrices* often have to travel very long distances to reach parents and girls, especially in the season when pastoralists move with their herds. One *animatrice* in Gao had to walk for 16 km with a baby on her back to catch up with a moving community (*ibid.*: 14).

Animatrices work closely with communities and have had great success in increasing the numbers of girls attending school. Within the first two years of the pilot phase, the number of girls in schools in the Gao programme had increased from 749 in 1999–2001 to 1260 in 2001–02, and 1423 in 2002–03. However, the programme has not been long established, and the sustainability of these gains is still to be tested. In addition, *animatrices* have had limited training in gender issues and analysis. Some held attitudes which actually compounded gender inequalities, and their promotion of girl-friendly classrooms in some cases led to increased work loads for women, such as keeping the school clean; targeting only women and girls with messages about hygiene and sanitation, the *animatrices* have reinforced the traditional gendered division of labour. In schools, girls carry out more of the tasks such as cleaning, fetching water, and washing dishes that are traditionally seen as 'women's work' (Terry 2002).

More research is needed to improve understanding of the messages used by *animatrices* in their sensitisation work, and to ensure that these communicate the need for equity and the right to education, rather than emphasising purely instrumental arguments that may be unsustainable and inequitable in the long term. Training conducted with local government officials in Mali indicated a familiarity with the 'instrumental' arguments for girls' education, where it is seen as a contribution to the well-being of the girls' future family and children. However, Terry (2002) found that the 'equity/rights' rationale was less likely to be accepted, and that, moreover, *animatrices* did not mention gender-equity arguments during the review interviews.

Earlier initiatives in the region to promote schooling for pastoralists have included the provision of mobile schools. These were short-lived, however, because few teachers came from nomadic backgrounds, owing to the lack of formal education requirements among pastoralists. The teachers, finding the challenge of moving with pastoralist communities difficult, dropped out in order to work in towns and in settled, permanent schools. The government discontinued the mobile schools programme, because it was too expensive: teachers had to be paid incentives over and above their salaries.[5] In-school feeding programmes have been implemented and have proved successful in attracting pastoralist children to schools. However, they are often short-lived and dependent on external funding, so that when a donor withdraws its support, the supply of foodstuffs – and the programme – comes to an end.

These experiences suggest that, rather than the government imposing one model of schooling for the whole country, there is a need for flexibility and a diversity of approaches to cater for and support the fragile demand for schooling in different contexts (see also Leggett's chapter in this volume). The *animatrice* model is one approach which appears to be achieving success with Touareg communities in the Gao region. But it is not a panacea for all the problems involved in providing a good-quality basic education for girls. There are other models, other initiatives, that should complement the work of the *animatrices* in order to ensure that, for the increasing numbers of girls attending school, their experience of schooling and their learning is of value for them.

Animatrices are lobbyists within the local communities and schools in which they work. The Oxfam project is concerned to make an impact at several levels, so that change can be sustainable. Therefore the programme needs to be working and lobbying for change at other levels simultaneously. For the *animatrices* to succeed in making schools 'girl-friendly', there need to be changes in other areas of education, including the curriculum. Curriculum reform is strongly influenced by processes at the national level. A new curriculum is being trialled by the Centre for National Education in some select schools throughout the country, though not yet in the Gao area. The Oxfam programme has been working to influence the national curriculum-reform process. The next section of this chapter examines the complementary and parallel work being carried out to influence gender equity and quality in the design of curriculum materials.

Curriculum reform in Mali

Mali is one of the countries in the sub-region to have embarked on a process to reform the 'classical' French-derived curriculum. (Niger is another, more recent, example.) This reform challenges the current *status quo* whereby all children throughout the country are taught in French as the exclusive medium of instruction. The fact is that only 10 per cent of Malians speak French (Public World 2004). As a Malian NGO commented: 'Children go to school and are taught in a language that they do not think in'.[6] There are two reform processes currently taking place: bilingual education (*pedagogique convergente*) and curriculum reform. A new competency-based curriculum has been developed, based on the principle that children need a less theoretical way of learning and a more practical curriculum, and that they should develop skills to equip them to live and work in their communities and in Malian society. The curriculum recognises the cultural, geographical, and linguistic diversity of the country.

The curriculum-development process started in 2000 with a series of consultations throughout the country. The government then opted for a competency-based and skills-based curriculum, aiming to cater for academically inclined students whose aim is to pursue higher studies and, at the same time, offer relevant skills to children who wish to or are obliged to terminate their education at the end of the primary-school cycle and find work. Hence the result is a curriculum which offers a 'common core' of subjects for all students – including academic subjects – as well as practical subjects which are designed to cater for people living in different contexts and with different needs. These practical subjects are intended to be flexible, so that teachers themselves can design lessons in their own schools to suit the cultural and geographical realities.[7]

A practical module known as 'familial economy' (home economics) includes topics related to environment, health, and sewing, which are taught to all pupils and are intended to be 'gender-sensitive'. But the Forum for African Women's Education

Mali (FAWE/Mali) challenges the extent to which the module and curriculum materials are indeed gender-sensitive. FAWE insists that both the module and the representation of women in textbooks 'fail[s] to empower girls and will in the long run contribute to gender inequalities' (quoted in Public World 2004). The Public World research also indicates that the quality or quantity of gender training for teachers is not sufficient to challenge conventional assumptions, and teachers are unable to apply the principles of gender equality to their teaching to create an environment more conducive to girls' participation (*ibid.*).

Women's and girls' roles

In order to address these weaknesses and the gender-blindness of the new curriculum, Oxfam and the Institute for Popular Education (IEP: Institut pour l'Education Populaire) launched a study in 2002 to analyse community attitudes towards change, and the images (visibility and roles) of women and girls, and boys and men, contained in school textbooks. The study examined 18 textbooks used in Malian schools, and draft learning units being produced by the National Centre for Education. The project also collected data on attitudes towards change and gender equity among Oxfam GB programme personnel, community groups, community stakeholders, and NGOs in the Gao Region and Menaka District. The research was carried out to survey the extent to which the curriculum reform was contributing to a larger project of social change, moving Malian society from dictatorship to democracy. Because gender equity is a fundamental dimension of a democratic society, Malian schools and curriculum have a role to play in orienting young people towards a democratic, gender-equitable society, built on respect for human rights (IEP 2002).

Data were collected by means of a range of survey tools and questions, and structured and semi-structured interviews with parents, NGOs fieldworkers, educators, and local government officials. A survey based on attitudes to the roles and relationships of women and men and girls and boys was used to form a picture of the kind of world that participants would like to live in. Participants fell into one of three categories:

- those who maintain present realities (the current role and *status quo* and parameters of possibility for women and girls)

- those who seek to reform present realities (institute modest changes which would make current realities more 'liveable', or would change individuals without changing the system that keeps the present realities in place)

- those who seek to transform present realities (make systematic change that reconfigures the roles, status, and parameters of possibility for women and girls) (IEP 2002: 12).

One such survey question presented three representational drawings, and participants were asked to choose the world that they would like to live in. One drawing showed a man standing on two women, the second showed a woman standing on two men, and a third a man and woman standing side by side. In a society where many men have several wives, the majority of respondents chose the first picture, which most closely represented the *status quo*. The few who chose the second picture were interpreted as indicating a willingness for reform of a situation where men dominated women. However, this choice – a woman standing on two men – was not an elimination of domination, but a transfer of domination from the man to the woman. Only one participant (a local government official) out of 75 participants chose the man and women standing side by side, a 'transformist' position, where domination was not present (IEP 2002: 21).

The overall analysis of attitudes towards change concluded that most participants had firmly held views that did not challenge existing conditions. The women field workers (*animatrices*) were not concerned with transformation, a fact which raised important questions about the extent to which they are able to change attitudes and beliefs about girls' education and girls' and women's roles. It was reasoned that if the *animatrices* promote girls' access to education but do not fundamentally challenge the *status quo* – when their role is intended to be that of 'change agent' – then it is unlikely that parents, teachers, and school head teachers would support reform (IEP 2002: 6-7). However, the study notes: 'The very presence of the animatrices is motivating to parents who see that these women who have not even completed high school have jobs and are receiving training. Parents look to them and think that possibly their daughters could have such a chance with schooling' (*ibid.* 18).

Women's and girls' representation in the school curriculum

The analysis of education materials indicated that while women and girls are visible in school textbooks, the images offered overwhelmingly portray current gender realities. That is, women are visible when they appear in traditional roles, but the teaching materials do not offer images of behaviour or attitudes which could break the routine patterns of gender inequality that characterise these roles and activities (such as cleaning, cooking, and maintenance tasks). An example in the textbook *Flamboyant* depicts a sick mother with her daughter, pounding millet while her brother stands by, looking on with his hands in his pockets (IEP 2002: 21). The study concluded that the materials are at best gender-blind, reflecting images which keep Mali women locked into inequalities.

In addition, the visibility of women and girls in text and illustrations varies. In several instances, women are visible in the illustrations but absent from the text that accompanies the illustrations. Similarly, any egalitarian messages are submerged in structurally sexist language.[8] Pastoralist women are always pictured 'behind' their men, and their destiny as wives and mothers appears unalterable.

In conclusion, the study showed that the attitudes of teachers, parents, and policy makers and the textbooks currently available for schools in Mali reinforce the gender inequalities present in Malian society today. The challenge for those seeking change in both school and society is to use the environment created by Mali's Ten-Year Plan for Transforming Education and the curriculum-reform process as an opportunity to enable children – girls and boys – to begin to experience a different reality (in terms of gender relations) from the day they enter school. The IEP study concludes that legally mandated processes – particularly government decentralisation and the education reform – are causing significant social change in all sectors of Malian society. 'In the same way that decentralisation is taking over traditional structures of governance, public discourse and community control, education reform is threatening to replace classic colonial-model schooling with the classroom as a more democratic and relevant to life space' (IEP 2002: 19). However, it remains to be seen whether the national plans and reforms will be implemented on a scale that will ensure impact, and with a strong enough commitment to gender equality, which will not only promote reform of present education inequalities but transform both educational and societal realities. The work of NGOs and *animatrices* at the grassroots level needs to take place within a broader context of dialogue, discussion, and debate about gender equality in relation to citizenship, democracy, and cultural and geographical diversity. For this to begin to happen, there needs to be a greater level of awareness of gender inequalities and ways of addressing them through training for teachers and education officials, with sufficient resources committed to ensure that transformative change happens.

Conclusion: a joined-up sustainable approach

The overall conclusion from the work of Oxfam's programme for Gender Equitable Education in West Africa is that more girls are attending school – a fact which suggests improvements in terms of gender parity in basic education. However, this chapter has raised questions about the need for more fundamental change in terms of the nature of education that girls are offered, their experience of education, and their academic achievements. It also raises the question of what girls can do with their learning and skills in the wider social environment in which they live.

Animatrices have a strong focus on increasing access and retention in schools, but they are not sufficiently engaged with questions about the quality of the education that girls are receiving. This is also true of teachers. The IEP study demonstrated that teachers prioritise access/retention without questioning their own practices within the classroom. Any changes introduced into the school system that may affect relevance or quality (for example, replacing French with mother tongue as the medium of instruction in classrooms) were resisted by schoolteachers for both boys and girls (IEP 2002:11). It would seem, therefore, that a recurring effect of the decade-old movement in Mali for girls' education is little more than an appropriation of slogans – Education For All and Girls' Education. Education for girls is still about gender parity – equal numbers of girls and boys – and falls short of being about equality and quality education for all. It does not ask what this means in terms of classroom relations, learning and teaching practices, and curriculum content. To move beyond access, the *animatrices* need to promote understanding and commitment to girls' rights to a good-quality education which challenges pastoralists' patriarchal gender relations and those of the wider Malian society.

Great steps have been taken in Mali at the national level to develop a skills-based curriculum, but the reformers do not propose specific measures that target girls' needs. Moreover, the locally developed practical subjects do not question gender inequalities in the pastoralist context. For pastoralist girls in the Gao region, the teaching continues in French under the 'classic' system, which is gender-blind and instrumental, reinforcing rather than challenging gender inequalities.

The Oxfam programme, with its partners, Adessah, Tassaght, and GARI, is nevertheless attempting to unravel the web of inequalities and discrimination that girls experience, by working through *animatrices* to achieve increased enrolment, through working with teachers, parents, and policy makers to provide more girl-friendly schools, and through influencing change in the education system through curriculum reform. This analysis of the *animatrice* model illustrates that gender inequalities need to be tackled through several different interventions and a diversity of approaches simultaneously: inside and outside the school, at both the local and national levels. It illustrates that change can and does take place, and that girls are now attending school in greater numbers than before. However, we need to understand why this is so, in order to sustain the trend. It illustrates furthermore that the changes in national legal frameworks and institutional organisation – such as decentralisation and education reforms – also need to be part of gendered processes. The active engagement of girls and women in their own schooling, promoted by the *animatrices*, is an important starting point.

Salina Sanou is the Education and Gender Specialist for the UN Millennium Project, based at The MDG Centre in Nairobi. Previously she was Regional Education Co-ordinator for Oxfam GB in West Africa. She is currently studying for a doctorate in Comparative Education at McGill University (Canada).

Sheila Aikman is the Global Education Policy Adviser with Oxfam GB, and co-ordinator of the DFID-funded 'Beyond Access: Gender, Education and Development' Project.

Notes

1   In the Gao Region, Oxfam supports partner schools in three districts: Bourem, Gao Central, and Menaka. The NGO partners in these districts are Adessah, Tassaght and GARI respectively.

2   Fatimata's story is part of a series of stories documented by Adessah, Oxfam's partner in Bourem.

3   Story documented in Oxfam's impact report, 2003. All names have been changed to preserve confidentiality.

4   The Gao programme has a total number of 20 schools. Each school is supposed to have an *animatrice*; but, given these difficult conditions, partners were able to recruit only 18 *animatrices* and two animators.

5   Interview with Abou Diarra, the Director of the National Center for Education, Ministry of Education. For discussion of mobility and pastoralist schooling see for example, Aikman and El Haj forthcoming; Carr-Hill and Peart 2002.

6   Interview with Debra Fredo, IEP, Kati.

7   Interview with Abou Diarra, the Director of the National Center for Education, Ministry of Education.

8   The school textbooks analysed in the IEP study include *Flamboyant, Mamadou and Bineta, Horizons d'Afrique, Djoliba Collection,* and *La Pedagogie Convergente Rencontre 4&5.* All these texts illustrate the point that women are less visible in textbooks than men, but the visibility that they are given reinforces roles that conform to current gender realities.

References

Aikman, S. and H. El Haj (forthcoming) 'EFA for pastoralists in North Sudan: a mobile multigrade model of schooling' in A. Little (ed.) *Education For All: The Challenges of Multigrade Teaching,* Kluwer Academic Publishing

Alainchar, F. (2003) 'Peer Review of Oxfam GB Education Programme in Mali', Oxfam GB Peer Review of Gender Equitable Education Programme in West Africa, unpublished

Carr-Hill, R. and E. Peart (2002) 'Study on Education for Nomads and Pastoralists of Eastern Africa: review of the literature', IIEP, UNESCO/IICBA, UNICEF/ESARO

Institut pour l'Education Populaire (IEP) (2002) 'Working Through Change in Education to Change Gender Realities in Mali: Recommendations for Action by Oxfam GB', Oxfam GB unpublished research report

Ministry of Education (2003) Mali National Statistics for Primary Education (First Cycle)

Ministry of Education (2005) Mali National Statistics for Primary Education (First Cycle)

Oxfam GB (2003) 'West Africa Impact Report', Oxfam GB, unpublished

Oxfam GB (2004) Oxfam GB Strategic Plan 2004/2005 – 2006/2007, Oxfam GB unpublished

Public World (2004) 'Mali Case Study: Education Services in Mali', unpublished draft report, Oxfam GB

Roche, C. and C. Roseveare (2001) 'Social and Economic Rights', unpublished paper, Oxfam GB

Sanou, S. (2001) 'Breaking the chains: girls' education in Mali' in *Links*, Oxfam Newsletter on Gender, June 2001

Sanou, S. (2003) 'Pastoralist education in Mali and Niger', in *Links*, Oxfam Newsletter on Gender, October 2003

Terry, G. (2002) 'Gender Review of Oxfam GB Gender Equitable Education Programme in Niger and Mali', unpublished report, Oxfam GB

Part Three

The Challenge of Local Practices – Doing Policy Differently?

10 Learning about HIV/AIDS in schools: does a gender-equality approach make a difference?

Mark Thorpe

Is HIV education based on the principles of gender equality possible in practice? If so, can it make a difference to gender relations in a society? This chapter considers these questions through reflection on two gender-based HIV-education interventions in South Africa and Mozambique, which took place between 2001 and 2003.

In my recent experience of working in Africa for five years, I have spoken to many teachers about HIV messages in school. Teachers are concerned with HIV education both as part of a formal curriculum and as a topic brought to the students through the actions of an external body. The question of how to mobilise teachers in the fight against HIV with their own students is one of the greatest challenges to HIV education in the developing world. But HIV education should also be a professional activity in which those who have proven skills and adequate training in this area work side by side with class teachers and are supported, rewarded, and mobilised to help young people to face the enormous challenges ahead of them in the wake of the HIV pandemic. If teaching about HIV in school were the responsibility of trained staff who were fully aware of the gendered elements of HIV education, we could ensure that young people in school were given the space to explore, reflect, debate, and ask questions. Offering such an opportunity to young people is just as important as verifying that everyone knows the facts about HIV transmission and how to prevent it.

There is a need for HIV to be mainstreamed into school subjects such as Geography, History, Religious Studies, and Science. This would help to address the problems created by a state of denial or the provision of misinformation. But mainstreaming does not necessarily address the issue of gender equity, which requires facilitative approaches that go beyond the training generally given to teachers. The widespread application of a process approach which focuses on the identity of individual teachers and learners, and develops their motivation and skills with regard to HIV prevention and gender dynamics, may be difficult but is not impossible, as the work done in South Africa and Mozambique, and discussed in this chapter, indicates.

I worked with gender-focused HIV workshops in Southern Africa for three years. Firstly, I took the dual role of participant and evaluator in a one-month intervention in 2001 in two former township secondary schools in greater Durban. I assisted an intervention by Dramaide, a South African NGO specialising in life skills and HIV education, using drama and participation. The workshops were adapted from a pilot programme called 'Mobilizing Young Men to Care', which was based on an understanding of the importance of engaging men and boys in the fight against HIV. The project with the Durban schools took a gender-focused approach, using participatory methods to challenge and work towards gender equity with students and staff. The Dramaide facilitator and I led the same sequence of 12 workshops, spread over one month, in two different schools, with a group of 30 girls and boys aged 13–15 in each.

At the time, South Africa had initiated a response to HIV in schools through a life-orientation syllabus as part of the new curriculum, and interventions such as this one were part of a multi-sector prevention response. Critiques of some of these initiatives identified problems in assumptions about behaviour change, dissonance between policy at national level and educational materials available locally, and an underestimation of the cultural strength of unsafe practices. Nevertheless, large sums of money were invested in HIV prevention from the late 1990s (Campbell 2004; Unterhalter 2002). Dramaide advocated the use of interactive approaches to HIV and life skills regarded as relevant for young people. In the Durban schools, children were not merely given information and told what to do. They were given opportunities to explore the issues raised by the HIV epidemic for themselves in order to develop an understanding that would be deep enough to affect their behaviour (Moletsane *et al.* 2002).

The second intervention was the training of a university-based HIV-education group, 'Juventude Alerta' (Youth Alert), in Beira, Mozambique, between 2001 and 2003 as part of my placement with VSO (Voluntary Service Overseas). Building on my experiences in South Africa in 2001, I invited university students to form an HIV-education group at the University of Beira. In the teacher-training college, there was an opportunity to carry out this training alongside core courses. It was even possible to do this on a very low budget. Over ten weeks I trained facilitators to use participatory techniques and activities to engage teenage students in discussion on HIV-related issues, including complex issues of gender relations.

In the next term we undertook interventions in five secondary schools in rural areas of Sofala province. These usually lasted half a day. We had a general format for school interventions: six workshops running concurrently in different parts of a given premises, using three facilitators in each group. Sometimes sessions took place within the time periods allotted for the main curriculum; at other times sessions were an extra-curricular event. Classes (usually consisting of 60 or more students) were generally split into two. In 2003, the first group of facilitators trained a second group of facilitators and undertook more workshops in schools in the urban setting of Beira.

Although the objectives and general approach of the workshops were consistent, there were many variations, because we did not necessarily know in advance what we would encounter. Sessions took place in classrooms or outdoors; teachers were sometimes absent and sometimes present; equipment such as a flipchart was sometimes available; students were of similar or varied ages. Some of these factors had an impact on the workshops themselves, including gendered aspects; for example, girls would often sit at the back or not sit on the chairs unless encouraged to do so; or groups, particularly those with higher numbers of boys, were sometimes dominated by older boys, and girls were consequently not able to speak. All these aspects had to be monitored by facilitators.

Gender in HIV education

The work with Dramaide and Juventude Alerta raised some key issues about gender equality and work on HIV/AIDS. In both contexts, issues about gender identities arose as a common concern, often centred on adolescent assumptions about femininity and masculinity, including the attitude among boys that it was desirable to have several sexual partners. Young men expected to be told in detail about their girlfriends' movements, but were very secretive about their own affairs. They regarded violence as an appropriate 'punishment' for the 'bad behaviour' of their girlfriends, and this attitude had been internalised by many girls too. There was a sense of risk inherent in male lifestyles, and an expectation that women could and should accept or tolerate this kind of behaviour.

An internalised sense of conflict between the boys' and the girls' interests was thus displayed. One consequence of this was the 'trading' of sexual intercourse (often seen as conquest) for goods or lifestyle benefits, and an unspoken contract which defined what each partner expected from the other. This conflict was played out many times in heated discussion during workshops. HIV-education sessions gave space for this conflict to be expressed, and for approaches to dealing with these views to be developed. For example, the trainers encouraged the students to develop mutual respect for each other's views, and they asserted ground rules such as the avoidance of personalising opposing views, and ensuring that everyone's views were heard.

As in the Durban workshops, very strong expectations of appropriate masculinity and femininity were expressed in sessions organised by the Youth Alert project in Mozambique. In one discussion, concerning the use of condoms, gendered reasons dominated the list of reasons expressed for not using one:

To be a man it must be 'flesh to flesh' [a reference to unprotected sex]

He will say I am a prostitute.

She will not accept them.

He will not let me.

We cannot talk about it.

The first and second statements listed above imply that the masculine or feminine identity is threatened by condom use. In the third and fourth statements, participants' views reflect power dynamics at play. The use of *'not let'* vs *'not accept'* is evidence of the imbalance of that dynamic. In the fifth statement, the problem of communication about condom use within a relationship is evident, and the notion of trust becomes central. These very firm assumptions about masculinity and femininity in connection with the crucial issue of condom use indicate that gender cannot be left out of the equation when designing or implementing HIV education. In fact, gender relations are often at the heart of the problems that a project in this area tries to confront.

In both South Africa and Mozambique, we believed that if a gender-equity approach was having any effect, it would not be surprising to find that there was tension or resistance to the ideas being explored. In Mozambique, a fellow volunteer set up a group for the older girls in her classes for the discussion of issues important to them as young women. The idea was well received by the girls, and the volunteer provided a good model of an independent, thinking woman, able to encourage the girls to assert their sexual rights. After three weeks, the Principal said to the volunteer teacher: '*We like what you are doing, encouraging these girls to work harder and be good, but please be careful, we don't want them having these ideas that they are not to be cooks and cleaners of the house...they must still know their place.*' It is obviously unrealistic to expect that an approach that actively seeks to challenge male power in heterosexual relationships will always be popular.

In a school in Beira, we sat down for our customary Coke and cake after finishing the workshops. The group looked pleased with the morning's sessions, a little tired in the growing summer heat, but satisfied – except that in one corner sat a seemingly deflated member of the team. When I asked him what was wrong, he replied: '*We start getting the kids all enthusiastic and they take what we're saying...but he just undoes everything we say.*' '*Who?*' I asked, aware that sometimes students get a bit 'showy' and start trying to be controversial. '*The teacher!*' he continued. '*He just contradicted everything...he didn't want them to learn about this stuff at all, just made out it was all rubbish.*' On further discussion, it emerged that this male teacher had been expounding a common male response to HIV: not taking it seriously, and using the debates as a chance to reaffirm male dominance.

This was a moment of realisation for me. I had had the notion that if a teacher was willing to stay in the classroom and join in the interaction, then at least he or she would tacitly support the aims of the workshop, and we welcomed this as a way of encouraging more 'ownership' of HIV education among teachers. There was always room within our workshops for debate, but for a teacher to contradict the aims at each stage of the workshop made me realise that HIV/AIDS as a topic was still contested ground. Some teachers wanted to deny its importance; others opposed the teaching of the topic, or preferred to make light of it.

In a Durban staffroom I watched a female teacher attempt to chastise a male colleague. He had passed her class – whose students he knew on fairly familiar terms – and commented: *'Oh, I am sorry for you all…you will not know the pleasures of "flesh to flesh" like our generation!'* He intended it as a humorous comment, but the female teacher tried to point out that his remark undermined HIV education and set a very bad model for youth. Both examples illustrate the fact that adult teachers can reverse the effects of important HIV-awareness work.

Many of these examples raise questions about whether school is an appropriate place to teach about HIV. Alex Kent's study of a Durban school (where Dramaide had worked) described it as a place 'where sexualities were schooled and also performed' (Kent 2004). She drew on ideas of Epstein and Johnson (1998), who looked at the way in which the informal curriculum has a far-reaching influence on the sexualities developed through schooling. She also drew on the writing of Karlsson (2002), who has illustrated how school space – that is, the organisation of spatial practices in South African schools, linked to racial inequalities – has changed much more slowly than the enrolment statistics. Kent draws attention to several ways in which masculinities and femininities are reinforced, maintained, and policed, reproducing gender inequalities in school. Male groups or female groups congregate in different places, with different meanings of power. Women teachers are generally given nurturing responsibilities within the school, while power in the hierarchical school structure is given to men. Men (and some women) believe that it is a girl's responsibility to avoid pregnancy, and they see risk as a normalised part of male behaviour (Kent 2002). At the extreme end of the gender–power dynamic, teachers regularly have sexual relations with young girls (according to some female students), thus adding to the risk associated with girls' attendance at school. All of these elements combine to make the school a problematic place to be talking of gender equity in the course of work on HIV.

Nonetheless, although a school may be a problematic domain for a form of HIV education that engages with gender-equity issues, schools can be enormously important places for the development of young people's perspectives on HIV. Boler, in a study of HIV education in schools in India and Kenya, found that school was the place that most students, parents, and teachers believed was appropriate for young people to learn about HIV (Boler 2003). A national study in South Africa revealed that 'some 85.9% of children (aged 12 to 14) and 75.7% of youth (aged 15 to 24) reported that their main source of HIV/AIDS education was their school' (Shisana 2002).

Unterhalter, while acknowledging the dangers of school as a space for gender inequality, also acknowledges its transformative power (Unterhalter 2002). Mannah, noting that, despite its problems, the school is a crucial setting in the fight against HIV/AIDS, presents six concrete reasons for this in the South African context: learners' daily contact with the school; the availability of skilled staff and personnel; the extreme vulnerability of young people in an area of high HIV-infection rates; the fact that schools are best located to establish good practice; and the influential position of a teacher in the community (Mannah 2002: 14). School is thus seen to be a place of importance in learning about HIV and related issues, and is highly influential in the orientation of young people towards the problem (Boler 2003: 5). Young people's schooling does have an impact (and will continue to do so) on their emerging beliefs and practices in relation to HIV: hence the importance of ensuring that the HIV education that is offered in schools, in both the formal and informal curricula, is positive and helpful in the fight against HIV and gender inequality.

Working for change

Given the significant barriers imposed by the attitudes of learners and teachers, and the problems of introducing a gender-equitable approach to HIV education in schools, what lessons were learned through the work in South Africa and Mozambique?

Using drama

One successful approach was to use drama and role-play, inspired by the work of the Brazilian drama practitioner, Augusto Boal. Boal used drama as a tool for empowerment in the 1960 and 1970s in poor Brazilian communities (Boal 1979). In his form of community theatre, 'Forum Theatre', roles could be played by any member of the audience, stopping the scene with a clap at any point where he or she thought that a 'turning point' in a sequence of events had been reached, and substituting himself or herself in a role within the drama, to play the part again – differently. This method offers the chance to see scenarios unfold differently and to 'rehearse for life'. 'The joker' is the name that Boal gave to the facilitator who helps the group to draw out conclusions from what they see and experience.

The Mozambique project, which lasted longer than the South Africa project, gave us time to develop this technique. The facilitators became accustomed to using Boal's techniques as a tool. In the workshops in schools, as students saw alternatives in each scene, discussion grew. When gender stereotypes emerged, they could be challenged. The 'sugar daddy' arriving at a school gate in a new car could be ignored, or different attempts at effective responses could be offered by girls. A school teacher, after flirting with a female student, could affirm clearly his duties as a teacher, rather than just later plead later on that it had not been 'his fault'.

Team work

The 'Youth Alert' project drew on a wide range of people. A local dramatist from the cultural centre in the city helped to develop the dramatic skills of the group. An HIV trainer gave key insights into the issues and their context. A few women had worked in HIV education before, and we were able to incorporate their knowledge into the training sessions. One member of the group, who was particularly gifted in public speaking, began to give the short introductory speech that many schools requested. Another member had experience in theatre and took on the role of drama director. Yet another was effective at translating from English (a language in which there tends to be more material) into Portuguese. One of the young women, recently out of school, led workshops with a large number of girls. She encouraged them to express their resentment of the fact that if they showed knowledge about sex they were immediately seen as morally inferior to boys (who were speaking about the same issues).

We took part in HIV festivals and marches and made strong links with students at the university. After a year, the group was represented by a woman member on the provincial government's HIV body. By making this a project with the support and involvement of others, we were able to strengthen its capacity to work on gender issues in a multi-faceted way with schools, the university, and civil society.

The workshop approach

A 'workshop approach' was very useful. As gender relations need to be raised, considered, challenged, discussed, and analysed, the subject does not lend itself to examination through didactic teaching methods. Participants had to be encouraged to think for themselves and to respond to each other and the facilitator's prompts. The skill of the facilitator lay in moving from awareness of the gender dynamics within the group to challenging them. In South Africa an example of this occurred when the facilitator asked a boy who was advocating an oppressive form of masculinity: '*What would you say if your own sister was in this kind of situation?*'

Our approach was to weave a gender-equality theme through all sessions. To keep moving forward on the theme of gender relations meant considering a wide range of issues. In South Africa, for example, there were sessions on 'risk' and on 'social assumptions'. A game was played to illustrate the ease with which HIV can be spread through unprotected sexual intercourse. The activity concluded that if one is not aware of the dangers or does not heed them and carries on without any change to behaviour, then one is at high risk. The facilitator, however, did not stop here, but continued with questions such as *'Do boys take risks less seriously than girls? Who is responsible in a relationship for making sure you don't take risks: a boy or a girl?'* The gender-related dimensions of risk were thus highlighted. Similarly, in the session on 'Messages of society', participants explored conflicting messages offered by different members of their community – doctors, teachers, brothers, and the media. The facilitator questioned what different community members say about the roles of boys and girls, whether there are positive images and expectations of boys and girls, and where these come from. The theme of gender equality was brought out in sessions that were not overtly about gender.

Involvement in the sessions varied, but most girls were initially reluctant to expose themselves by offering detailed responses, challenging boys, or being the first to improvise in dramas or respond to questions. As a result, when sessions took place in short 'school periods' it was sometimes difficult for facilitators to encourage equal engagement when working with mixed-sex groups. However, when an intervention lasted several weeks, as was the case in South Africa, there was time for relationships to be formed. By the mid-point of the series of sessions in South Africa, the girls were able to voice their concerns with equal conviction and greater clarity of argument than the boys. This illustrates the importance of structuring interventions over periods of at least a month, to allow those who may have been silent initially to develop confidence and take the opportunity to speak about issues like sexuality and gender equality.

Our pedagogic approach was concerned with developing a climate of gender equality. As facilitators we encouraged girls and asked mixed groups to allow them to finish off the points they were making if boys tried to block them. We asked boys to answer with their own argued responses, rather than merely expressing shock or disdain. For example, boys often assumed that they were justified in being angry if a girl in any way 'showed them up', but at the same time they did not hesitate to humiliate their girlfriends by their own sexually promiscuous behaviour. They found this contradiction hard to 'argue for'. A workshop approach created spaces for important debate and discussion about gendered power dynamics, which in turn allowed boys to be challenged, and created opportunities where girls could speak directly to boys about their attitudes and behaviour, an outcome that could not have been achieved through a didactic approach.

In mixed-sex groups, girls were often more articulate than boys when given the opportunity. They were able to challenge some of the boys to think again about the way they perceived and treated girls. *'We listened to her in the end...her arguments were good, even if we don't always agree'*, commented one boy at the end of a workshop in South Africa, as participants were evaluating what they had learned. The workshop format had allowed stereotypes to be examined.

Attention to the space created within a group was important. Sometimes, particularly in Mozambique, an outdoor group would increase in size, and there would be some on the outside (often girls) who could not see or be seen very well. When this happened, the outsiders were asked to come forward, and girls were sometimes asked individually for their offerings in the dramas, if they seemed to be inhibited by the gender dynamics.

Gender and power

Issues of gender and power were evident not only among the students, but within our own group also. In time the members became more aware of gender issues within the group, in the workshops that they ran, and in schools more generally. We tried to address those dynamics and explore them as a group, so as to be more aware of them and incorporate them into the work. We aimed to integrate the issue of gender relations into our approach to HIV education, and this aim was enhanced by relating gender issues to ourselves. Through discussion, activities, and role-play among ourselves, we examined stereotypical images of men and women, and the power dynamics present in everyday situations. In one improvised scene, a young woman was allowed to travel in a minibus taxi although she could not pay the fare; this was followed by scene in which a man who couldn't pay was thrown off. Rather than dismiss this as a scene showing gender issues the 'wrong way round', we considered who was exploiting the situation and ultimately benefiting from it, and we were able to frame that within other aspects of gender in wider society. We contrasted it with other scenarios, such as a man talking to a woman in a bar and expecting sex at the end of an evening.

To provoke thought about power within society, we used 'The great game of power', devised by Augusto Boal, which illustrated the gender dynamics that influence men's and women's perceptions of power. In this activity, we asked participants to arrange five chairs, a bottle, and a table so that one item held power. Participants then entered the frame set by this furniture, each acting as a 'more powerful' character than the previous person. The group thus created a collective frozen image of many elements expressing 'power'. Through discussion this tableau can be used to illuminate various types of power, such as economic/resource power, oppressive power, responsible power, physical power, personal power, and sexualised power. Male participants often adopted the most overtly dominating stances, such as a man looking over a woman, or they expressed physical power, for example by miming violent gestures. Women, on the other hand, expressed themselves through facial expressions of defiance or postures of independence. The facilitator aimed not to identify particular forms of power as gender-specific, but to encourage discussion of the term 'empowerment'. This entailed finding ways to overcome, resist, or challenge the dominating or oppressive power. For example, a woman stepping in after a man had assumed a 'mighty' position of total control over other members stood aside, laughing at him, thus demonstrating the man's position as ridiculous.

For equal representation and facilitation, we aimed to assemble a group with equal numbers of men and women; but as women constituted barely 15 per cent of the students at the university, this posed considerable problems for us. This obstacle could thus never completely be overcome in a voluntary project, but in public appeals for volunteers we emphasised the need for women. There were always more men than women, but we ensured that no workshop was facilitated without a woman being present.

Much of the material that we used was adapted from resources previously used in similar contexts. Some of the material used in South Africa in the Dramaide intervention was adapted, through discussion with group members, for the Mozambique context. In South Africa, the manual that the facilitator used was entitled 'Mobilizing Young Men to Care'. It challenged certain assumptions common among South African men, such as their assertion of a need for several partners, and beliefs about the rightness of 'following in a father's footsteps'. The activities in the workshops, however, developed a concern for gender equality, rather than simply aiming to provoke thought about male identities. In Mozambique, this focus developed to include relationships between boys' and girls' identities. Although a handbook was used, we quickly learned the advantages of knowing the material and being able to adapt it to different situations.

Helping adolescents to make sense of their culture

'Culture' relates to personal identity and thus one's sense of well-being, and it is a crucial determinant of views about gender and equity. Mozambican culture has been undergoing change in the past 15 years, after a communist government which sought to resist alien Western cultural influences was replaced by one that embraced the Western economy, and the cultural elements that are linked to it. The changes create new frictions in daily life, expressed in forums of debate from bus-stop queues to television talk shows. The ways in which ideas about 'culture' are contested often relate directly to issues of gender and sexuality. Topics such as 'bride price', responsibility for safe sex, the role of the extended family in teaching and initiating sexual activity, the desire for multiple partners as a biological need or cultural right, and the role of women in modern Mozambican society all provoke much debate and make gender equality a topical issue, even when such a term itself is not often used.

Students trying to make sense of their cultural worlds need a forum in which to work through such issues, with the help of the skilled facilitation of older people who have had the chance to consider these issues for themselves in the light of the HIV epidemic. In Mozambique one member of our group had encountered negative family responses to her commitment to higher education, and she feared that studying at this level would make her less desirable as a marriage partner for Mozambican men. However, she was adamant that she wanted this level of education and she assured girls in groups that this was their right too. One of the male members of the group, who was seen as a stylish and 'cool' kind of personality, was enabled in workshops to reconcile this image of himself with the concept of 'being safe' and using condoms.

University students are generally highly respected as having succeeded in society, and they already have a voice that is likely to be taken seriously. Girl pupils heard strong testimony from a woman who had been able to make her own decisions about sexual activity and use condoms without losing her attractiveness. Teenage boys welcomed accounts of someone able to assert himself as an 'African man' without the need for 'flesh to flesh' or multiple partners. These are key issues for many young people in trying to move beyond the *theory* that safe sex is in their long-term interests. The confusing impulses and half-made resolutions that are often the realities of youth, and the need to work through their identity and lifestyle choices, mean that issues of sexuality and gender are sometimes complex or confusing for teenagers. We wanted them to be discussed by young people in ways that emphasised the development of critical thinking that is often lacking in those who completely neglect the threat of HIV. University-level students had this capacity.

The need for training

Training of facilitators for this type of work is no easy task, but is perhaps the most crucial aspect of attempts to implement HIV education in Southern Africa. Techniques and methodology used in projects such as Reflect, Stepping Stones, and 'My Future is My Choice' all emphasise the importance of providing appropriate training in order to facilitate the participation of young people. Training must highlight the importance of helping young people to move from awareness to behaviour change, and to challenge the gender relations in society that exacerbate the spread of the virus. Such work needs an approach that is skills-based rather than content-oriented; the training should focus on the process and not only the product, so that trainee facilitators reflect on their own changes of perspective and on difficult questions relating to identity, culture, and sexuality, and learn to develop through critical self-analysis. Appropriate selection techniques are essential. Good training is a long-term, on-going process which needs to be adequately planned and managed, because there are no short cuts to high-quality outcomes.

Conclusion

In this chapter I have used my experiences in two HIV-education interventions to demonstrate the gendered nature of HIV education and the sexuality issues embedded within it. These gender relations are often unequal and can be reinforced during HIV education if they are not challenged in an adequate way. A gender-equity approach, as attempted in both interventions described, seeks to do this through its focus on gender in the various different aspects of the intervention, such as training, workshop methodology, and the development of a gender-equity 'culture' within the group. Thus, despite many difficulties encountered in attempting such an approach in schools, the projects were able to make a difference to the participants, and they formed part of a response to HIV that regarded the gendered nature of the HIV/AIDS pandemic as central.

Mark Thorpe has been working for several years on HIV, education, youth, and participation. Most recently he has worked with the International HIV/AIDS Alliance on participatory assessment; for Save the Children on stigma, HIV, and child participation in OVC (Orphans and Vulnerable Children) projects; and in 2005 on a participatory study of adolescents and youth in Mozambique for UNICEF to inform programming there.

References

Boal, A. (1979) *Theatre of the Oppressed*, London: Pluto

Boler, T. *et al.* (2003) 'The Sound of Silence: Difficulties in Communicating on HIV/AIDS in Schools', London: ActionAid

Campbell, C. (2004) 'The role of collective action in the prevention of HIV/AIDS in South Africa' in D. Hook, N. Mkhize, P. Kiguwa and A. Collins (eds.) *Critical Psychology in South Africa*, Cape Town: Juta/ University of Cape Town Press

Epstein, D. and R. Johnson (1998) *Schooling Sexualities*, Buckingham: Open University Press

Karlsson, J. (2002) 'Redesigning schools and the problem of school space in South Africa', in S. Marks (ed.) *Education In South Africa – 1994 and Beyond*, Siyafunda Education Conference Report, Canon Collins Educational Trust Southern Africa (www.canoncollins.org.uk/publications/publicationsMain.shtml)

Kent, A. (2002) 'Let's Talk About Sex, Baby! Negotiating Space, Performance and Sexualities within a Compulsory Heterosexual School Regime in South Africa, in the Context of the HIV/AIDS Epidemic', unpublished dissertation, MA in Education and International Development, Institute of Education, University of London

Kent, A. (2004) 'Living life on the edge: Examining space and sexualities within a township high school in greater Durban, in the context of the HIV epidemic', *Transformation: Critical Perspectives on Southern Africa*, 54: 59–75

Mannah, S. (2002) 'South Africa: the complex role of teaching about HIV/AIDS in schools', *Prospect* 32/2, June 2002

Moletsane, R., R. Morrell, E. Unterhalter, and D. Epstein (2002) 'Instituting gender equality in schools: working in a HIV environment', *Perspectives in Education* 20/2: 37–53

Shisana, O. (2002) 'Nelson Mandela/HSRC Study on HIV/ AIDS in South Africa', commissioned by the Nelson Mandela Foundation and the Nelson Mandela Children's Fund, conducted by the Human Sciences Research Council (HSRC) in collaboration with the Medical Research Council (MRC) and the Centre for AIDS Development, Research and Evaluation (CADRE)

Unterhalter, E. (2002) 'Gender, schooling, HIV and violence in Kwazulu Natal, South Africa', *EID Review* 6 (7–8), Institute of Education, University of London

Unterhalter, E. (2003) 'The capabilities approach and gendered education. An examination of South African complexities', *Theory and Research in Education* 1/1:7–22.

11 Gender, education, and Pentecostalism: the women's movement within the Assemblies of God in Burkina Faso

Alicia Zents

Among the technological advances, intellectual and economic trends, and social movements of the twentieth century, few would have predicted the emergence and subsequent growth of Pentecostalism. From its small beginnings in the early 1900s, the movement has grown enormously. Accounting for a quarter of all the world's nearly two billion Christians, comprising 14,000 denominations, spanning 8,000 ethno-linguistic cultures and some 7,000 languages, and growing at a rate of 54,000 new members per day, or 19 million per year, the Pentecostals now represent a significant social and religious force (Barrett in McClung 1993: 35). Whether it is because of their emphasis on personal redemption through the 'born-again' experience, their reliance on faith healing, their dynamic communities, their well-oiled organisational machinery, or the fact that Pentecostals offer a comprehensive system of coping with life, given the enormous burdens of poverty, their culturally adaptable message is having its effect. People, especially in developing countries, are flocking to Pentecostal churches. And women are doing so in greater numbers than men.

From the beginning, Pentecostalism was marked by a high degree of participation by women, and still today women are generally acknowledged as its most dedicated and committed adherents. However, in terms of confronting gender hierarchies and transforming gender roles, the movement is noted for reinforcing the subordinate position of women and confining them to traditional gender roles in the household. What, then, accounts for this large, voluntary movement of women in developing countries within these rapidly expanding, conservative, evangelical churches?

To seek answers to this question, I travelled to Burkina Faso, to hear how women defined themselves and their church involvement, and to try to understand the space in which their lives, work, and faith merge. During the field research in Burkina, I met with the leadership, conducted individual interviews with women involved in the movement, held focus-group discussions, and attended a variety of meetings and seminars in different parts of the country in an effort to gain a contextual perspective on their organisation, *l'Association des Servantes de Christ*. Specifically, I wondered if, in context of the women's movement, education, literacy, and training were encouraged and, if so, what was the impact on women.

And more broadly I asked: is the Pentecostal movement reinforcing traditional gender roles, or transforming them? In the context of women in the church in Burkina Faso, are women acting as agents of social change?[1] In other words, does this movement have anything to offer those in the development community who are committed to improving the lives of women by increasing their access to education and redressing vast gender disparities?

This chapter, then, examines the role and activity of African women in an emerging branch of Christianity. At the intersection of gender and religion, it investigates how women experience their Pentecostal faith, and explores the impact of their activities and organisation in the context of education, gender relations, and development of women. I begin by providing an overview of my research motivations and limitations, considering some aspects of faith in the African context, educational trends in Burkina Faso, and the Pentecostal church's presence there. Following this introductory sequence, I discuss the promotion of education and learning in the Pentecostal context; the Church's encouragement of women's self-development (within certain parameters); and the extent to which gender relations can change.

Background information

A personal perspective

My interest in exploring Pentecostalism arises out of my own history. I am the daughter and granddaughter of former Assemblies of God missionaries to Burkina Faso. The memory of six childhood years spent living in Burkina can still evoke the smell of the early mango rains in my nose, the taste of sorghum porridge in my mouth, the sound of its language on my lips, and the lingering impression in my heart of a rich culture that I only vaguely comprehended. In the course of researching the life of my grandmother, who worked for 36 years as a missionary in Burkina, I encountered the literature that documents the Pentecostal movement and its emergence in its African context. When I realised how little was written about women's experience within the movement, it proved to be too tempting an area for me not to explore further. Thus I returned to Burkina as an outsider, wishing to critically assess the impact of work in which her family played a role. But I was welcomed as a daughter. My status afforded me access to the local church and its leadership, as well as the international missionary community. Everywhere I travelled, I met Christians who had worked with or been affected by the ministry of my parents and my grandparents. My reception by the women was warm, and my quest for information was energetically accommodated. I was being honoured for the work of my family—a fact that I found both disconcerting and humbling. Grateful though I was for the access provided, underlying my open reception and the women's willingness to divulge information was a tacit assumption that this trust would not be abused. I am unsure what exactly an abuse might entail, but the pressure that it brought to bear on the interpretation and analysis of my data must be acknowledged. Although I had considerable access to women in the Assemblies of God during my time in Burkina, the limitations of the study must be acknowledged. These include a relatively short field-work period and no discussion with development workers outside the Church.

Faith and gender in Africa

The inter-relationships of gender, spirituality, and development in the African context represent a fascinating and intriguing area of research, for several reasons. Too often, scant attention is paid by the development community to the way in which faith and spirituality affect the development process and the people in it. Faith is an all-pervasive force in societies around the world and it can serve as a significant factor in promoting change, and a filter for individual decisions about whether or not to engage in risky social action (see Ver Beek 2000). Only recently have international development institutions come to acknowledge this fact. One illustration is the publication of *Faith in Development: Partnership between the World Bank and the Churches of Africa* (Belshaw and Calderisi 2002). The reality in Africa is that Christianity continues to play a crucial and dynamic role. Africa registers around 4000 new converts daily, and out of a total population of 450 million roughly 200 million are recognised as Christian (Barrett in Niringiye 1996:115). This has led historian Adrian Hastings to comment that '[b]lack Africa today is totally inconceivable apart from the presence of Christianity' (1990: 208).

If Christianity has become a permanent feature of the African landscape, then so too has Pentecostalism, a term used to define those Christian churches or groups who hold 'the distinctive teaching that all Christians should seek a post-conversion religious experience called the Baptism in the Holy Spirit' (Barrett 1982: 838). Pentecostalism, in Africa and elsewhere, focuses on encouraging what is described as an individual and direct experience of God, a spiritual rebirth, and the expression of that experience of being 'born again' in oral testimony. For Pentecostals, their ultimate authority on life is the Bible, and they are noted for their evangelistic zeal and missionary fervour. They practise what has been termed a 'seven-days-a-week' form of Christianity, and their church services are marked by expressive and exuberant forms of worship, energetic singing, hand-clapping, raising of hands, and the practice of what are termed 'the gifts of the Holy Spirit', such as speaking in tongues and prophecy. Their growth in Africa is attributed to a willingness to acknowledge the force of the supernatural and to confront the world in terms of demons and spirits; to their strong organisational structures; and to a social and economic network that has flourished in conditions of poverty, breaks down boundaries of class and ethnicity, and helps in the creation of a modern identity (Gifford 1998; Meyer 1998; Marshall 1991; Laurent 1994; Marshall-Fratani 1998). Today the topic of Christianity in Africa can hardly be addressed without discussing the changes brought about by the growth of the Pentecostal churches (Gifford 1998: 33).

Commentators remark on the importance of women in maintaining church vitality and growth. Women's prayer groups and efficient and energetic lay organisations have furnished the church with a powerful vehicle for expansion and provided its most dynamic core (Hastings 1979; Gaitskell 1990, 1997; Oduyoye 1995). Unfortunately, the impact of spirituality and faith on the lives of women is too often defined by others, and rarely articulated by women themselves (King 1991). This is particularly true of women's involvement in African Pentecostal churches. Very little has been published about the gender implications of the Pentecostal faith in Africa, although one author, on the basis of small-scale qualitative research, maintains that women in the Nigerian Pentecostal church are provided with a role that is both attractive and transformative, and this in spite of the Pentecostal Biblical teaching on the subordination of women to men (Marshall 1991). Before considering the relevance of this possibility to the women's Pentecostalist movement in Burkina Faso, let us first place it in the context of development trends in Burkina and the growth of the Pentecostal church there.

Education and Pentecostalism in Burkina Faso

Burkina Faso poses a severe challenge to the development community's commitment to improving the lives of women and girls in sub-Saharan Africa and increasing their access to good-quality education. Although gains have been made recently, one need glance only briefly at the statistics to note the improbability of Burkina Faso reaching the education goals outlined in 2000 in the Dakar Framework and the Millennium Development Declaration. UNESCO's *Education for All Global Monitoring Report 2003/4* shows that the net enrolment ratio for primary school is 36 per cent, and the gross enrolment ratio for secondary school is only 10 per cent. The figure for tertiary education, at 3.6 per cent, is even more revealing. The same report notes that there is still no legal guarantee of free primary education in Burkina, and that adult literacy stands at only 24 per cent. If the education prospects for Burkinabé children in general look uncertain, the same report also indicates that for girls the prospects appear even more discouraging: the female literacy rate is only half that of the men, and the ratio of girls to boys at both primary and secondary levels is still well below 1 (.71 and .64 respectively). This serves to highlight the fact that Burkina's chances of achieving gender parity by the international target date of 2015 remain tentative at best. According to the *Human Development Report* for 2003 (UNDP 2003), poverty continues to affect more than half the nation, with 61 per cent of the people living on one dollar or less a day. In addition, women are generally under-represented at the political level and with some notable exceptions are largely absent from positions of leadership and management. Although the country has laws in place to ensure equal treatment of women in civil affairs, women's civil rights in matters of marriage, divorce, and inheritance are generally not respected (Ouedraogo and Dakoure 1998: 38). Women must therefore find alternative ways to cope with the extreme demands that poverty and culture place on them. Thus, in spite of these difficulties (or perhaps because of them) the Burkinabé woman, although poorly represented in official contexts, has more than 100 organisations, NGOs, and societies established exclusively to promote her political, social, and economic rights and interests (*ibid.* 43). It is not surprising, then, that Burkina's Pentecostal church has a thriving women's organisation.

On 1 January 1921, six Assemblies of God (AG) Pentecostal American missionaries arrived in Ouagadougou, now the capital city of Burkina (AHPAC 1996). By the 1950s, the AG in Burkina had 'acquired real local roots' (Hastings 1979: 109), with their largely Africanised liturgies, ceremonies, and music (see also Skinner 1974). Today, the *Assemblées de Dieu*, or AD, of Burkina number around 550,000 members and adherents (DFM 1998). They also contribute to educational opportunities in the nation by running and/or maintaining a total of seven Bible schools, a distance-learning extension programme that serves 580 students, 41 primary schools, and eight *collèges* and *lycées* (middle and high schools) (Lagengo 1999). The church experienced phenomenal growth between 1971, when it registered some 25,000 believers (Zents *et al.* 1971: 40), and 1996, where it grew on the average by 20,000 new converts a year.[2] Although it occupies a minority status in the country, the Protestant community is a dynamic one, exerting an influence that far exceeds its size in proportion to the other religious communities and the population in general (Laurent 1994; Otayek and Dialo 1998). Laurent (1994: 155-77), in the course of fieldwork conducted in one Burkina province, found the AD to be forging itself into a powerful and cohesive community—a trend, he claims, that rests on a willingness to embrace change and on a capacity for organisation. In general, he noted that the Protestant AD communities in the village had higher literacy rates than the community as a whole, were economically better off, due to a strong commitment and engagement with good agricultural practice/techniques, and were frequently to be found in positions of responsibility or leadership in the community.

The women's movement within the church represents a significant part of the church's growth. Founded in 1979, the *Association des Servantes de Christ* (ASC) is led by a national bureau with nine executive members, and by offices at the regional and local levels (Assemblées de Dieu 1996). The ASC's primary objectives, according to its statutes, are as follows: to bring souls to Christ, to participate in the spiritual and material development of the church, to sustain and encourage each other with good works, and to work towards helping the Burkinabé woman reach her full potential[3] (*Statuts de L'ASC* 1997). There are some 200,000[4] women active in the movement, and for several years the ASC was able to mobilise 80,000 women across the country who met weekly for prayer and fasting for the growth of the church in their country (Blumhoffer 1996:54). Although the women did not officially organise themselves until 1979, the foundation had been laid many years before. There are records from the 1930s of missionaries meeting with women for prayer and Bible study, and early on women began planning their own efforts to contribute to the church by planting peanut crops and selling the harvest from pieces of land that they called 'God's Peanut Patch' (AHPAC 1996: 4). The results of these early roots in terms of the nature of women's involvement and activity in the movement today will now be examined in more detail.

Learning in faith, faith in learning

To determine how the Pentecostal faith culture affected women and how this in turn shaped their engagement with education, learning, and development, I conducted research with ASC throughout Burkina Faso. Although my base was the capital, Ouagadougou, I also travelled to the city of Bobo-Dioulasso in the south-west and the rural towns of Po in the south and Kaya in the north. I held open-ended focus-group discussions in both Po and Kaya, with women who represented some twenty different churches. I interviewed members of the church and ASC leadership. I also had opportunities to make observations and speak formally and informally with men and women in the church in such diverse settings as choir practice, the ASC's national bi-annual council meeting, teaching sessions for women leaders, and the national church's tri-annual administrative session. In addition, I conducted in-depth interviews with twelve ASC members, who gave me an oral history of their lives and involvement with the ASC. The women, whose ages ranged from 23 to 69, were originally from different religious backgrounds (Muslim, traditional African, and Christian), lived in rural communities (with the exception of two), were all married, and together had a total of 65 children. What emerged from the discussions during my field study is that learning and education play a prominent role in the Pentecostal experience.

A culture of learning, or an atmosphere in which learning is encouraged and reinforced, seems to be fostered by the ASC by a range of means. First and foremost, informants identified the emphasis placed by the church on reading the Bible and reflecting on its principles, instructions, and stories as a key factor in encouraging women to learn to read. Several of the women whom I interviewed had become literate in the local language of Mooré because they were taught by someone in the church. Informants described how literacy skills are maintained and reinforced through regular practice, with an immediate, relevant application. The women read their Bibles independently, the scriptures are read aloud and reflected on in church, and in their own sessions women read passages aloud and discuss them. One 41-year-old pastor's wife teaches literacy in her church and said it was important because it enabled a woman to read the Bible and 'encourage her family' through the sharing of Bible verses. It also encouraged an independence of spirit, in that a woman who reads, she told me, can see for herself what the Bible says; otherwise, she is dependent on what others say and what she hears. One of the members of the national bureau said that her impression of a literate woman was one who can better understand ideas, think at a higher and more effective level in her life and work, and more consistently accomplish for herself what she needed to do. There were no statistics available regarding the literacy rate among women in the church, but I speculate that it could very well be higher than the national average of 15 per cent (UNDP 2003: 313).

Secondly, informants reported that learning is encouraged and literacy reinforced through the teaching sessions, seminars, and Bible Camps arranged at local, regional, and national levels. In one leadership seminar that I attended, the women took copious notes during the sessions, because many would take the ideas back to their churches and share them with those who could not attend, thus becoming in the process both learners and teachers. They said they enjoyed these teaching sessions because they learned new things and were given something to think about. They claimed to be spiritually refreshed by these gatherings: sometimes by the teaching itself, which they found encouraging and personally applicable, and sometimes by the group community and the chance to meet with other women, talk to their friends, and hear reports and testimonies of what was happening in other churches and areas.

In addition to this, I was told that, although being literate is not a requirement for joining the ASC, the women are strongly encouraged to learn to read and write, particularly those who wish to be a member of a local bureau. For presidents, secretaries, and treasurers, literacy is virtually obligatory. Two of the women were secretaries of their local ASC chapters, and they both told me how much they enjoyed the job because, as one put it, '*it raises my level of intelligence*'. She said that it forced her to think, and she could see the progress that she made in organising her local chapter's plans and goals. The other mentioned that she liked to write down all the activities and plans that the women intended to accomplish, and then at the end of the year she would take note of the progress they had made.

Thirdly, informants commented that the ASC community functions as an information-exchange network where women can share new ideas and learn from each other. One Burkinabé woman, who worked for a local NGO, described her culture as one that does not actively seek out information. Instead, she claimed, people wait for information to come to them – women even more so than men. Within the ASC, with its local, regional, and national offices, conferences, seminars, and teaching sessions on various topics related to health, small credit loans, and small business practices, information passes from one woman to the next and new ideas are encouraged. In addition, the ASC is a member of both national and international organisations, with strong ties to sister churches in neighbouring countries. Often delegations are sent to attend conventions in Côte d'Ivoire, or Mali, or Togo in an effort to expand and strengthen these links.

Finally, there is evidence that education and skills acquisition are seen by the ASC as a key tool in promoting and encouraging some forms of women's personal and economic independence. To that end, the ASC runs a *Centre de Formation*, or training centre, just outside of Ouagadougou. There, 140 women and girls of various religious and ethnic backgrounds receive training in sewing, embroidery, weaving, and knitting as well as classes on health-related issues (AIDS, family planning) and literacy and numeracy. The teacher, an energetic and lively woman, described her satisfaction when she saw former pupils established and earning money. For her, financial independence was the means for the girls to improve their lives and shape their own destinies. She said that the classes at the Centre place emphasis on the girls taking control of their own sexuality, and in the context of her faith she encouraged the girls to recognise their value as human beings created by God.

These opportunities to study and learn indicate a number of ways in which women might be able to change existing gender relations. First of all, it appeared to me that studying raised women's level of confidence and bolstered their sense of self-worth. Secondly, possibly as a result of an increased feeling of pride and personal accomplishment, women feel able to assert themselves in public. In the group discussion, the women from one rural community told me that many of them felt intimidated when they had to speak in front of people in the church. They acknowledged that it was still a problem for them, but could also proudly recount how they had organised two *Journées de l'ASC*. The 'Day of the ASC' occurs on the first Sunday of May each year, when the women plan and conduct the entire service, including the preaching. This is an important event for the women, since it raises their visibility in the church community, increases awareness of their activities, and pushes them into more public roles. Finally, the emphasis on learning and thinking for oneself also, I believe, encourages the women to be more openly critical. I saw evidence of this in one teaching session, where women openly discussed and criticised comments made by the (male) pastor who was teaching their session. In another group discussion, women commented critically on the church's (and ASC's) micro-credit programme, listing its benefits but also pointing out areas where the programme had failed. All of this self-development is linked to their concerns with spirituality.

Pentecostalism and women

The reason given to me to explain the women's motivation for learning to read and write and train is linked with what lies at the heart of the Pentecostal movement: the conversion experience. In Pentecostalism the spontaneous and creative outpouring in prayer and oral testimony that the 'born-again' experience elicits becomes a vehicle for self-expression and affirmation. According to Pentecostalists, it is the learning in faith that makes faith in learning possible. The journey of learning begins from the moment when conversion takes place. Joining the church calls for no less than a redefinition of one's sense of self, for it is in the born-again Pentecostal community of the AD of Burkina Faso that the women could be seen to place their identity. Every woman to whom I spoke could point to the year, the day, and the hour when she got 'saved'. It was within this space that they had located a power that they found life-changing. When asked what they enjoyed most about their involvement in the ASC, the women overwhelmingly gave answers that pointed to this fact. They described themselves as *'women of God engaged in God's work'*. They explained their commitment to the ASC as a *'calling of the Holy Spirit'*, not on behalf of the women but for God. Their deliberate choice to convert was made clear to me when I asked the women who came from Christian backgrounds if they felt that it had given them an advantage. In admonishing tones I was informed that one is not born a Christian, no matter what the background, but one makes a choice to become one – a choice that still carries a certain risk: six out of the twelve women were banished from their families following conversion, some for several years, others for months.

The tangible aspect of this new status is evidenced through a dialogue of prayer and testimony, first with God and then with others. When asked what they enjoyed most about the ASC and which activities were most important to them, they answered 'prayer'. Seven out of the twelve women specifically named prayer as their favorite activity, and every other woman mentioned it at some point in our conversations. Prayer, they said, helped them to cope with the demands placed on them as mothers and wives, encouraged them in sickness, offered refreshment from fatigue, and guidance in the making of decisions. ASC, they said, was also about establishing a network of support and a safe environment in which to discuss problems and needs. Women described communal prayer times at Bible Camps as their *'best times together'*. Additionally, many women spoke of being encouraged by the testimony of others. Every time they meet together, whether for prayer, Bible study, or choir practice, time is taken for testimonies. For them, the testimonies affirmed each individual's experience as special and unique; her testimony becomes a narrative, a story, told and retold, and the fact that it inspires others becomes in itself an affirmation for the woman telling the story.

The conversion experience and its evidence in prayer and testimony appeared to be translated in social action. In the group discussions, the women described a myriad of activities through which they support each other and the church community in general, in times of marriage, death, sickness, childbirth, general hardship, the building of churches, teaching of Bible studies and Sunday school, and installing new pastors. That these social activities were meaningful to the women was clear from their own comments. Second only to prayer, these were the activities that the women enjoyed the most. They told how they liked to visit the sick, sing together, meet together for singing, prayer, or just talking and encouraging each other. They told the story of a believing woman who had been expelled from her home, for one reason or another, by an unbelieving husband, and told how she was provided with immediate support. In one town, I was told of how a woman involved in a small prayer cell was evicted from her home with her small children by her husband. Within a day, her cell group had collected money, found housing for her, hired a taxi to transport her and her few belongings to her new home, and provided a small donation to set her up in a small business selling food. When I asked the women how they found the time to engage in all these activities in addition to their demanding roles as mothers, housewives, and family providers, they insisted that although it was difficult they were happy to do all these things for each other, and would get up even earlier than usual to do their household chores, in order to have time to meet at the church. It is here within this sisterhood that the women focus on their concerns and their needs.

There appeared to be other aspects of this social action, however, than mere sisterly support. In a sense, the ASC is building the capacity of its members to take part in development initiatives to help others. The President of the ASC specifically reported that the ASC encouraged every woman who did not already have a salaried job to undertake some form of economic activity, to enable her to provide for herself and the needs of her family, and to establish some measure of independence. With one exception, each woman whom I interviewed was thus engaged. Some women shared with me how the money that they earned in their business enabled them to take financial decisions on their own, such as buying clothes for a woman in the church who was particularly disadvantaged, or deciding to give financial assistance to a pastor. The ASC also runs a micro-credit programme specifically for widows in the churches, and provides small loans to help them to establish some form of economic independence. Every ASC member was encouraged to pay dues, called *cotisation*. The amount did not matter; what counted was the effort. With their funds, the women engaged in a wide range of communal activities, including purchasing roofs for churches, building doors and windows in the churches, supporting Bible School students, preparing cereal banks in order to have produce to sell in time of need, and financing special trips to conventions or seminars for members of their groups.

It is this emphasis on economic independence that sets the ASC apart from the other women in Pentecostal churches described in the literature and provides a particular dynamic to the way in which the ASC addresses the needs of women. Of course, economic activity in the areas of agriculture and animal husbandry is key to women's roles in agricultural production in West Africa in general; but the ASC specifically emphasises the importance of income generation for individual independence and community contribution.

Impact on gender roles

What is the outcome of the learning opportunities and the activities of the ASC: do they transform gender roles, or reinforce the traditional gender hierarchy? I believe that the examples provided thus far have illustrated how the ASC is meeting women's 'practical interests', through satisfying basic needs, and also is addressing their 'strategic interests', those that play a role in transforming social relations and improving the condition of women's lives (Molyneux 1998: 75). More specifically, I would argue that although tensions are evident in several areas, the women are pushing against gender hierarchies and expanding their traditional roles, if not dramatically transforming them.

At first glance, however, this does not appear to be true. The AD church teaches the submission of women to men and is, in this sense, no different from Pentecostal churches around the world. The women themselves informed me several times of the Bible's teaching on the need for the wife to submit to her husband. Secondly, there is the striking absence of women in leadership positions of the national church. The day after I arrived in Ouagadougou, the national church met for one of its tri-annual business/administrative meetings, and the only woman present was the President of the ASC, who came to represent the organisation and give a report on its activities. Woman are denied ordination and cannot serve as pastors (and therefore in leadership roles, since all leaders are pastors), although they can within limited contexts preach and evangelise. Thirdly, most of the activities in which the women engage reinforce their traditional roles as care givers and housewives, and as agricultural providers for the family. Even the name of the organisation, the Servants of Christ, does not in itself seem to make a challenging statement, but serves to reinforce women's subservient role.

However, in spite of the above, I believe there is evidence of tension within the church setting that points to the subtle, if not dramatic, ways in which women are pushing against traditional boundaries and slowly expanding their roles. In the first place, the fact that the ASC is encouraging women to be more independent, take on some limited leadership responsibilities, even learn to speak confidently in public (whether in women's groups, or up in front of the whole church, as they do on the Day of the ASC), is significant in a society (and to some extent a church as well) where, as one church woman told me, '*women are encouraged to be silent*'. In a supportive environment, women are learning to read and write, to think and plan and set goals for the future, and learn the leadership and management skills necessary to enter the public, modern sphere. Secondly, some of the activities in which the women engage bring them into conflict with traditional views of the place that women should occupy. At one teaching seminar that I attended, a heated discussion took place on the question of which should come first, duties or family. One of the leaders of the ASC described how one pastor was quite upset about the amount of time his wife spent engaged in activities in the group, insisting that she had a responsibility first to her husband and then to her duties. Because women see themselves as part of 'God's work' and consider their contributions as vital to ministry of the church as a whole, they are becoming more assertive in public.

Finally, the ASC is concerned with issues of gender relations. One member of the ASC's national bureau recounted to me how the ASC has identified the need to have special, separate sessions for young girls where they can freely discuss issues relating to sex and marriage, and any other concerns that they might have. The ASC's efforts to provide training for girls has been resisted by the all-male leadership of JAD (*Jeunesse des Assemblées de Dieu*), the youth programme of the AD church, who have interpreted the ASC's efforts as an attempt to encroach on their territory, to undermine their control. At the time when I conducted my interviews, the women had not yet succeeded in obtaining girls-only programmes or classes.

Thus, I believe, does this anecdotal evidence support my claim that in subtle ways the women in the ASC are actively seeking to improve the conditions of women, and expanding the space for women to advance economically and educationally. But their scope for progress is constrained by the church's teaching on the submission of women to men. The ASC is officially under the leadership of the national church, although they are financially self-sustaining and admin-istratively independent. In times of prayer and discussion together, they discuss their visions, plans, and ideas for the future, and sometimes, as we have seen with the case of initiating special courses for young girls, their ideas come into direct conflict with male leadership. Even the idea for the Day of the ASC was initially rejected by the national church leadership, but over time the women were able to convince them otherwise. One member of the ASC leadership told me that although the idea is now accepted and endorsed by roughly 80 per cent of the churches, the remaining 20 per cent are still resisting the idea of giving women control of the service and allowing them to preach.

Ultimately, this all points to another important issue concerning the ASC: the women appear to have carved out a considerable niche in church life and have made themselves indispensable to the success of the Pentecostal movement in Burkina. With all their outreach activities, they have significantly enhanced the church's social capital, as described by Laurent, in the community. Several pastors to whom I spoke recognised this fact, and commented that the women were far better organised than the men, and more effective in accomplishing their goals. Even the ASC's financial contribution to the church should not be underestimated: in a period of twenty years, the ASC gave a total of 64 million cfa (or approximately \$183,000)[5] to the national church (ASC 1999).

Conclusion

What are we to make of the impact of Pentecostalism on the women drawn to its churches? I would argue that the religious experience that typifies Pentecostalism is clearly creating spaces to which women are drawn and in which their lives are changed. The women to whom I spoke identify strongly with their own individual religious experiences, and the narrative testimony arising from those experiences becomes an empowering, life-affirming story. Moreover, this faith-based narrative has provided a space for women's education in the Pentecostal movement in Burkina Faso. Education and learning, along with reading, writing, planning, organising, and critical thinking, are viewed as essential elements of both personal faith and women's participation in the church. The research suggests that the power of the Pentecostal experience can change the lives of women and provide an increased sense of self-esteem, through the growth of communal organisational networks and social group support, and through encouraging financial independence. The women still face institutional constraints in the church context in terms of their aspirations to leadership. The women in the ASC in Burkina appeared inspired by their faith to actively change the world in which they lived, and improve their lives in the process. As development agencies, both foreign and local, search for partners to improve the education of girls and women throughout the world, religious movements and groups like the ASC could well prove to be allies.

Alicia Zents grew up in Burkina Faso and Côte d'Ivoire. She has worked in Mali, Honduras, and Kenya and is currently living in Kenya. The research for her chapter was conducted as part of her work for her MA at the Institute of Education, London University.

Notes

1 I am indebted to the perceptive work of Elizabeth Brusco (1995), who researched the gender and household impact of conversion to evangelical, Pentecostal Christianity in Colombia. In trying to reconcile contradictions between her own anthropological training and the knowledge of religious ideology as an instrument of patriarchy, she found it more useful to ask how women in their traditional roles could be agents of change and even bring about gender-role transformations, rather than asking from a Western feminist perspective how Pentecostalism might inspire women to take on new roles in society.

2 I base these figures on my own calculations using the statistics available to me.

3 Elsewhere this final objective is described as 'ameliorating or improving the conditions of the Burkinabé woman' (AD 1996: 74).

4 Exact figures are hard to come by, since the church does not distinguish between the sexes when counting members, but I am assuming that women make up at least half the number of adherents. The figures may well be much higher than those that I have quoted. Leaders that I spoke to, pastors, etc., often had the impression that women were more numerous than men in their assemblies.

5 This is a rough estimate, since the exact amount, due to the fluctuation of the cfa and the devaluation in 1994, is difficult to determine. Even so, this is a significant sum for the women to have raised, especially considering many women's lack of resources.

References

AHPAC (Africa Harvest Projects and Coordination Office)(1996) 'The Ladies Page' (Assemblies of God publication), Springfield: Division of Foreign Missions

ASC (1997) 'Statuts de l'Association des Servantes de Christ'

ASC (1999) 'Situation d'execution du Budget 1998 et Projet de Budjet 1999 Dieu veulant' (budget of the ASC)

Assemblées de Dieu du Burkina Faso (1996) *75ieme Anniversaire des Assemblées de Dieu du Burkina Faso 1921–1996*, Ouagadougou: Imprimerie des Assemblées de Dieu

Barrett, D. (ed.) (1982) *World Christian Encyclopedia*, Oxford: Oxford University Press

Belshaw, D. and R. Calderisi (2002) *Faith in Development: Partnership between the World Bank and the Churches of Africa*, Regnum Books and World Bank Publications

Blumhofer, E. (1996) 'Pentecostal mission and Africa,' in Christopher Fyfe and Andrew Walls (eds.) *Christianity in Africa in the 1990's*, Edinburgh: Centre of African Studies

Brusco, E. (1995) *The Reformation of Machismo*, Austin: University of Texas Press

Division of Foreign Missions (DFM) (1998) *1998 Annual Statistics*, Springfield: DFM

Gaitskell, D. (1997) 'Power in prayer and service: women's Christian organizations,' in Richard Elphick and Rodney Davenport (eds.) *Christianity in South Africa*, Oxford: James Currey

Gaitskell, D. (1990) 'Africa women's Christianity' in Cheryl Walker (ed.) *Women and Gender in Southern Africa to 1945*, London: James Currey

Gifford, P. (1998) *African Christianity*, London: Hurst & Company

Hastings, A. (1979) *A History of African Christianity 1950–1975*, Cambridge: Cambridge University Press

Hastings, A. (1990) 'Christianity in Africa' in Ursula King (ed.) *Turning Points in Religious Studies*, Edinburgh: T & T Clark

King, U. (1991) 'Introduction' in Ursula King (ed.) *Religion and Gender*, Oxford: Blackwell

Lagengo (1999) Statistics from the AD church headquarters in Lagengo, Ouagadougou

Laurent, J.-P. (1994) 'Prosélytisme religieux, intensification agricole et organisation paysanne,' in J.-P. Jacob and Lavigne Deville (eds.) *Les associations paysannes en Afrique*, Paris: Karthala

Marshall, R. (1991) 'Power in the name of Jesus', *Review of African Political Economy*, 52: 21–37.

Marshall-Fratani, R. (1998) 'Mediating the global and the local in Nigerian Pentecostalism', *Journal of Religion in Africa*, 28/ 3: 278–315

McClung, G. (1993) 'The Pentecostal "trunk" must learn from its "branches"', *Evangelical Missions Quarterly*, 29/1: 34–9

Meyer, B. (1998) ' "Make a break with the past". Memory and post-colonial modernity in Ghanaian pentecostalist discourse', *Journal of Religion in Africa*, 28/3: 316–49

Molyneux, M. (1998) 'Analyzing women's movements', in C. Jackson and R. Pearson (eds.) *Feminist Visions of Development*, London: Routledge

Niringiye, Z. (1996) 'Parachurch organizations and student movements', in C. Fyfe and A. Walls (eds.) *Christianity in Africa in the 1990's*, Edinburgh: Centre of African Studies

Oduyuye, M. (1995) *Daughters of Anowa*, Maryknoll: Orbis Books

Otayek, R. and D. Dialo (1998) 'Dynamisme protestant, développement participatif et démocratie locale,' *Afrique Contemporaine* 185: 19–34

Ouedraogo, E. and H. Hakoure (1998) *Situation des femmes au Burkina Faso*, Ouagadougou: RECIF

UNDP (2003) *Human Development Report 2003*, New York: Oxford University Press

UNESCO (2003/4) *EFA Global Monitoring Report*, www.efareport.unesco.org

Ver Beek, K. (2000) 'Spirituality: a development taboo', *Development In Practice* 10/1: 31–43

Zents, R., P. Chastagner, and D. Compaoré (eds.) (1971) *Les Assemblées de Dieu Haute-Volta: 50ème Anniversaire*, Accra:

12 Enabling education for girls: the Loreto Day School Sealdah, India

Ruth Doggett

The government of India's Ministry of Human Resource Development lists the fifth goal of Education For All in India as 'The creation of necessary structures and the setting in motion of processes, which could empower women and make education an instrument of women's equality' (Ministry of Human Resource Development 1997). It has been suggested that one structure to increase female participation in education may be single-sex secondary schools (Brock and Cammish 1998: 56). While in decline in the Western world, girls' schools are common in India, attracting about one third of all enrolments (Malhotra 1982). Yet there appear to be no studies of students' experiences of single-sex schools in India. This chapter provides a snapshot of one such school in Kolkata which, in its attempts to embrace 'Education For All' and widen the scope of education for girls in urban India, is inconsistent with the prevailing image of private, fee-paying, single-sex schools as the domain of the upper classes.

The chapter draws on a recent case study of Loreto Day School Sealdah (LDS), which analysed the meanings and values that girls attach to their single-sex schooling, and considered the ability of a single-sex school to effect social change (Doggett 2003). The study built on previous work conducted by Jessop (1998), which identified the school's elements of best practice, and by Greene (1996), which examined its approach to education from a religious standpoint. My study was developed from analysis of documents referring to or published by the school; observations made during my time working at the school; interviews with the school principal; and questionnaires administered to 183 students by their teachers in August 2002. These questionnaires, containing a number of open-ended questions, were administered to girls from six classes, one class from each of Years 7–12. This combination of research tools was designed to elicit students' perceptions and views of their schooling, in response to the fact that students are often silent in the public sphere and hold little power (Ribbens and Edwards 1998: 153). This sample was chosen also to reflect the reality that, in the literature on single-sex schools, there is more debate about this form of schooling in the context of girls reaching adolescence (Halstead 1991; UMO 1975: 14). It is also at this age that girls often drop out of school in India (Stromquist 1998: 572), which makes it pertinent to examine how adolescent girls were relating to their education in this particular school.

My interests in these questions arise partly from my own experiences and the contradictions that I have experienced in growing up and being educated in single-sex environments in Ireland. I first became aware of societal influences on girls' education in my teens, when a father of three girls expressed surprise that I, a girl, was studying (and doing well in) higher-level mathematics. Later I questioned why I eventually became channelled into studying the humanities and traditionally 'feminine' studies, despite taking 'masculine' subjects for my final-year exams at secondary school. If I had attended a co-educational school, would my choices of subjects and career have been different, and what possibilities would I have seen as being open to girls like me?

As a teacher in a wide range of different types of school in Ireland, the UK, and New Zealand, I have witnessed diverse experiences of students in single-sex and co-educational environments. For example, I have seen the streaming of boys and girls into feminised and masculinised forms of study and have noted the interactions between boys and girls in their co-educational schools, and their teachers' expectations of them. I have watched as boys and girls are pitted against one another in competition, and lined up in separate lines outside their classrooms. I have observed girls being told to report class 'troublemakers' to the school authorities. I have heard boys whistle at girls and tell them 'I'll break you in soon, yeah?'. I have noticed my own biases towards boys and girls in class, invariably reporting afterwards that I have spent more time addressing the 'boisterous' boys. In short, I have become aware of teaching as a political exercise in a gendered terrain.

These experiences, as well as working as a volunteer teacher in Loreto Day School, Kolkota, in June and July of 1997 and 1999, have raised for me the question of whether single-sex schools widen educational opportunities for girls. The aim of this chapter is to provide a portrait of the Loreto Sealdah's learning environment and examine the impact of girls' gendered identities on their response to education.

Loreto Day School Sealdah: a brief history

Loreto Day School Sealdah belongs to the Institute of The Blessed Virgin Mary, an order of Catholic nuns more commonly known as the Loreto Sisters. Representatives from Loreto Ireland arrived in India in 1842. Charged with the task of schooling the daughters of the colonial administration, they swiftly set about opening English-medium schools for girls. Their arrival in Bengal coincided with the time of Brahmo Samaj, a religious movement which promoted social reforms that sought the controlled emancipation of women and paved the way for the establishment of educational institutions for women

(Karlekar 1994). They saw within these reforms the possibilities of further widening the provision of education 'for the upper classes as well as the poor' (Colmcille 1968: 7). In this way it can be said that Education For All has always been a central premise of the Loreto's 'mission' in India.

Loreto Day School Sealdah (LDS) began life under the direction of Sister Catherine Cantopher in 1857, but in 1938 the arrival of Mother Dorothy Maher, described as a 'woman of vision, clear sighted, strong willed and utterly fearless' (Colmcille *op.cit.*: 280), changed the Loreto's provision of education for ever. In the spirit of their revolutionary founder, Mary Ward, the Loreto Sisters challenged restrictions and sought ways to open education to all, rejecting discriminations inherent in policies such as the code for Anglo-Indian schools that dictated that no more than 25 per cent of students in such schools should be Indian (*ibid.*; Doggett 2003: 62). Today there are seven Loreto schools in Kolkata, within a network of 19 across India. The current principal, Sr. Cyril Mooney, took up her post in 1979 and set about extending the scope of the school, which at that time was a private school catering largely for the daughters of elite Bengali society, with only 90 out of 790 students coming from poor backgrounds. LDS therefore belongs to an elite English-medium academic tradition, very different from the types of single-sex school in (for example) rural Pakistan, which cater for some of the poorest girls in areas where co-educational schooling is not an option.

On arrival, Sr. Cyril embarked on a mission to foster a school with students from all financial, social, and religious backgrounds, because there was 'a certain uneasiness felt at being part of a formal education system imparting quality education to a privileged few, while millions of their less fortunate peer group get virtually nothing at all' (Cyril 1997: 3). The school today has 1,400 girls, ranging from the Nursery class to Year 12, half of whom do not pay fees on account of their families' financial circumstances. LDS has become a multicultural educational setting, providing for Hindu, Muslim, and Christian students, and in doing so has been recognised as 'a model of best practice' (Jessop 1998). Alliances and networks have been formed between the school and organisations such as UNICEF, Save the Children, the British Council, Rotary Club, Ashoka, Childline, and Round Table, ensuring that LDS has a vast network from which to draw experiences, lessons learned, and opportunities for advocacy on the rights of the child. It challenges conventional assumptions that private fee-paying single-sex schools are exclusively for the middle and upper classes, and thus raises questions about the potentials of this form of school organisation.

Loreto schools have a distinguished reputation in India, and Loreto Sealdah is no exception. On International Literacy Day 1994, it was awarded the UNESCO Noma Literacy Prize for spreading literacy and education. Each year since 1998 it has won the Telegraph Better Calcutta Contest, as an acknowledgement of its work towards achieving social excellence. More recently it was chosen out of 600 schools for the Telegraph 2002 award for the Best School in Calcutta, to mark its work on social, health, and environmental issues. Such a reputation means that politicians, business people, and the wealthy send their daughters to Sealdah, paying tuition fees of up to 740 rupees per month. But despite the fact that it is a private school, it does not perceive education as a profit-making exercise. In late 2002, when private schools were forced to increase their tuition fees by a reduction in the State government's Dearness Allowance, which provides a percentage of the salaries of teachers of registered private schools, the school discussed the matter with parents and guardians and it was agreed that 160 out of the 700 fee-paying students could continue studying at the old rate of 440 rupees per month.

The school has also been successful in reaching out to families living in the nearby slums, on railway stations and pavements. Students from such underprivileged families study free of charge at the school and are often provided with school uniforms, textbooks, and meals. They are supported by overseas sponsors and the generosity of wealthy families associated with the school. The tuition fees are covered by the fees of other students and by donations from overseas sponsors and aid agencies, and the State-administered Dearness Allowance. As a strategy for the integration of all children into the school community, uniforms and colour coding of classes were introduced to eliminate social differences. Throughout LDS, most classes are mixed-ability and include both fee-paying and non-paying students.

This chapter discusses data from questionnaires gathered from both fee-paying and non-fee-paying students (see Table 1).

Table 1: a summary of the fee status of pupils in Years 7–12 of Loreto Day School Sealdah

	Year					
	7	8	9	10	11	12
Non-fee-paying	9	12	6	9	5	6
Fee-paying	22	20	16	20	23	25
Unspecified	0	4	2	2	2	0
Total	31	36	24	31	30	31

Apart from the students attending the regular lessons, the school caters for approximately 250 street children – or 'rainbow children', so named by the school principal because they 'drop in like rainbows, colourful as they are, giving joy as they appear' (Cyril 1997). These rainbow children attend the school's 'Rainbow

School' and night shelter, which, as explained below, consists of an informal teaching programme for street children, provided by LDS students.

The success of such a school depends on the creativity and commitment of the staff. In the past, Loreto schools were staffed mainly by ordained sisters, but over time they have been replaced by lay teachers. Today, Loreto Sealdah has a staff of 65: 62 female teachers and three men, many of whom have been through a Loreto education themselves and come from a range of social and religious backgrounds. Some teachers are first-generation learners. The unique ethos of the school requires that teachers are constantly challenged and involved in a training programme which involves their participation in reflective workshops. In addition, initiative and personal investment are expected, thus ensuring that a sense of ownership of school activities is fostered among the staff (Jessop 1998: 15).

Towards an enabling curriculum

Ethos

Loreto Sealdah's unique status among Bengali schools is born out of its philosophy and ethos. The vision of LDS is to create 'dynamic people, with the values of giving, sharing and extended love – a vibrant living instrument for human change' (Cyril 1997: 3). This type of education, it is stressed, depends on ensuring that students do not receive an insular elitist education, but one which involves their interaction at all levels of society. The school has developed not only an academic curriculum, but also a curriculum of non-academic activities, such as working with street children, which support students' interaction in the public arena. These activities occur alongside the academic curriculum and are equally valued; they may therefore be called co-curricular programmes, as opposed to extra-curricular programmes. The focus is on education for community and solidarity, not competition. This is seen as a way to tackle privileges and hierarchies within Indian society which divide rich and poor, men and women. The vision is based on a belief that, through exposure to life experiences, 'the regular school child learns at first hand what real destitution is and will be less likely to dismiss the poor when she holds a position of power later on, and if the regular child is herself poor, then she learns the need to work for her own community and is challenged to share rather than climb up the social ladder and be lost to her own people' (Majumdar 1999: 3). In this way at LDS 'Compassion is Compulsory', just as maths is compulsory (*ibid.*). This commitment is made explicit at enrolment, which is accompanied by a value test. While most schools assess the students, this entrance test also evaluates the parents' values: they are reminded that their daughters must attend the school's various co-curricular programmes, and that the education that the school provides aims to be dynamic and potentially liberating (Cyril 1997: 2).

The academic single-sex schools, of the tradition from which LDS emerges, have been identified as places for the academically oriented, with little on offer for those not so inclined (Arnot 1983: 79). For LDS, however, the value system and ethos present the academic side of school as 'one of the tools for intellectual development on par with but never taking precedence over the formation of mind and heart necessary to produce an agent of human change' (Cyril 1997: 12). Academic achievement is expected, but is presented in a context that stresses co-operation and the holistic development of its students, in contrast to the extremely competitive nature of the contemporary Indian education system. An education which promotes individual competition is rejected. This is reinforced by a request that no student should receive extra tuition outside the school. Instead, students with difficulties are encouraged to seek help from within the school.

Exam results suggest that this approach has not been to the detriment of academic achievement. Loreto Sealdah achieves good results in the public examinations – the Madhyamik Pariksha at Year 10 and the Higher Secondary Exam at Year 12 – by both fee-paying and non fee-paying students, with 50 per cent of students attaining a first-class pass annually (Jessop 1998:13). This is comparable to the achievements of other private schools in Kolkota. However, it is achieved in a school where students are admitted through a lottery system, not through competitive examinations, as is the case with other private schools.

Sarmistha Sarkar is a former pupil of the school, now involved in a peace initiative in Kolkota. Interviewed in 2003 about her experience of LDS, she attributed her activism to empowering experiences provided by Loreto Sealdah, and commented that 'we were never expected to compete for marks and ranks. What was stressed instead was our ability to reach out, to try and solve a problem if we saw one. It was only when I went to college that I realized how paranoid everybody was about academic performance!' (Ray 2003). The school's vision is to awaken the consciousness of everyone who plays a part in the school. This awakening happens through reflective participation in the variety of remarkable programmes described below.

Co-curricular programmes

In 1979 LDS established a rural programme in co-operation with the Children in Need Institute. Following negotiations with the village head teachers of suburban Amgachia district, it was agreed that LDS students would teach in the village schools once a week (Jessop 1998: 9). It is now well-established practice that each Thursday, 150 regular students give up their day off and teach. I had the privilege of accompanying students on one such weekly trip in July 1997 and was impressed by the confidence and commitment with which students related to their peers and taught them through participatory techniques using song, story telling, and art.

Students are taught teaching methods and class planning from Year 5 onwards, by their Bengali teacher. Teaching topics, selected in consultation with the village head teacher, mainly consist of topics such as vocabulary building, environmental and practical science, and practical maths (Cyril 1997: 5). At Year 11, students begin teaching English in the village high school. The direct impact of their work was the establishment of a junior high school for girls in Amgachia district, and an increase in the number of girls attending the 'boys'' school in 1979 from 7 to more than 800 currently studying in the new girls' junior high school, funded by LDS through overseas sponsorship. The involvement of Sealdah students in the village schools increased the visibility of girls in education and set a positive example for parents who were contemplating sending their daughters to school.

While the rural programme was initiated by staff, the 'rainbow programme' is an initiative led by a group of students who approached Sr. Cyril in 1985, concerned about the numbers of children and young people on the streets who were not receiving an education. From their ideas grew the concept of 'a school within a school'. The dynamism of LDS can be seen in the progression of the rainbow programme from an *ad hoc* weekly afternoon programme, run by volunteer students, to one which is now an integral part of the school, involving all students from Year 5 to Year 10. When a rainbow student was abused on the streets, students again approached the school principal, and from their concern the concept of a night shelter developed.

As part of this programme, children living on the streets and on the platforms of nearby Sealdah and Howrah railway stations, both male and female, are invited into the school for lessons. They are also provided with facilities to sleep and wash, and they have the services of a nurse and social worker. The programme operates efficiently, due to the use of 'work education' slots within the school. From Year 5 onwards, the school timetable is divided into ninety-minute slots of 'work education' per week, with one class participating in it during every period of the day. Work education is a curricular subject, preparing students for employment in the workforce. This means that at every period there are at least fifty potential teachers from the regular student community, ready to teach and play with the 'rainbow' students on a one-to-one basis. Their educational programme includes literacy, numeracy, life skills, dancing, yoga, singing, painting, and crafts such as pottery and tie dye which may later be used to generate income (Cyril 1997: 4). The success of this programme is apparent through the integration of some 'rainbow' students into the regular school and other schools in Kolkata. One of the earliest rainbow students is herself teaching in the rainbow school and in the villages of Amgachia. A property next to the school was acquired in 1997, and the night shelter for rainbow students is currently expanding to accommodate up to 300 students.

The Hidden Domestic Child Labour Project began as a survey led by students from years 5 to 7, which established that 4,900 children were involved in domestic labour in the Sealdah area. In response to this, students established social clubs for the children, currently involving more than 300 children. Students' activism includes approaching employers on Anti Child Labour Day to demand the day off for child labourers, who are subsequently treated to an organised trip. Further advocacy is carried out by the school through its involvement in the Shikshalaya Prakalpa movement. Sr. Cyril is convenor of the State Resource Group for the Education of Deprived Urban Children, which began its work in January 1999 by surveying street children and discovering 44,646 street children out of school. Approximately 50 NGOs and government agencies are working in partnership to identify and enrol all Kolkata's children in regular schools. As part of this movement, the school has trained more than 552 teachers, who work in pairs and collect the children in groups of 50 in areas where there is either no school or no vacancy for the children in existing schools ('Ripples and Rainbows', September 2001).

Recognising India's need for more teachers, the school developed a Barefoot Activity-Based Teacher Training Programme in 1988. This is a two–four week programme held every month, designed to train teachers in child-centred educational methods. The participants are young men and women who have dropped out of school before reaching Year 10 and are consequently ineligible for places at teacher-training colleges. As many of the participants work in rural villages without access to sophisticated teaching materials, the programme focuses on encouraging participants to develop learning and teaching aids from locally sourced materials. Aside from designing aids, the trainee teachers also undertake observation of Sealdah's teachers, and learn about teaching methodologies and self-evaluation.

Academic curriculum

Loreto Sealdah is affiliated to the West Bengal Board of Education, the West Bengal Council for Secondary Education, and the National Open School. These affiliations allow the school to design its own academic curriculum, as long as students are prepared for the State exams: the Year 10 Madhyamik Pariksha exam and the Year 12 Higher Secondary Examination. Up to Year 10, students study science and maths, Bengali, English, history, and geography, and they also receive physical education, work education, and values education. In years 11 and 12, students choose between commerce, humanities, and science. In Sealdah the most popular option is commerce, a phenomenon explained by Sr. Cyril in terms of the financial rewards on offer in the IT industry. Other activities include Indian dance, yoga, Indian singing, karate, sports, and team games such as basketball.

'Enabling' activities

My research in 2002 drew on the work of Mukhopadhyay and Seymour (1994), who developed the analytical concept of a 'patrifocal family structure and ideology' to account for the way families regulate gender-differentiated access to and control over resources both material and social, such as education, in India. This concept implies subordination of individual goals to collective welfare, which reinforces the centrality of men and the subordinate status of women. For example, they identified that intrinsic to this ideology is a series of sanctioned structural features, such as patrilocal residence or patrilineal inheritance, which marginalise daughters and create a concern to regulate female behaviour (Mukhopadhyay and Seymour 1994:3). This results, for example, in the commonplace observation that educating girls is equivalent to 'watering a tree in your neighbour's courtyard' (in Stromquist 1998:581; see also the chapter by Janet Raynor in this volume), which betrays families' conviction that their obligation to a daughter consists primarily in getting her settled in marriage. A daughter's education must be tailored to the opportunity of finding a suitable husband, rather than enabling her to pursue what she herself wants to do.

In contrast to the subordination to which girls might be subject in the coeducational school (Drudy and Uí Chatháin 1999; Spender 1980), Loreto Sealdah tries to present students with the space to identify their own and others' realities through the various school programmes and activities. LDS also encourages girls to engage in activities that acknowledge their power to change what is taking place around them. During their time at LDS, they become involved in the public domain, participating in all sorts of rallies, competitions, and social initiatives which address issues ranging from environmental health to child rights. These activities are a vital component in the school's attempts to increase the visibility of girls, develop students' critical capacities, and aid their future employment prospects: they may therefore be called *enabling activities*.

The students' exposure to the examples of strong women in positions of power, such as their teachers, helps to reinforce the positive messages that they receive through the school's programmes. The first LDS newsletter was dedicated to three women at the school and another to 'women who have touched our lives' ('Ripples and Rainbows', September 1997). Attempts are made to provide robust non-stereotypical messages and images about women's roles in life (as can be seen in the Value Education Books, *We Are The World*, edited by Sr. Cyril, which portray women as surgeons, construction-site managers, scientists, etc.).

It is within this supportive atmosphere that girls gain skills and confidence which, it is hoped, will enable them to claim their rights. It is hoped that they will realise that 'we don't have to settle for small meaningless lives – we can set realistic meaningful goals, and do the things to make them happen' ('Ripples and

Rainbows', September 1997).The research found that students are aware of structural inequalities, with comments such as *'We all together can draw out remedies for the women in poor families who are deprived most in this male dominated world. Males do not accept this'* (Year 10), showing a firm resolve to challenge the position of women in India.

The Value Education curriculum is seen as fundamental for the formation of students who are reflective and want to promote social change. It also encourages dialogue about life experiences. Analysis of the sequential curriculum materials reveals a collaborative and participatory pedagogy with a strong emphasis on reflection:

- **Key in** (where students gather their own thoughts)

- **Share it around** (sharing with friends)

- **Pass it on** (sharing group work with the class)

- **Talk it over** (class discussion)

- **Think it through** (self-reflection)

- **Take it in** (Scripture-guided reflection)

- **Carry it through** (plan and carry out action)

Within these classes, the girls' own experience and knowledge are validated and used as building blocks for reflection, discussion, and action, nourishing students' critical abilities and their *'capacity to form and express an opinion, the courage to express and form an opinion which people may not agree with'* (Cyril, interview, 2002). Each lesson ends with the students developing an action plan which reinforces the message that the girls themselves can be active agents. They are provided with practical strategies at the end of each lesson, such as encouragement to contact UNICEF or find out about and help a local women's organisation. That many students do become agents of change may be illustrated by the participation of a ten-year-old student in the 2001 National Conference on Domestic Labour in Mumbai, where she spoke about her experiences as a former child labourer. She was accompanied by a fellow former LDS student, herself a first-generation learner, who had gone on to become a qualified teacher and now co-ordinated the LDS project on Hidden Child Domestic Labour.

The 'enabling' activities and the school ethos, therefore, are part of the reason why *'we don't have drop outs because we don't let them drop out, we provide them with alternatives'* (Sr. Cyril, interview, 2002). This is also achieved by avoiding 'disabling' educational experiences or experiences of failure, by providing additional tuition for students experiencing difficulties, encouraging participation in the National Open School, and allowing some students to sit one examination at a time. These strategies help girls to transform their lives and empower them in their struggle against deprivation.

An LDS education – and the response of students

An education at Loreto Sealdah can therefore be seen to consist of two strands: the academic curriculum, which supports the academic development of all students and prepares them for State examinations, and the 'curriculum of agency', which attempts to build confidence and a sense of capacity within students through participation in the co-curricular programmes and other enabling activities. This section uses questionnaire data (Doggett 2002) to examine students' responses to their education.

Responding to questions about the academic curriculum, and asked to name favourite subjects, students appear to align themselves with the traditionally 'feminine' subjects such as languages and the arts, whose favoured status appears to be rooted in their practical applications. See Figure 1.

Figure 1: Students' favourite subjects

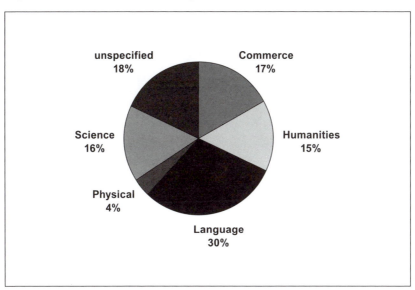

As can be seen in Figure 1, the majority of pupils in the survey chose languages, which included English and Bengali. After this, favour was spread across Commerce (Business, Maths and Accountancy), Science (Computers, Biology, and General Science), and the Humanities (History, Geography, Political Science, Nutrition, and Home Science).

However, closer analysis revealed that the response of students to the academic curriculum appears to be influenced by two factors: social position and increasing awareness of women's gendered roles in life. As Figure 2 shows, social position affected the favoured status of subjects. Those students who showed some ability to move beyond stereotypical 'female' areas of study were invariably fee-paying. In contrast to the fee-paying students, who expressed interest in a range of subjects, non-paying students clustered around the humanities and languages. Similarly, every student, bar one, who gave either Nutrition or Home Science as her favourite subject did not pay fees. In contrast, every student who chose Accountancy, Political Science, or Maths as her favourite was fee-paying. It could be that while poorer students may have greater aspirations in private, they fear that these aspirations may be imprudent and threaten their future marriageability or family reputation. Consequently they opt for subjects leading to jobs which will provide them with security.

Figure 2: Favourite subject areas – fee-paying status

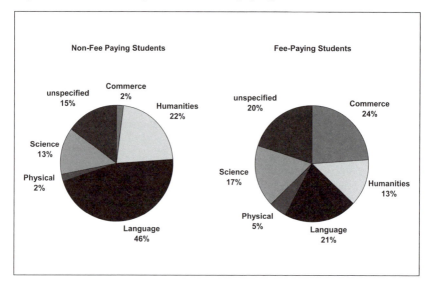

The co-curricular programmes, particularly the educational ones, evoked varied responses from students. Commitment ranged between those who expressed little connection with the programmes, seeing them as *a 'waste of energy (for me) but it helps the poor children to learn about general knowledge'* (Year 9) to those who expressed a sense of ownership, pride, and genuine excitement in the school's achievements: *'I am proud to be part of such a unique institution. I plead to all the other schools around the world to communicate with us and build up a chain to reach out for the less privileged group. I hope the mission of our school would reach the apex of success and prosperity and we will be able to feel all the more proud'* (Year 10).

When invited to describe the skills that their participation in the programmes has developed, many students spoke of confidence and being taught *'to become self independent and build a character of our own'* (Year 8). Most students chose to focus, not on personal gains, but on how the programmes are about learning to *'Sacrifice, to co-operate and to be compassionate towards others'* (Year 10), and to become *'a complete countryman and … know how to serve the country'* (Year 9).

In cases where students said they had developed practical skills, these were linked with becoming teachers or parents, by learning *'how to control children and how to behave with children'* (Year 9). This element of service appears to be closely linked with their identification of women as nurturers and givers. Commenting on her single-sex education, one Year 11 student asserted, *'I strongly feel that it develops our feminine identity and helps us to develop the feminine qualities like perseverance and adjustment to our family members'*. Such a strong assertion suggests that this student sees her education in terms reminiscent of the old 1920s education-reform slogan 'Educating a girl means educating a family' (Mukhopadhyay and Seymour 1994: 38). It orientates girls towards family duties and suggests that a girl's own needs, and perhaps goals, should be subordinated to those of her family. While the school's outreach programmes give the girls exposure to the realities and consequences of the patrifocal ideology and encourage them to reflect and speak out, there is only tentative engagement in and a certain resistance to the parameters of behaviour imposed on them by this ideology. For some, the programmes seem to be equating femininity with ideals of self-sacrifice and service.

This definition of femininity was echoed by many of the students, and reinforced by statements such as *'from Loreto Sealdah we have learnt to give and give our knowledge, love, respect, kindness and a helping hand to the needy persons but in return we just want love, love and love'* (Year 8). The school's philosophy of nourishing students' critical abilities and confidence to pursue justice for girls and women around them appears here to be subordinated to students' definition of femininity. In stressing their capacity for self-sacrifice and their loving natures, they are once again maintaining the ideology of appropriate female behaviour that the patrifocal ideology demands in order to maintain group harmony and welfare (Mukhopadhyay and Seymour 1994: 3).

A single-sex school and responses to sexuality

Regardless of the school's academic record, enabling activities, and high reputation, many parents continue to send their daughters to this school to ensure maintenance of female purity. This is confirmed by Sr. Cyril and senior students. Across all year groups, the data suggest that students have internalised an ideology which considers boys and girls to have distinct natures which necessitate separation in education, with single-sex schools providing the safest option for girls. Comments such as *'Nowadays not all boys are good so it is important to a girl to study in an all-girls' school'* exemplify perceptions of boys' innate ill intentions, which must result in the restriction of girls' movements. Such an emphasis places all the responsibility for action on girls, with male accountability a non-issue.

Further to these discourses, some students commented that the single-sex school actually helps them to learn their distinct roles: *'School is a period when children grow up. Boys and girls are to grow up according to the manners suitable to them, which is different from one another'* (Year 12). Asked what 'manners' are suitable for girls, the students varied in their replies, according to their age. Ninety per cent of Year 7 students questioned thought that girls should be modest and obedient, while only 23 per cent in Year 12 agreed, which suggests that senior students had become more critical and questioning through Loreto's programmes. For some students, perceptions of the 'appropriate' behaviour of girls govern the range of topics that they can discuss. Some talked openly about their future husband and the numbers of children they wanted, while other deemed this 'unladylike'. However, some Year 12 students acknowledge this treasured space, saying *'girls have their own problems and their own views of life so it is better and easier to share these when in an all girls' school'*, and they *'can discuss feminist matters freely'*. It is this opportunity for girls to discuss realities away from the presence of men that has been prized by many feminists (for example, Deem 1984; Mahony 1985; Scott and Spender 1980).

Reflecting on Loreto Sealdah's programmes, one 15-year-old student spoke of her increased awareness of women's subordinate positions in India: *'girls have always been treated badly, especially in the villages... Girls are also being hit, kicked, burnt and killed by their husbands and in-laws and some women are ill-treated by other men. The children from poorer families are given in marriage under-age and they suffer all their lives.'*

However, the ability to negotiate a strong position after school was questioned by some students, who stressed that the regulation of their sexuality and social interactions through single-sex schooling may impede their success in future life, because *'it sometimes leads to fear and hesitation for some of the girls to commu-nicate with the masculine world in their coming days'* (Year 11). This is made all the more significant as senior students consistently identified life after school as being within a masculine realm, within which they had yet to negotiate a space. Students spoke of being *'faced with a whole new world'* (year 10) and, repeatedly, about *'obstacles'* ahead of them in the outside world.

Life after Loreto – finding a place in 'a whole new world'

LDS also appears to function as a sanctuary where *'We can be ourselves (in our school) without any second thought for our actions'* (Year 11). This is in contrast to life beyond school, the masculine world, where girls feel that their behaviour is under constant scrutiny. Students, particularly the older ones, mention their teachers in the same sentence as friends and identify them as their allies. One aspect of this openness towards teachers is the ability to approach teachers and ask for help or advice on school matters or personal life. A Year 8 student declares: *'All girls should be given equal rights as boys. Nowadays in an all-girls school, they are treating girls equally. People must not think that girls are the weaker sex. Today a girl can do all the things that a boy can. I feel each and every girl should be allowed to go to school.'* It is suggested that the single-sex school is the structure through which this may be achieved.

As with choice of subjects, when students were encouraged to look beyond school and focus on future careers, there was little evidence of moving beyond culturally sanctioned female occupations, such as nursing and teaching. This is not surprising, considering how strongly they perceive life after school as being full of obstacles which advantage men. But some fee-paying students identified a diversity of desirable careers, including those in science (6 per cent), law (4 per cent), medicine (9 per cent), the military (2 per cent), and business management (6 per cent), but they still showed little evidence of interest in risk-taking through (for example) entrepreneurship, despite the school's valuing of initiative. Non-paying students were significantly less imaginative: legal careers were not mentioned, and only 2 per cent wanted to be nurses, while 7 per cent mentioned business management, usually of small family businesses.

As students become increasingly aware of the limited opportunities open to girls in a male-dominated labour market, they see teaching as a reliable career: 12 per cent of the students named it as their chosen career (8 per cent of fee-paying students, 17 per cent of non-paying students). Such a choice does little to threaten the prevalent ideology, but it provides the necessary social and cultural capital to maintain status and provide economic stability, while allowing them time to tend to their families. It may also demonstrate the function of teachers as role models, some themselves first-generation learners, offering practical examples of education leading to social mobility. This would clearly be important to the non-paying students, for whom teaching would provide the financial security denied to their parents. It is also a career of which all students have some experience through their involvement in the school's programmes, as mentioned previously, and one which allows them to give something back to their community – a very strong aspect of the school's philosophy.

Focusing on future careers appeared problematic for the 34 per cent of students who chose not to answer this question. It may be that many girls see their future roles within the home or that, for the wealthier students, education is about building or maintaining status through qualifications, not careers. The fact that only small numbers of students appear to be heading into 'male' environments points to the continuing dangers that women can incur through damage to their social reputations in a male-dominated society. Modest aspirations may also indicate increasing awareness of the constraints imposed on girls, and the limited time that they have in school to establish confidence in themselves. Students therefore cherished their time at school, and 90 per cent agreed that 'Education helps to improve a woman's position in society'. The strength of this conviction may be reflected in the decision of 22 per cent of students surveyed to pursue some form of higher education.

Conclusion

The form of schooling exemplified by Loreto Day School Sealdah presents numerous advantages as a means for increasing the participation and retention of girls in education in India. Its single-sex nature, combined with the levelling strategies employed since 1979, ensure that students from a diverse range of backgrounds participate fully in quality education. Once they are engaged in education, Loreto Sealdah provides girls with the support and encouragement that they need in order to remain in school and gain qualifications. Students are encouraged to reach their full potential through the academic curriculum, at which they are expected to succeed, and through the innovative co-curricular and enabling activities, which provide girls with a range of opportunities to exercise leadership and initiative, question the social position of women in India, and develop practical strategies to effect change and achieve their goals. This study has revealed that the students at LDS directly linked their reflection to the challenges posed by social equations with the single-sex environment of their school. However, although they are vociferous critics of the inferior position of many women in India, their desire for independence and female autonomy appears to be tempered by an internalisation of the ideals of female behaviour and roles that are embedded in a wider patrifocal ideology. The study also indicates that girls respond in different ways to the challenges ahead, according to what they believe to be the possibilities for change in their future lives.

The case of Loreto Sealdah illustrates how students' responses to their education and their ability to maximise its benefits are conditioned by gendered identities formed inside and outside school. It illustrates the complexity and the interrelatedness of internal and external expectations and social pressures on girls.

The LDS education is designed to provide its female students with the opportunities and abilities to challenge gendered identities that limit and constrain the ways in which girls can respond to their education – an education that Sr. Cyril describes as a true education: liberating girls from the fear which prevents them from achieving their full potential spiritually, intellectually, and emotionally (Sr. Cyril in Green 1996). Loreto Sealdah provides, therefore, an example of a valuable approach to education, which offers girls from all backgrounds in urban India the opportunity to achieve greater equality as women.

Ruth Doggett is a qualified teacher who has taught in Ireland, the UK, and New Zealand. She gained her first degree in Mater Dei Institute of Education, Dublin, and a master's degree in Gender, Education, and Development at the Institute of Education at the University of London. She is currently co-ordinating a programme addressing educational disadvantage and early school leaving in Dublin.

References

Arnot, M. (1983) 'A cloud over co-education: an analysis of the forms of transmission of class and gender relations', in S. Walker and L. Barton (eds.) *Gender, Class and Education*, New York: Falmer Press

Brock, C. and N. K. Cammish (1997) *Factors Affecting Female Education in Seven Developing Countries*, London: Department for International Development

Colmcille, M. (1968) *First The Blade: History of the IBVM (Loreto) in India 1841–1962*, Calcutta: Mukhopadhyay

Cyril, Sr. (ed.) (1989) *We Are the World – Experience Based Value Education for Schools*, Kolkata: Orient Longman

Cyril, Sr. (1991) 'Nurturing to Freedom: Loreto Education in India', paper presented at the Loreto Education Meeting at Dhyan Ashram

Cyril, Sr. (1995) 'A School for Justice', Newsletter, Calcutta: Loreto Day School Sealdah

Cyril, Sr. (1997) 'Ripples and Rainbows in a Regular School', Calcutta: Loreto Day School Sealdah

Deem, R. (1984) *Co-education Reconsidered*, Milton Keynes: Open University

Doggett, R. (2003) 'The Single Sex School as an Agent of Social Change – The Case of Loreto Day School Sealdah', unpublished MA dissertation, Institute of Education, University of London

Drudy, S. and M. Uí Chatháin (1999) *Gender Equality in Classroom Interaction*, Kildare: NUI Maynooth

Greene, E. (1996) 'From Dirt Streets to Rainbows: An Analysis of Loreto Sealdah's Dynamic approach to Education', unpublished paper, Pontifical University of Maynooth, Dublin

Halstead, M. (1991) 'Radical feminism, Islam and the single sex school debate', *Gender and Education*, 3/3: 263–77

Institute of The Blessed Virgin Mary website: www.IBVM.org

Jessop, T. (1998) 'A Model Of Best Practice At Loreto Day School Sealdah, Calcutta, India', London: DFID Education Sector Group

Karlekar, M. (1994) 'Woman's nature and access to education in Bengal' in Mukhopadhyay and Seymour (eds.) (1994)

Mahony, P. (1985) *Schools for the Boys – Co-education Reassessed*, London: Hutchinson

Majumdar, G. (1999) 'At this school, compassion is compulsory', available online at www.humanscapeindia.net/humanscape/hs1099/hs10995t.htm

Malhotra, A. (1982) 'Problems of girls' education – future course of action', in *Educational Development of Women in India*, New Delhi: Ministry of Education and Culture, online at the Education Portal of the MHRD at www.shikshanic.nic.in/cd50years/s/3N/EP/3NEP0501.htm

Ministry of Human Resource Development Government of India (MHRD) (1997) 'Goals of EFA', online at the Education Portal of the MHRD at http://shikshanic.nic.in/cd50years/r/2R/7Q/2R7Q0401.htm

Mukhopadhyay, C. and S. Seymour (eds.) (1994) *Women, Education and Family Structure in India*, Oxford: Westview Press

Ray, A. (2000) 'Sister Cyril's army of barefoot teachers', *Changemakers Journal*, August 2000, www.changemakers.net/journal/00august/ray.cfm

Ray, A. (2003) 'Rainbow children: dissolving differences', *Changemakers Journal*, October 2003, www.changemakers.net/journal/03october/cyril.cfm

Ribbens, J. and R. Edwards (1998) *Feminist Dilemmas in Qualitative Research: Public Knowledge and Private Lives*, London: Sage

'Ripples and Rainbows', Quarterly Newsletter of Loreto Day School Sealdah (1996–2001) Sealdah, Calcutta

Spender, D. (1980) *Learning to Lose: Sexism and Education*, London: Women's Press

Stromquist, N. P. (1998) *Women in the Third World – An Encyclopedia of Contemporary Issues*, London: Garland Publishers

UMO (Union of Muslim Organisations of United Kingdom and Eire) (1975) *Islamic Education and Single Sex Schools*, Jamadi-al-Awwal: UMO

13 Conclusion: policy and practice change for gender equality

Sheila Aikman and Elaine Unterhalter

What have the contributors to this book offered in terms of improving understanding, practice, and policy making to ensure that education for girls and women is gender-equitable, that it transforms the structures that shape their lives, and contributes to their empowerment? How can we use the learning generated here to influence not only the development of good policies – for it should be acknowledged that many good policies exist already, at least on paper – but to influence the implementation of good policies which translate into high-quality educational experiences for girls and women and men and boys?

The chapters in this book illustrate a vision of a transformational education that is currently being put in practice in a number of places. This is an education that promotes social change and contributes to building a just and democratic society. It is a view of education as a human right, a right which we are ethically obliged to provide for each other. The right to education is itself nested in other human rights. These include the right to live in health, without the indignities of poverty; and the right to an education which is free from violence and free from discrimination – not only gender-based discrimination and injustice but ethnic, economic, cultural, and social forms of discrimination. Where peoples such as indigenous Quechua groups of Peru (Chapter 7) or Somali pastoralists of Kenya (Chapter 6) experience negative discrimination in their education, women and girls find themselves doubly or triply marginalised, with less access to education, a poorer quality of education, and education of shorter duration than that on offer to boys and men. These chapters help to expand the concept of rights and capabilities presented in Chapter 1. Rights to education are not fulfilled simply because a set of laws at national or international level confers them. Women's and girls' rights to education are won through active processes of discussion and negotiation, to which research makes a contribution. Rights, seen in this way, are thus much like capabilities, and securing rights in education is bound up with ensuring the freedoms against violence and discrimination that will enable rights to be fulfilled.

We are calling for a transformation of policy and practice so as to achieve this empowering education for all, irrespective of their sex. But what will it take to achieve it?

In broad terms, there are three ways in which the Millennium Development Goals (MDGs) can promote gender equality over the next ten years. In the first scenario – a 'business as usual' approach – we continue with the current patchy implementation of policies and programmes for gender equality, concentrating primarily on improving access, and leaving the responsibility for fulfilling human rights, promoting social change, and building a just society to short-term projects located (for example) in small units within education ministries, or to a handful of NGOs and groups of concerned teachers and education officials. Larger numbers of children will come into school, but only some will learn in ways that help them to thrive, and a considerable number will be subject to threat and violence in school. Some innovative and transforming programmes will be implemented, but funding and support for them may remain unreliable and limited, provided through committed teachers, NGOs, and community-based organisations with little institutional support or follow-up. This scenario is a revitalisation of a 'Women in Development' (WID) approach, with small projects engaged in 'Gender and Development' (GAD) work, or the development of thinking about gender, education, and human rights.

In the second scenario we will have achieved Education For All, as proposed in the Dakar Framework for Action (itself a considerably enlarged vision compared with that sketched in MDG 2), and all children will be in school. But the links between improved education quality and gender equality will be made only in part, because attention will be focused on the formal education system, to the exclusion of wider societal considerations. Schools may receive resources to implement education reforms, and school–community relations may be improved through the work of school councils and by enhanced training for teachers in gender equality, as well as increased numbers of female teachers. But the vital linkages across and between sectors will remain fragile. This second scenario would see the expansion of GAD concerns within the formal education sector, and some concerted efforts by governments to treat gender equality as a human right. However, the links between gender equality in education and wider gender-equality agendas would be limited.

In the third scenario the full vision for gender equality, as presented in the Beijing Platform for Action, will be realised, together with the resolutions made at other key international forums such as the International Conference on Population and Development at Cairo in 1994, and the World Summit for Social Development in 1995. This means that gender-equitable education will be based on broader societal change for gender equality, with implications for the sustainability of practice, and girls and women will be empowered to demand that their rights be respected and their positions in society strengthened. They will benefit from an education which provides them with the capabilities to achieve the freedoms and the kind of life that they have reason to value. This third scenario would bring together the insights of all four frameworks discussed in Chapter 1: WID, GAD, post-structuralism, and 'capabilities and rights'.

Achieving no more than Scenario 1 in the next ten years would be extremely unsatisfactory. It would mean that MGD 2 and MGD 3 were not achieved, and the expanded policy visions articulated in the 1990s would have been abandoned. Achieving Scenario 2 would be a good outcome, because it could provide the conditions that would generate Scenario 3. If Scenario 2 were achieved by 2010, therefore, we could push for a substantive change in social development in order to reach Scenario 3 by 2015.

What have we learned about transforming policy and practice?

Because we believe that good learning and good research can guide good policy making, this book documents good innovative practice. However, it also documents problems, weaknesses, and shortcomings in practice and policy making. The book indicates that there are no quick fixes to the deep-rooted and often widely accepted forms of gender discrimination that affect education and schooling, but it does highlight key areas for change.

The *participation of women* and girls in decision making about their own education is a fundamental aspect of developing an education which transforms women's lives in the way that they desire. Such participation would put into practice the concept of rights and capabilities that we believe will guide transformative policy. The school-based work on HIV/AIDS (Chapter 10) illustrates how young people – both girls and boys – need opportunities and space to explore, reflect, debate, and ask questions about their sexuality and HIV/AIDS; it emphasises that the space needs to be safe, so that young people can challenge gendered power relations and develop their own understandings, which will enable them to change their behaviour.

Transformational education needs *transformed teachers*. It is important therefore that the training of teachers and adult educators not only raises their status and self-esteem but is empowering for them and, through their teaching, for their students. In addition, the structures that shape teachers' lives, salary scales, career ladders, and conditions of work need to address concerns about gender inequality if the GAD vision is to be realised. Failure to attend to the consequence of gender inequalities in the employment and training of teachers created the conditions for the reproduction of gender inequality. Where a teacher transmits gender inequalities that are 'hidden' in the curriculum (for example in Mali, see Chapter 9) or discriminates against female students because of the teacher's own prejudices and lack of awareness (for example in Peru, see Chapter 7), change is urgently needed – change of a type illustrated in the enabling aims of Loreto Sealdah School (Chapter 12), where teachers and students engage in structured reflection. Raising women's status through their participation in the Total Literacy Campaign (see Chapter 8) is a step towards empowerment which needs to be supported by government and by society. However, these small-scale changes at the project level need to be sustained and enhanced by attention in policy and practice to address the deep-seated structures of gender inequality that will always constrain anything that the most transformative teacher can do, unless they are supported by access to equal pay, good working conditions, and secured rights to participate in political, economic, and social decision making.

But we are not suggesting that policies and practices which work in one context can be replicated in others wholesale. On the contrary, what works in one context may fail dismally in another. We are suggesting, however, that there is a need to look beyond the confines of the school or the literacy class and understand the bigger social, cultural, economic, and geographical environment in which it is embedded. The diversity of context, of learners, of teachers, as well as the diversity of frameworks for education and development within which we work (see Chapter 1), mean that we must develop flexible policies and flexible practices that take account of the different scenarios described above. The examples from Kenya (Chapters 5 and 6) remind us not only of the need for *flexibility within national policies*, but also of the need for a *range of different strategies* for change, each tackling different and interrelated aspects of education and gender equality.

The processes of learning and influencing that enrich policy and practice can only flourish if there are good partnerships between practitioners, policy makers, and researchers. The foregoing chapters recognise the importance of civil society working in small-scale and innovative projects and programmes, linking with government and intergovernment organisations charged with policy making. They also recognise the extent to which NGOs themselves influence policy, and the way in which governments responsible for national policy can also learn from their own practice. We are not necessarily dealing with discrete categories – practitioner or policy maker – but we should recognise that there is often a large degree of overlap and also of movement between the two: policy makers sitting in government ministries may have been teachers, or they may have worked with an NGO or UN agency – and *vice versa*. A change of government, such as that which took place in South Africa in 1994, or the successive regime changes in Peru during the 1990s, means that an influential lobbyist from the NGO sector can overnight become an influential policy maker in the ministry of education or finance.

NGOs and civil-society actors have an important part to play in influencing the policy and practice of government. And good documentation of innovative, good-quality, and small (or not so small) education programmes is key to successful advocacy and lobby for change. MDG 8 calls for developing a global partnership for development and recognises the importance of civil-society participation in change for the achievement of the MDGs themselves. Civil society, and especially the work of national education coalitions of civil-society organisations (see, for example, Chapters 2 and 5), have a very important role to play in partnering government for successful education. The work of women's organisations in promoting transformative agendas is crucial, and here we find that there is more work to be done across sectors (see, for example, Chapter 8) and at all levels of the education system, to foster respect and facilitate negotiation of aims and objectives. There are organisations and groups of concerned and involved women, teachers, communities, and parents which need more space and greater voice in policy-development processes. As Elimu Yetu in Kenya illustrates (see Chapter 5), NGOs and national coalitions are lobbying to gain this space.

Strong political will and leadership in a range of social sectors and settings is important, and there is evidence that political commitment is beginning to achieve change. While that change may not be as extensive or transformative as we desire (see Ahmed and Chowdhury 2005), it provides us with evidence of what is possible and with examples of how to proceed where high levels of political commitment are accompanied by civil-society action and dynamism. In countries where there has been significant political commitment to change at all levels, we see how dramatic actions, such as the abolition of school fees, can result in huge numbers of girls attending school, and the first steps being taken towards gender equality in education. There may be a process of moving from WID to GAD to rights and capabilities, but it is important that the momentum of that process is maintained, and equally important that policy should extend beyond a narrow focus on access.

As this book has shown, the evidence of political will and social mobilisation does exist. We do know a lot about what good-quality, gender-equitable education looks like, and what needs to change in order to achieve it. The Millennium Development Goals provide an opportunity to galvanise new resources, new partnerships, and collective energies and commitment to overcome the difficulties and to achieve really significant results.

Reference

Ahmed, M. and R. Chowdhury (2005) 'Beyond Access: Partnership for Quality with Equity', Institute of Education and Development, BRAC University; Campaign for Popular Education, CAMPE), www.ungei.org

Index